THE GREAT
MISTAKE

THE GREAT MISTAKE

THE BATTLE FOR ANTWERP AND THE
BEVELAND PENINSULA, SEPTEMBER 1944

PETER BEALE

SUTTON PUBLISHING

First published in the United Kingdom in 2004 by
Sutton Publishing Limited · Phoenix Mill
Thrupp · Stroud · Gloucestershire · GL5 2BU

British Library Cataloguing in Publication Data
A catalogue record for this book is available from the British Library.

ISBN 0-7509-3286-4

Typeset in 11/13pt Photina MT.
Typesetting and origination by
Sutton Publishing Limited.
Printed and bound in England by
J.H. Haynes & Co. Ltd, Sparkford.

Contents

Maps

Foreword

Armies throughout the world are notoriously inefficient and wasteful of resources. These faults arise from many different causes, but two are of major importance. These are an inability to learn from past experience and a lack of clearly defined and realistic objectives. To the British Army's major faults can be added a third, and that is the contempt it has for the competence of other armies, be they those of the enemy or those of their allies.

It has been a disadvantage for the British Army to have emerged on the winning side in the two major conflicts of the twentieth century, the First and Second World Wars. Being one of the winners gives rise to the complacent thought: 'We won, so we must have done it right'; or alternatively, 'We beat them, so we won't have to worry about doing it again.' These attitudes were proved tragically wrong in the years 1919–39. The British Army took more than ten years to evaluate its performance in the First World War, and British politicians, even if they were made aware of the deficiencies revealed, did little or nothing about them until it was too late.

The second major fault, the lack of clear objectives, is a political rather than a military fault. That does not absolve the armed services of blame. At the level of Grand Strategy the politicians are responsible, but at the operational level the service chiefs have that responsibility. This work is concerned primarily with the Army, the objectives given to the Army by the politicians, and the operational objectives formulated to carry out the country's political will.

In the Second World War the British Army's principal opponents were the Italians, the Germans and the Japanese. The Italians were considered to be cowardly, non-battleworthy, and generally lightweight troops. This judgement was not altogether wrong, although Italian troops under Rommel fought well in the desert. However, the British Army had some respect for the quality of the German soldier, based on the experience of the First World War. The Japanese were thought of as funny little men with spectacles and bad teeth, whose factories could make only second-rate products. This attitude was mirrored in the British Army's contempt for them as soldiers – until the two armies met in combat. Wavell was a commander who had a particularly low opinion of Japanese military competence.

The principal allies of the British in the Second World War were the Russians, the French, the Americans and the countries of the Empire – Canada, Australia, New Zealand and South Africa. The Russians were seen as disorganised hordes whose only strength lay in their numbers; the French had large forces and a long military tradition, but they were considered decadent.

The Americans and the armies of the Empire were all considered to be amateurs in war – a reflection on their colonial past. It was thought that they could not comprehend or execute strategic concepts, but they could provide large numbers of fit, even if amateur, soldiers. The contempt for American ability for military command was strongest at the highest level of the British Government and its military apparatus. Two of the most outspoken critics were Alan Brooke, Chief of the Imperial Staff, and Montgomery, Commander of the British 8th Army and subsequently 21 Army Group. Both of these two were equally contemptuous of the strategic ability of the Commander of the 1st Canadian Army, Gen Harry Crerar.

It was the belief of the British that it was only possible for professional soldiers to understand and execute military campaigns at the highest level. This arrogant attitude had little justification, considering that the British Army had won only two campaigns in the first three years of the Second World War (North Africa 1940, Gen O'Connor, and East Africa 1941, Gen Cunningham), both against ill-trained and poorly supplied Italians.

This book makes clear how these faults affected the course of the campaign in north-west Europe, particularly around Antwerp in the autumn of 1944. The central purpose of this work is not to impute blame, but to identify the causes of one of the major tactical blunders of that campaign. A very powerful tool for improvement is the evaluation of mistakes. To use that tool, the mistakes must be acknowledged, and their causes and cures sought with objectivity.

Acknowledgements

My thanks to Cornelius Ryan, who used the phrase 'The Great Mistake' in *A Bridge Too Far* to describe the failure of 21 Army Group to drive north from Antwerp on 4 September 1944. Curiosity as to the reasons for this mistake led to the research that formed the basis for this book.

Several people helped with research and production, and I would like to thank in particular Jonathan Falconer at Sutton Publishing for his encouragement and continued support; Christopher Dawkins of the Library of the Australian Defence Force Academy for preparing a very extensive list of references; and Stephen Bond for research at the National Library of Australia.

Living in Australia, it is of course not possible to access primary records held in England, and for his research at the National Archives and the Imperial War Museum my most grateful thanks go to my cousin Nick Beale. His intelligent appreciation and selection of relevant documents was invaluable.

Finally, my loving thanks to my wife Shirley, who has as always supported my work with patience, understanding and love.

Peter Beale
Valentine, New South Wales

Chapter One

WHAT WAS THE GREAT MISTAKE?

On 4 September 1944, units of 11 British Armoured Division entered Antwerp after a whirlwind advance through northern France and Belgium. With considerable help from the local Belgian Resistance, they captured the essential installations that controlled the operations of the docks, and occupied the dock area and the city up to the Albert Canal. But in spite of pleas from the Resistance, the British advanced no further for two days.

Had they immediately crossed the Albert Canal before the bridges across it were blown, their tanks could have moved north against light opposition and reached the Woensdrecht isthmus within hours. Such action would have sealed the isthmus, trapped 15 German Army to the west of the isthmus, and made the task of clearing the banks of the Scheldt estuary relatively easy and quick before the retreating Germans could rally and regroup.

The failure to cross the Albert Canal and advance north was called 'The Great Mistake' by Cornelius Ryan. What were the reasons for the mistake, and are there lessons we can learn from it? This part of the campaign had as its starting point the crossing of the lower reaches of the River Seine. The force under the command of 21 Army Group when they closed to the Seine was very mobile, consisting as it did of five armoured divisions, five independent armoured brigades and eight infantry divisions (see Appendix 2).

CROSSING THE RIVER SEINE

After the closing of the Falaise–Argentan pocket and the annihilation of much of the German forces in it, Allied forces advanced to the River Seine. The original plan for Operation Overlord envisaged that the Germans would have established defences along the river, and it would need set-piece attacks to cross it. But the German collapse allowed the Allies to close up rapidly to the river and make assault crossings on the run.

The crossings by 21 Army Group took place in the last days of August. The British 2nd Army crossed at two places: 43 Division of XXX Corps on

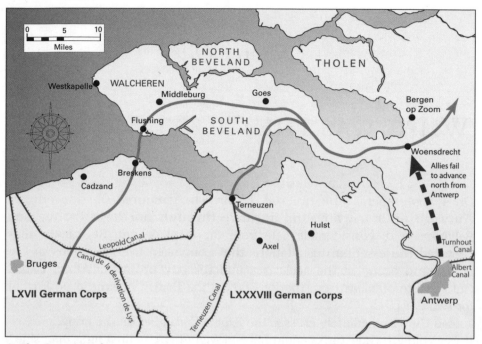

1. The Great Mistake.

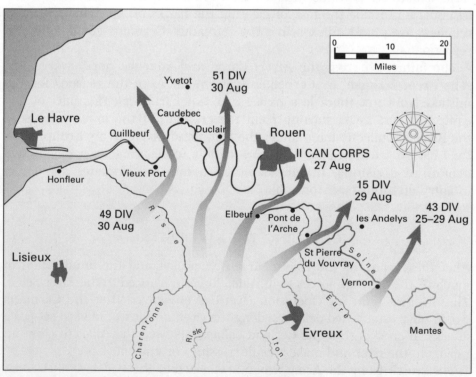

2. 21 Army Group Seine crossings, 26–31 August 1944.

26 August at Vernon; and 15 Division of XII Corps at St Pierre de Vouvray, where a firm position was established on the east bank on 29 August.

The 1st Canadian Army consisted of II Canadian Corps and I British Corps. The Canadian Corps crossed between Pont de l'Arche and Elbeuf on 26 and 27 August, and entered Rouen on 30 August. Downstream from Rouen, 51 Division of I Corps pushed patrols across the river on 30 August, and further downstream again 49 Division, accompanied by the Royal Netherlands Brigade, got elements over the river on the same day.

XXX CORPS CROSSING AT VERNON

The crossing furthest upstream and nearest to Paris was that made by 43 Division of XXX Corps at Vernon. The leading brigade started their crossing at 1900 hr on 25 August. Although the Germans had no prepared positions on the northern bank, they still put up determined resistance. It was not until 28 August that the division was able to construct a class 9 bridge, followed by a class 40 to allow passage of tanks across the river. On 28 August, 11 Armoured Division, accompanied by 8 Armoured Brigade, moved over the bridge, and the next day they began their advance north-eastward on two parallel axes.

On the first day, 29 August, the pace of the advance was restricted by bad weather, demolitions and pockets of enemy resistance. On 30 August, the Guards Armoured Division took over the right-hand axis, and that evening the Corps Commander, Gen Horrocks, ordered a night advance to seize bridges over the River Somme at or near Amiens. This was achieved early on 31 August.

The advance continued at great speed, and by 2 September the Guards Armoured had captured Douai and Tournai and 11 Armoured had by-passed Lille. Orders were now issued directing the Guards on Brussels and the 11th on Antwerp. In the early hours of 3 September the Guards crossed the Belgian border, and before nightfall the whole division was in Brussels with units fanning out round the city to control the main approaches. On the next day, 4 September, elements of the division entered Louvain.

On the left axis, 11 Armoured fought through opposition on 3 September to reach a position to the east of Alost by nightfall. The next day they advanced on Antwerp, capturing the city and the docks. They were thus firmly established in Antwerp, with very effective support from the Belgian White Brigade, on 4 September.

XII CORPS CROSSING AT ST PIERRE DU VOUVRAY

The advance from the XII Corps bridgehead began on 30 August, with 4 Armoured Brigade leading and 53 Division close behind. The armour moved 25 miles during the day, reaching Gournay by nightfall. The next day, 31 August, 7 Armoured Division passed through the leading troops, and by the end of the day was within 20 miles of the River Somme. On 1 September, 7 Armoured drove on and, in spite of opposition, secured a bridge over the river between Amiens and Abbeville. Opposition became stronger during the next two days, and on 4 September the division bypassed Lille to the east so that it could advance more rapidly. It was thus able to reach Oudenarde and then Ghent on 5 September.

II CANADIAN CORPS CROSSINGS, ELBEUF–PONT DE L'ARCHE

On 30 August, 3 Canadian Division cleared the line of the River Seine into Rouen. Patrols pushed into the city and beyond, and on the next day 9 Canadian Brigade moved through the city in a triumphal procession and then on to the coast. They reached and captured the coastal town of Le Treport on 1 September.

On the same day, 2 Canadian Division captured Dieppe, the scene of the tragic raid on 19 August 1942 in which the raiding force, most of them Canadian, lost 3,600 out of 6,000 men. On the next day, the division stayed in Dieppe, partly to absorb 1,000 reinforcements and partly to prepare for a memorial ceremony on 3 September.

4 Canadian Armoured Division moved out of the bridgehead and reached Buchy, one-third of the way to the Somme, on 31 August. There the Corps Commander, Gen Simonds, received orders to make a night march to the Somme at Abbeville where, so Montgomery told him, there was a bridgehead over the river that had been captured by XXX Corps. Simonds decided that the advance should be made by the Polish Armoured Division and 3 Canadian Division, leaving 4 Canadian Armoured to refit and reorganise.

On arrival at the river on 1 September, they found that there was no bridgehead, and it was not until 3 September that the engineers of Polish Armoured were able to construct a class 40 bridge to take their tanks across. By the evening of 4 September, the Poles were 25 miles north of the Somme, but were held up by determined anti-tank opposition.

On 4 September, 3 Canadian Division moved over the Somme at Abbeville and advanced to the outskirts of Boulogne. The next day, part of the division moved on to Calais, with the intention that both ports should be invested and captured. 4 Canadian Armoured reached the Somme on 2 September, and concentrated astride the river, ready to move forward to assist the Poles.

CROSSINGS BY I CORPS

I British Corps consisted of 49 and 51 Infantry Divisions. 49 Division crossed the Seine between Caudebec and Vieux Port, and immediately swung left so that it could advance westward to invest and capture Le Havre, known as Operation Astonia. 51 Division was also to take part in this operation, but was first given the task of liberating St Valery. It was there on 12 June 1940 that the then commander of the division, Maj Gen Fortune, was forced to surrender with 8,000 men of his division to 7 Panzer Division and its leader Erwin Rommel.

On 1 September 1944, 51 Division avenged the disaster of 1940, and then turned westward to join 49 Division at Le Havre. Both divisions of I Corps, together with 33 and 34 Armoured Brigades, were therefore outside Le Havre on 4 September. They remained there during the preparations for the assault, which started on 10 September and was successfully completed on 12 September.

THE DAY OF THE GREAT MISTAKE, 4 SEPTEMBER 1944

The positions of the main formations of 21 Army Group on 4 September 1944 are shown below. The right flank of 21 Army Group was covered by the 1st US Army. The English Channel coast of north-east France had been reached between St Valery and the mouth of the Somme. Le Havre

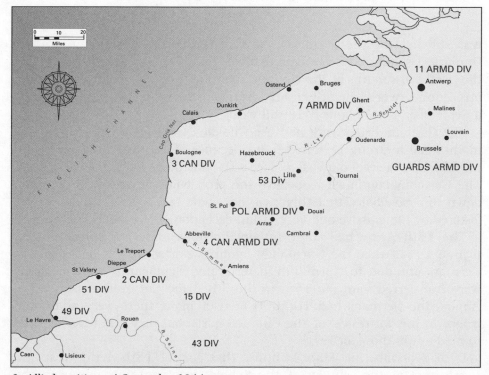

3. Allied positions, 4 September 1944.

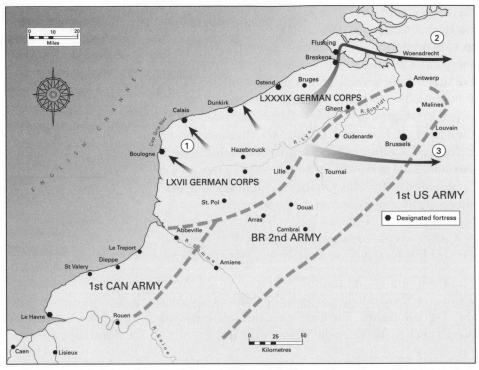

4. Situation of German 15th Army, 4 September 1944.

was still held by the Germans, as were the ports of Boulogne, Calais, Dunkirk, Ostend and Zeebrugge. Antwerp had been captured, but as yet the northern suburbs of the city and the road to Woensdrecht and Bergen op Zoom were in German hands. But on this vital day, 4 September, those hands were still weak.

The German 15th Army had been holding the Pas de Calais, and had maintained a strong presence there because of the fear that the Allies would mount a second invasion across the narrowest part of the Channel. The Germans continued to believe the probability, progressively winding down to a possibility, that this invasion would take place. The belief was fostered by the massive and very skilful deception of Operation Fortitude.

The 15th Army had some fifteen divisions under its command on 6 June 1944, when the Normandy landings started. It was not until the German situation in Normandy deteriorated significantly that divisions were transferred from the 15th to the 7th Army. But even at the end of August the Germans had 100,000 men or more; there were additional troops in the 'fortresses' of the Channel ports, but they had been ordered to hold out in those fortresses.

By 4 September, as Map 4 shows, that part of 15th Army west and south-west of the estuary of the Scheldt was contained between the

English Channel, the 1st Canadian Army pushing east from the Somme, and the strong thrust of the British 2nd Army from the Seine, across the Somme at Amiens, reaching the Scheldt at Antwerp. This thrust cut off any possibility of the 15th Army escaping to the south and east of Antwerp.

Map 1 shows the situation closer to Antwerp. The 15th Army was falling back from the Somme towards the Leopold Canal and the towns of Breskens and Terneuzen. It still held the Walcheren–South Beveland peninsula in strength. On 4 September the area between Merxem and Woensdrecht was held lightly.

The 'Great Mistake', then, was the failure by the Allies to send whatever force could be mustered to seize a crossing over the Albert Canal at Merxem (as the Belgian White Brigade encouraged and implored them to do), and send an armoured column with all possible speed to the isthmus 2 miles west of Woensdrecht. This column would have had to be reinforced promptly to put in place a block to prevent the escape of the 15th Army. But had this been done, and then followed up once again very promptly with more troops, there could have been an opportunity to sweep up the Beveland peninsula during the very short period that existed until the resilient Germans reorganised themselves.

The Great Mistake was to lose this fleeting opportunity.

COMMENTS BY MILITARY COMMANDERS AND HISTORIANS

In *A Bridge Too Far*, Cornelius Ryan records how 11 Armoured Division under Gen Pip Roberts reported on 4 September that the city of Antwerp had been captured with the docks intact:

The thirty-seven-year-old Roberts had brilliantly executed his orders. Unfortunately, in one of the greatest miscalculations of the European war, no one had directed him to take advantage of the situation – that is, strike north, grab bridgeheads over the Albert Canal in the northern suburbs, and then make a dash for the base of the South Beveland peninsula only 18 miles away. By holding its 2-mile-wide neck, Roberts could have bottled up German forces on the isthmus, preparatory to clearing the vital northern bank. It was a momentous oversight. The port of Antwerp, one of the war's major prizes, was secured; but its approaches, still held by the Germans, were not. This great facility, which could have shortened and fed Allied supply lines all along the front, was useless. Yet nobody, in the heady atmosphere of the moment, saw this oversight as more than a temporary condition. Indeed, there seemed no need to hurry. With the Germans reeling, the mop-up could take place at any time. The 11th Armoured, its assignment completed, held its position awaiting new orders.

The person who could have given immediate orders to move forward
with all possible urgency was the XXX Corps commander, Lt Gen Brian
Horrocks. In his autobiography, *A Full Life*, he says that the Antwerp
docks seemed the obvious objective, but he subsequently realised that this
was a serious mistake. His excuse was that his eyes were fixed entirely on
the Rhine. It never occurred to him that the Allies would not be able to
use the port until the banks on either side of the estuary had been cleared
of enemy troops and the mines swept. He goes on to say:

> If I had ordered Roberts, not to liberate Antwerp, but to by-pass the town on
> the east, cross the Albert Canal and advance only 15 miles north-west
> towards Woensdrecht, we should have blocked the main German escape
> route. The meagre force in front of him was spread out on a 50-mile front
> along the canal. And on 3 September we still had 100 miles of petrol per
> vehicle, and one further day's supply within reach.

In his *History of the Second World War*, Liddell Hart comments on what
he calls 'an extraordinary oversight':

> When the 11th Armoured Division raced into Antwerp on September 4 it
> had captured the docks intact, but made no effort to secure the bridges over
> the Albert Canal, and these were blown up by the time a crossing was
> attempted two days later, the division then being switched eastwards. The
> divisional commander, Roberts, had not thought of seizing the bridges
> immediately he occupied the city, and no one above had thought of giving
> him orders to do so. It was a multiple lapse by four commanders: from the
> top Montgomery, then Dempsey, Horrocks, and Roberts, four commanders
> who were normally alert to tactical opportunities.
>   Moreover, barely 20 miles north of Antwerp is the exit from the Beveland
> peninsula, a bottleneck only a few hundred yards wide. During the second
> and third weeks of September the remains of the German 15th Army were
> allowed to slip away northwards from the Pas de Calais. They were then
> ferried across the mouth of the Scheldt and escaped through the Beveland
> bottleneck. Three of the divisions arrived in time to strengthen the Germans'
> desperately thin front in Holland before Montgomery launched his drive for
> the Rhine at Arnhem, and helped to check it.

The German General Eugen-Felix Schwalbe was put in charge of the
operation for ferrying the 15th Army units across the Scheldt. He
achieved this task to his own enormous satisfaction, and presumably that
of his superiors. He has this to say about the Allied inaction:

> I was in constant fear that the Allies would cut off the Beveland Isthmus by
> an advance north of Antwerp and thereby trap such troops as were in the

process of moving out. If this had happened our alternative plan was to evacuate the troops through the Dutch islands to Dordrecht and Rotterdam. But such a journey would have been slow and dangerous. It would have meant a twelve-hour voyage by sea rather than the three-quarters of an hour needed to cross from Breskens to Flushing. We could not have hoped to rescue anything but the troops themselves had it been necessary to adopt this course.

In his *Defeat in the West*, Milton Shulman is critical:

If there be one criticism to make of Allied tactics at this stage of the campaign, it was the failure to push on beyond Antwerp shortly after the port had been taken. From 4 to 21 September no serious effort was made to cover this stretch of 20 miles from Antwerp to the base of the Beveland isthmus, thereby depriving 15 Army of their only reasonable escape route. True, the small British armoured spearheads that reached Antwerp were tired after their headlong dash from the Seine, and the long supply haul from Normandy had affected the availability of petrol, food and ammunition for any large-scale operation. Nevertheless, with little to oppose them but the hastily assembled infantry troops in Holland, a gamble of this kind might well have paid handsome dividends. Had the Allies bottled up 15 Army in the Beveland peninsula, or even forced them to take the hazardous sea voyage to Rotterdam, there could never have been an effective German position south of the Maas River. And had this position not existed there might have been a different outcome to the airborne operation at Arnhem. The fact that no determined effort was made to seal off the escape route of 15 Army is probably a measure of the surprise with which the Allied Supreme Command received the news that Antwerp had been taken.

In *The Second World War*, John Keegan looks back at the operations after the Allied victory in Normandy:

In retrospect it can be seen that the failure to clear the Scheldt estuary, and thus to open the way for the Allies' fleet of cross-Channel supply vessels to deliver directly to Antwerp in the immediate rear of 1 Canadian, 2 British, and 1 American Armies was the most calamitous flaw in the post-Normandy campaign. It was, moreover, barely excusable, since Ultra was supplying Montgomery's headquarters from 5 September onwards with intelligence of Hitler's decision of 3 September to deny the Allies the use of the Channel ports and waterways; and on 12 September Montgomery's own intelligence section at 21 Army Group reported that the Germans intended to 'hold out as long as possible astride the approaches to Antwerp, without which the installations of the port, though little damaged, can be of no service to us'.

It would be fair to call Maj Gen Pip Roberts, commanding 11 Armoured Division, the Liberator of Antwerp. His division had distinguished itself in Normandy, and in a brilliant sweep north-east from the Seine it had ended its run by capturing most of Antwerp up to the Albert Canal, saving the vital sluicegates and port installations before they could be destroyed by the Germans.

There they stopped. The tanks had just completed one of the fastest advances in history, moving sometimes all through the night. Men and vehicles were fatigued, though not exhausted. Nearly forty years later, in 1983, Roberts insisted that he could have gone on across the Albert Canal on 4 September, resistance being still so feeble:

> Monty's failure at Antwerp is evidence again that he was not a good general at seizing opportunities. My thoughts, like Horrocks' and Monty's, were east to the Rhine on 4 September. We should have looked west towards Walcheren.
>
> Unfortunately, I did not appreciate the significance of the fighting on the Albert Canal, and the Germans did not blow the crucial bridge for another twelve hours. If briefed before, I would have crossed the Albert Canal with tanks to the east of Antwerp and closed the Germans' route into Beveland and Walcheren.
>
> At that time petrol was coming up regularly on lorries, and we saved space on lorries by not using much ammunition. I had enough petrol to continue my advance.

The importance of having free access to the docks of Antwerp was understood at the very highest level. In Churchill's memoirs covering this period the Prime Minister says: 'Without the vast harbours of this city no advance across the lower Rhine and into the plains of northern Germany was possible.' And in a despatch of a few days later, sent while he was at sea on his way to the Quebec Conference to be held on 10 September, Churchill wrote: 'It is difficult to see how Twenty-First Army Group can advance in force to the German frontier until it has cleared up the stubborn resistance at the Channel ports and dealt with the Germans at Walcheren and north of Antwerp.'

This point was emphasised at the Quebec Conference, where the Combined Chiefs of Staff underlined the urgent need to open the port of Antwerp. Admiral Sir Bertram Ramsey was the Naval Commander-in-Chief of the Allied Expeditionary Force, Eisenhower's senior naval commander. His sailor's eye discerned the importance of opening supply ports, and on 4 September he sent a signal to Eisenhower, Montgomery, the Admiralty and the Commander-in-Chief, Nore:

> It is essential if Antwerp and Rotterdam are to be opened quickly enemy must be prevented from:

* carrying out demolitions and blocking ports
* mining and blocking Scheldt and new waterway between Rotterdam and the Hook
* both Antwerp and Rotterdam are highly vulnerable to mining and blocking. If the enemy succeeds in these operations the time it will take to open the ports cannot be estimated
* it will be necessary for coastal batteries to be captured before approach channels to the river routes can be established.

On the next day, Ramsey wrote in his diary: 'Antwerp is useless unless the Scheldt is cleared of the enemy.'

The capture of Antwerp with its docks intact was of paramount importance, since it offered an early improvement to the deteriorating logistics system. But as Ramsey said, it would be of value only if the approaches were cleared. Yet not one senior Army commander made this necessity clear to his subordinates, nor did they realise it themselves. Eisenhower's directive of 4 September called for 'securing' of Antwerp without emphasising the need for its use. Montgomery, with his eyes fixed on the far side of the Rhine, paid it but scant attention, although his supply situation was becoming difficult. As a result, no instructions were given by 1st Canadian or British 2nd Army to subordinate formations to give priority to clearing the approaches. This was in spite of the above-quoted signal from Admiral Ramsey.

Montgomery did not at once exploit beyond the Antwerp docks, and the bridges leading north over the Albert Canal were not captured. The subsequent arrival of German reinforcements ensured a prolonged defence of the estuary, which could have otherwise been freed in a matter of days. The battles to free the estuary lasted into November and caused heavy casualties, most of them Canadian. In the early days of September, those Canadians were concentrating on capturing the Channel ports, most of which were severely damaged.

Chapter Two

GERMAN FORCES,
AUGUST–SEPTEMBER 1944

GERMAN COMMANDERS IN THE WEST

There was a considerable difference between the actual German force available to oppose and attack from the West and the Allied perception of that force. We first look at the real situation of the Germans in the vicinity of Antwerp in the period late August to early September 1944, as well as the possibilities of reinforcing those formations.

The main problem in attempting to set down the facts of the German military situation at that time is that it was extremely fluid. This account cannot therefore pretend to be completely accurate, and it is unlikely that the Germans themselves were aware of the precise locations and strengths of all of their formations.

The German forces in north-west Europe were under the command of the Commander-in-Chief West, or to use the German designation, Oberbefehlshaber (OB) West. Field Marshal Gerd von Rundstedt had been OB West until he was fired by Hitler. At the beginning of July, when asked what should be done about the situation in Normandy, Rundstedt replied: 'End the war, you fools, what else can you do?' Somewhat naturally, Hitler considered this to be defeatist, and replaced him with Field Marshal Gunther von Kluge on 4 July. Six weeks later, on 17 August, von Kluge committed suicide, and was replaced by Field Marshal Walther Model.

As OB West, von Kluge had commanded Army Group B under Rommel and Army Group G under General Blaskowitz. Rommel was badly wounded by a strafing Allied plane on 17 July, and no one was sent to replace him. Thus, from mid-July until he committed suicide von Kluge fulfilled the dual roles of OB West and OB Army Group B. These two roles were taken over by Model. He was to concentrate on his northernmost formation, Army Group B, to meet the urgent threat posed by the Allied 21 Army Group and 1st US Army. Army Group G had in effect been written off. Following the second Allied invasion (Operation Dragoon) carried out by French and American troops in the area of Marseilles on 15 August, Army Group G had hurriedly left southern France and was falling back in disarray to the German border.

Model sent regular reports to the Chief of the Wehrmacht Staff (in German Oberkommando der Wehrmacht, or OKW). That officer was General Oberst Jodl, to whom Model sent his reports endorsed 'with request for submission to the Führer'. Three of these reports were sent on 24 August, 29 August and 4 September. They give a picture of a progressively worsening situation, and one in dire need of reinforcement. However, Model is still clearly in control of his depleted and battered forces, and makes such moves as are feasible given the pressures the Allies are inflicting on the ground and in the air.

MODEL'S REPORT TO OKW, 24 AUGUST

Model's report of 24 August, which was written before the Allies had crossed the Seine, describes the German positions along the river. Downstream from Paris they were held in sequence by LXXXVI Corps, LXXIV Corps, LXXXI Corps and XLVII Panzer Corps. Between them the four corps had twelve divisions or divisional battle-groups (this term implying a greatly reduced division). These included infantry divisions, parachute divisions (in German Fallschirm, or Fs), and field divisions of the German Air Force (in German Luftwaffe, or Lw). The divisions were: 711, 346, 3 Fs, 353, 271, 331, 344, 17 Lw Field, 49, 18 Lw Field, 6 Fs and 275.

Model goes on to say that in view of the strong Allied pressure it was probable that the Seine line could not be held, and he would have to fall back to the River Somme. That line needed to be constructed and occupied urgently, and for that purpose he had the very weak remnants of twelve divisions, which were: 352 (the stalwart defenders of Omaha Beach), 84, 89, 326, 363, 276, 277, 708, 272, 273, 343 and 5 Fs.

MODEL'S REPORT TO OKW, 29 AUGUST

Situation of the enemy

The British Army Group (25–27 Divisions) has started a rapid thrust across the Seine towards the north with the intention of driving our forces to the coast and taking possession of the V1 bases. They have powerful artillery support and total superiority in the air; they have up to 1,500 tanks that they can employ between the coast and Paris. [*Note*: with this number of divisions and tanks, and the location defined as 'between the coast and Paris', Model must have combined 1st US Army and 21 British Army Group in these figures.]

Situation of our troops

The divisions which came back across the Seine from Normandy after hard fighting and under extreme difficulty are armed only with few medium weapons, in general carbines, etc. Supply of personal and material requirements is completely inadequate. After five exhausted infantry divisions have been taken off to be used in the Fatherland, we can create four formations by combining the remnants of eleven divisions plus some reinforcements. These formations are in personnel only, all of whom will need equipment.

The armoured divisions each have between five and ten tanks ready for battle. In regard to artillery, only isolated guns are left with the infantry divisions and isolated troops of guns with the armoured divisions. Our soldiers are being considerably affected by the enemy's superiority as to materials, particularly in the air, and his great number of tanks, and by the fighting in pockets when encircled. *Remedial measures are being taken.*

The low degree of manoeuvrability of the infantry divisions, caused by the fact that they have been made mobile only by temporary expedients [horses], has had a particularly unfavourable influence in the unequal fight with the motorised enemy, all the more as the necessary reserves of assault guns and other heavy anti-tank guns are non-existent.

MODEL'S REPORT TO OKW, 4 SEPTEMBER

Enemy troops

The British Army Group is thrusting north-east towards Antwerp with the objectives of capturing the V1 bases and bottling up our 15 Army. The British formations are still considerably deployed in depth, but are closing up. French and Belgian resistance groups are taking part in the battle in increasing numbers. The anticipated large-scale air-landing appears most likely in the West Wall region.

Own troops

Our own troops have been very severely mauled in the period since my last report. They were no match for the enemy's military operations and high mobility, above all on the northern wing. They were continually overtaken and cut off, largely because they lacked the tanks, artillery, and heavy anti-tank weapons needed for setting up a defensive position from which to counterattack.

The troops we have available at present are: 15 Army, inclusive of Military District Holland, has four infantry divisions; in 15 Army area there are also the fortress garrisons; 5 Panzer Army has four Panzer divisions, and nearly two composite infantry divisions.

The course of the breakthrough battles of 15 Army cannot as yet be gauged. Only some sections will fight their way through. The line Albert

Canal–Meuse–West Wall can still be considered as a feasible defensive position for Army Group B.

COMMENTS ON MODEL'S REPORTS

As stated earlier, Model was still able to exercise control over this very difficult battle. He made reasonable forecasts about the movements of the Allies, and was especially prescient regarding the use of airborne troops. His assessment of the line of the Albert Canal as a defensive position was sound, it being some weeks before its entire length was in Allied hands.

MOVEMENTS OF THE GERMAN 15TH ARMY, 27 AUGUST– 5 SEPTEMBER

At the time of the Normandy invasion the Commander of the 15th Army was General Oberst Hans von Salmuth. He had the misfortune to be taken prisoner, and his place was taken on 27 August by General Gustav von Zangen. Von Zangen recorded what he found when he took over, and the actions taken by the 15th Army in the days immediately following. This is his account:

I assumed command of 15 Army on 27 August 1944. The Army area covered the Channel coast from the Scheldt estuary, including the island of Walcheren and North Beveland, up to the Seine estuary at Le Havre. LXVII Corps comprised 245 Infantry Division (on either side of Dieppe) and 226 Volksgrenadier Division (up to the Seine estuary).

The security garrisons of the fortresses and defence areas consisted in part of former coastal divisions or those now holding the coastal line, and in part of special fortress cadre formations. The fortresses were in need of further forces to be brought up for the occupation of the land fronts and for the creation of tactical reserves.

Our adjacent formation on the right was under the Commander-in-Chief Netherlands, and on the left the worn-out 5 Panzer Army, at that time fighting for the Seine crossings on either side of Rouen. The remnants of 5 Panzer Army were strongly mixed with divisions from the battles in the neighbourhood of Falaise. The majority of these belonged to 7 Army, which, as later experience proved, were just as inefficient in fighting qualities as the units of 5 Panzer Army. We gained this knowledge in the ensuing battles, at the price of heavy losses for us.

The mission of 15 Army on 26 August was still 'defence of the Channel coast', when it was now obvious that there would be no second invasion in the Pas de Calais. There needed to be a new decision on the use of 15 Army. Seeing that we had failed to master the situation on the Seine and then the

Somme, most of the tasks we subsequently undertook were on our own responsibility, although sanction was asked and obtained for those actions.

After crossing the Seine on 28 August, the enemy headed for the Somme in two spearheads on either side of Amiens. It appeared to us that we were unlikely to hold the Somme position, and in that case the enemy had at least two possible courses of action. He could advance on an axis Arras–Lille–Brussels, or he could attack the rear of our coastal defence works and the entire front of 15 Army. We were then without significant reserves, and there was a danger that we could be pushed up against the coastline and eliminated.

There was no longer any sense in staying at the coast. We had to try to withdraw all mobile forces from the Channel area and turn them to meet the danger threatening from our rear. On 28 August, 15 Army ordered missions for its two Corps as follows. LXVII Corps was to withdraw from the coast and to march to positions to defend the line of the Somme from its estuary to Picquigny, making Abbeville the centre of their defence. LXXXIX Corps was to move 59 Division to Arras and 712 Division to Douai, also establishing 64 Division at St Pol.

Beside the Channel fortresses, the only remaining coastal defence was the personnel needed to handle the stationary weapons; also the non-divisional artillery as well as all naval formations, security troops and emplaced antiaircraft and naval artillery.

30 and 31 August

LXVII Corps was withdrawing toward the Somme with both its divisions in small groups because of Allied aircraft. Many of the units were not accustomed to the hardships of marching, and every means was used to help them on their way. Every type of transport was used, including that of the Army coastal artillery and the naval artillery. 245 Division helped itself with motor vehicles it had procured.

Only on the southern wing of 245 Division south and south-east of Abbeville was light contact made with the enemy. In fact the Corps was carrying out a march parallel to that of enemy troops feeling their way forward on the sector of 5 Panzer Army. The enemy push to the north which we expected to follow their reconnaissance did not materialise; it would necessarily have cut off large portions of the Corps from the Somme. Apart from this there was only one intact bridge over the river near Abbeville, to which the main body of both divisions was pressing forward.

1 September

Amiens fell with surprising ease without any resistance. Abbeville was taken by the Polish Armoured Division against slight resistance by 245 Division. On account of the fall of Amiens, LXXXIX Corps was ordered to build up a defensive wing ahead of Doullens after the arrival of 64 Division from St Pol.

From there they could either mount a counterattack on Amiens or on the flank of the enemy advancing to Arras.

2 September

The situation near Arras and south of Bethune was vague. LXVII Corps was not able to resist the enemy any longer after they had crossed the Somme near Abbeville, and retreated to the line of the next river east of and parallel to the Somme, the River Authie. LXXXIX Corps built up a new front line with 64, 59 and 712 Divisions and one battalion of the 348th.

At Lille, Tourcoing and Roubaix the local resistance forces made themselves conspicuous to an increasing degree; their actions were thought by some to have been an enemy breakthrough. There were no local forces for subduing the resistance fighters, and their activities threatened to gain serious proportions in the rear of our combat elements.

The enemy attack at Arras initiated the break in the continuity of the front line just established. The decision was therefore made to withdraw slowly to the north-east, and to make a thrust from the area north of Lille to the east in order to make contact with 5 Panzer Army and possibly break through to the east.

3 September

In the afternoon an order from Army Group B by radio extended the sector of the Army to the left, practically to the full extent of the sector up to this time occupied by 5 Panzer Army. Additional forces for carrying out this order were not placed at our disposal. As a result of a representation made by phone to Model giving a description of our situation the order was withdrawn.

LXVII Corps was engaged in a heavy battle near Hesdin and Montreuil. The news of the fall of Brussels confirmed our belief that the main thrust of the enemy in that direction meant the envelopment of the whole of 15 Army. The plan of a breakthrough to the east was now about to be put into effect.

4 September

With the news of the fall of Antwerp, the envelopment of 15 Army seemed to be complete. To the Army, still comparatively strong numerically, but seriously impeded by low fighting qualities and lack of combat experience in some soldiers, the following possibilities remained:

1. Withdrawal to the Channel coast in order to reinforce the garrisons of the fortresses and the defence areas with the aim of allowing them to offer resistance for a longer period.

2. Withdrawal to the Scheldt estuary in order to cross the river there with the main body and to reach the mainland over Walcheren and South Beveland near Woensdrecht.

3. Break through to the east.

5 September

An order was received from OKW through Army Group B. Because of the strength of the enemy forcing his way to the north and north-east we were to suspend the plan for a breakthrough to the east, which had now become hopeless. Instead, we were to move the Army across the Scheldt to the mainland; the Scheldt estuary was to be defended vigorously by two divisions, one north of the estuary and one south; and the Channel fortresses were to be similarly defended by their occupation forces.

COMMENTS ON VON ZANGEN'S ACCOUNT

The role of the 15th Army from long before the Normandy invasion and at least up to the Allied break-out from Normandy in mid-August, was to repel an Allied invasion across the Channel in the Dover–Calais area. Its divisions, therefore, were generally stationed close to the coast and orientated in that direction. The great majority of these divisions were static or reserve formations, and lacked the mobility of the standard field divisions.

When Allied thrusts over the Seine threatened von Zangen from the south and south-east rather than from the north-west, his Army needed to change direction completely. This would have been easy for field infantry divisions or Panzer divisions, accustomed as they were to rapid movement and manoeuvre. But, as von Zangen points out, many of his troops were in reserve formations of lower quality than field formations; they had little or no combat experience; and their mobility was severely impaired by having to use horse-drawn wagons rather than trucks for much of their transport.

His account shows, however, that the movements of LXVII and LXXXIX Corps were reasonably well controlled; that he was in touch with his superior, Model, and through him to the OKW; and that he made realistic plans to deal with situations as they arose.

His comments made on 4 September present three plans, each of merit. Retiring to the Channel coast and strengthening the fortresses (Option 1) would have certainly made them much harder to capture. A break-out to the east to join up with 5 Panzer Army (Option 3) would have been a good move had it been done a week earlier; but at that time the probability of the Allies capturing Brussels and Antwerp within a week seemed extremely low.

The other problem with a break-out was the 15th Army's lack of mobility. The troops could march, certainly, although many of them had little experience of marching and would have suffered greatly; but the movement of field artillery and heavy anti-tank guns would have been slow, and in any case they were not particularly well supplied with those items.

The capture of Antwerp by the Allies on 4 September and the OKW order of 5 September meant that the course to be taken was the retreat across the Scheldt (Option 2), escape down the Beveland peninsula, and the placement of defensive forces to deny the use of the Scheldt estuary and the port of Antwerp. The slow retirement across country well-suited to defensive operations was a manoeuvre almost tailor-made for such a force as the 15th Army then was. That retirement, as we will see, was well executed and gave much trouble to the Allies, particularly the Canadians.

RESOURCES AVAILABLE TO GERMANY, 4 SEPTEMBER

There was a widespread feeling in the Allied armies during the rapid advance from the Seine to Antwerp that the German Army was a spent force, and that there would be little future resistance. Allied perceptions and intelligence summaries at this time will be examined later in this book; what we are concerned with here is to try to estimate the resources that the Germans could assemble to defend the western approaches to their country.

Available forces can, in the broadest terms, be grouped under three headings: physical resources, comprising men and material; organisational systems, which are used to group, assign and control those physical resources; and psychological resources, or the will to fight and the resilience to overcome setbacks.

Physical resources
While Army Group B might have felt totally inadequate to meet the Allied onslaught in the early days of September, the overall picture for Germany was not one of unrelieved gloom. The Wehrmacht, or the fighting force of Army, Navy and Air Force combined, could still muster ten million officers and men on its strength on 1 September. The Army had 327 divisions and brigades, of which 44 were armoured – although almost all of them were under-strength.

Surprisingly, even after five years of war, much of the time engaged in heavy fighting, German manpower resources had not been fully exploited. The hospitals could provide a steady flow of replacements. Physical standards for front-line service could be reduced; in the 15th Army, for example, 70 Division had many men who needed special diets, and as a result it was known as the 'Stomach' Division. The age of call-up could be reduced; the Navy and the Air Force were carrying on their strengths large numbers of men in excess of their needs. Men who had had their service deferred could be released from that deferment; men in the civil service and in the factories could be released for military service. The potential of women power had hardly been touched. A new mobilisation plan using some of these opportunities had in fact been instituted by Reichminister Josef Goebbels, and by early September these programmes were in full swing.

Goebbels had made his announcement on 24 August, and extracts from it show what new sources of manpower Germany was still able to call on.

The whole of Germany's cultural life has been maintained, even in the fifth year of war, to an extent which the other belligerents did not reach even in times of peace. The total war effort of the German people now necessitates far-reaching restrictions in this field as in others. All theatres, music halls, cabaret shows and schools of acting are to be closed by 1 September. All schools of music, academies, art colleges and art exhibitions will be closed down. Only scientific and technical literature, armament and school books, as well as certain standard political works will be published; all other types of literature will be suspended.

Trade schools of no direct war importance, e.g. domestic and commercial colleges, will be closed. At the universities male and female students who are studying subjects which are not of direct importance to the war will be available for employment in the armaments industry. These measures will make available a total of several hundred thousand persons.

In order to fully utilise all labour, working hours in public administration and offices in industry and trade have been fixed uniformly at a minimum of sixty hours a week. To bring civilians in line with the soldiers, a universal temporary ban on holidays is ordered with immediate effect. Women who will be fifty and men who will be sixty-five on 31 December are exempt from this ban.

As a result of the measures it was hoped not only to rebuild the divisions destroyed on the Eastern and Western Fronts, but also to form between twenty and twenty-five new divisions. These new divisions were to be called Volksgrenadier, or 'People's infantry' divisions. Their role would be to fill the bunkers of the Siegfried Line.

In terms of material, the quality of the German equipment was equal to or ahead of that of the Allies in several important areas, including some specifically important in defensive operations. The hand-held anti-tank weapon, the Panzerfaust, was every bit as good as the Bazooka or the Piat. The 88 mm gun, particularly in its anti-tank role, was devastating. The 150 mm multibarrel mortar, formally the Nebelwerfer but colloquially the 'moaning minnie', was a very effective and nerve-tingling weapon; it was also easy to conceal and quick to move, and presented a baffling problem for counter-battery action.

In respect of tanks, the German Tiger, Panther and Mark IVs H and J out-gunned all the Allied tanks except the Sherman Firefly, which was on limited issue only to British units. The Allies had a far greater quantity of tanks, but the Germans were still able, in spite of the vaunted operations of the vast fleets of Allied bombers attacking their factories, to produce an average of 1,500 tanks and assault guns every thirty days.

Some of the measures taken to restore the balance of strength for the Germans would not have immediate effect. However, at the critical juncture when the German resources were stretched to the limit in early September, the Luftwaffe came to the rescue. In the German military system the Luftwaffe commanded all military aircraft; Luftwaffe ground formations and Luftwaffe field divisions, basically used for defence of Luftwaffe installations; *and*, unlike most other national armies, all paratroop formations.

On 4 September Göring disclosed, to the complete surprise of the Army General Staff, that he had six parachute regiments in various stages of training or re-equipping, and that he could raise two more regiments from paratroops in convalescent depots, making a force of 20,000 men altogether. To these he could add 10,000 men from the Luftwaffe, aircrews and ground staff whose training or operations had been curtailed by the shortage of petrol. Few of these men were fully trained for fighting on the ground, but almost all were young, fit and fanatical – as indeed they proved.

Organisational systems

The overall command of the German forces was greatly complicated by Hitler's paranoia and simultaneous self-confidence. He had taken risks and succeeded on several occasions, sometimes without fighting, as in Austria and Czechoslovakia, and at other times with fighting, as in Poland and France. His paranoia gave rise to his mistrust of his generals, greatly increased after the 20 July bomb plot, and to the complex organisational structures he put in place. The way he used those structures aggravated their dysfunctional nature, particularly when he gave his 'no retreat' commands.

Even if in the end it was the interventions of Hitler that brought about Germany's defeat in the West, the actions of his operational and tactical commanders staved off that defeat for a long time in the face of great odds. The German General Staff had developed systems of versatility, flexibility and simplicity. In the hands of their immensely battle-experienced commanders, many of whom had been fighting continuously for three or four years (Poland, France, North Africa, Italy and especially Russia), their systems could absorb and react positively to almost any shock. In the débâcle following their defeat in Normandy, the German respect for organisation and discipline had preserved the machinery of command virtually intact. We have seen the actions of Model and von Zangen, and noted that even in the fluidity of those days they still retained reasonable control over their formations.

In the first week of September, the 7th Army and 5 Panzer Army had been reduced to skeletons, and the 15th Army had been considerably battered. But they all had divisional staffs capable of rounding up retreating and disorganised soldiers and restoring a measure of control. This philosophy had permeated throughout the German Army, and many small groups were anxious and determined to reunite themselves with larger formations, and thus once again feel part of their military family. This attitude, of course, applies to the armies of all nations to some degree; but the German Army possessed it to a greater extent than any other.

MORALE AND RESILIENCE OF THE GERMAN SOLDIER

The German Army was recognised by all its opponents as being a formidable fighting machine. The saying went: 'You have not fought in a war unless you have fought against the Germans.' There were several causes giving rise to its efficiency and performance. One was its command system, which we have just considered. The second was the way in which it trained its officers and soldiers to be confident and resilient in even the most adverse situations.

Germany had a rigorous professional educational system for its officers that had withstood the buffeting of the First World War, even if it had a lean time in the decade after the end of that war. The system tested and honed the skills of its officers, and ensured that they all, of whatever arm of the service, understood the needs and contributions of the other arms, and could work together to achieve joint objectives. The inter-arm understanding was especially important in operations requiring the coordination of infantry, tanks and aircraft. This was very much in contrast to the British system, in which infantry–tank cooperation was for many years abysmal.

In the use of military manpower, however, the one factor that gave the Germans the edge over every other army was their system for training NCOs. Anyone who has served as a private, trooper, gunner, etc., will recognise that to have a good platoon or troop sergeant gives a great boost to confidence. And regimental officers at all levels appreciate the power, strength and support that comes from a team of competent and experienced warrant officers and NCOs. The most junior level of officer, the platoon or troop commander, has an enormous amount to gain from the wisdom of a good sergeant, and may be for ever in his debt.

The fighting reputation of the British Brigade of Guards is based largely on the excellence of its NCOs, and it is a formidable and well-deserved reputation. The German system, however, amplified even further the value of its NCOs by incorporating in their training the 'mission system' – in German, the *Auftragssystem*. This system had been introduced into the

German Army in the late nineteenth century, and provided the backbone for its great military strength in the wars of the nineteenth and twentieth centuries.

The essential feature of the *Auftragssystem* was that a subordinate commander of whatever rank was accountable for carrying out the 'mission' of his superior officer, with or without orders. This meant at least three things: the junior commander – we will assume an NCO – is trained and indoctrinated to take over command automatically if his superior becomes disabled; the system of training gives him instruction and practice in how to do so; and he is made continuously aware of what his superior's mission is.

Part of this training must be, and was, to instil into the NCOs a great deal of initiative. The German NCO was thus able to react immediately and forcefully to any sort of reverse in battle. Such a reverse could be the loss of ground, loss of equipment or the death of a superior. The ingrained reaction was, 'When in doubt, attack.' This response was used time and time again in Normandy.

A gap might open up in the German line under an immense weight of artillery, air power, or infantry and tank attack. But then a single tank or self-propelled (SP) gun, a small group of soldiers with an anti-tank gun, a mortar or a machine-gun would immediately attempt to seal the gap, acting instinctively rather than having to wait for explicit orders.

Within the German Army there was also a sense of comradeship stronger than that in the Allied armies. Not that it did not exist in the American and British Armies, where it was an important contributor to performance and morale. But in the German Army, if something went wrong, the officer, NCO or soldier would feel responsible for doing something about it irrespective of danger, and do it immediately.

The effect of the combination of these various factors was continuously underestimated by the Allies, who had the concept that the Germans were inflexible robots – although the Allied soldiers at the sharp end would vehemently disagree. In the débâcle of the last days in Normandy, the German Army at all levels remembered its training, and reacted instinctively. The Allies appeared to be unaware or contemptuous of these inherent strengths. Contempt or wishful thinking about the enduring capability of the German Army during the pursuit across Flanders was a contributor to the Great Mistake.

The ratio of officers to all ranks in the German Army in the Second World War was between 2.5 and 3 per cent, compared with 7 per cent in the American Army. But the German officers were so capable of transforming individual soldiers into cohesive units that in the German Army the company, with a strength of 120 to 150 men, developed a sufficient sense of comradeship and solidarity to constitute the primary group. By contrast, in the Allied armies the usual primary group was the section or squad of 8–10 men, or at the largest the platoon of 30. Unit consciousness and solidarity makes an army an effective fighting force.

If we add a sense of dedication to a cause, we find that Nazism and the Fatherland were significant driving forces for the German Army, whereas democracy (and for the British, the Empire) were irrelevant for the Allied armies as motivators.

The combination of ability to absorb reinforcements and the dedication of those reinforcements is well illustrated in the massive expansion of 1 Parachute Army in the first days of September 1944. As we have seen, many of the reinforcements came from the Luftwaffe, unexpectedly supplied by Göring. The Luftwaffe, says Milton Shulman in *Defeat in the West*:

> yielded up some thousands of able-bodied, eager young men it had been retaining for the day when German planes would be available again. In one huge convulsion the bulk of their potential pilots, observers, navigators, and signallers were sent West to save the Fatherland. Arriving either as complete units, or organised into improvised battle groups with an army officer in command, they entered into the fray with the enthusiasm and will of the young. Although completely untrained for their new role – one battalion of four hundred men had gone into battle after doing one infantry exercise during which their commanding officer was killed – they nevertheless fought tenaciously and well, making up for their inexperience by their courage and zeal. This collection of fresh youth, picked from amongst the best manpower in Germany, had not yet suffered the disillusionment and carnage of the ordinary infantry soldier. Until they did, they were to prove a formidable opponent whose presence in the line played a significant part in slowing down the Allied advance from a gallop to a slow walk.

A report on the interrogation of a German officer shows that there was despair in some elements of their forces, but that the system was able to reassure and regroup soldiers into units and formations capable of determined resistance. The officer's account relates to an SS Panzer Grenadier Division which had retreated from Normandy back behind the borders of Germany:

> Only a few bedraggled remnants arrived in Merzig. No human account could ever describe the hardship, the sacrifice, the misery the men of this division alone experienced. No one who finished this retreat still alive will ever forget this Gethsemane, because each village, each road, even each bush has seared into the brain the memories of terrible hours, insufferable misery, of cowardice, despair and destruction.
>
> In the re-forming area all means were employed to get the division back on its feet. Every available officer of the divisional staff, including the divisional commander, went out cruising in the frontier area with

instructions to gather troops. The officers would stand at road crossings and shanghai every passing soldier who did not have a ready answer to an inquiry after his destination.

In one instance I was directing traffic into the divisional area. The army men, not quite satisfied about the prospect of being impressed into an SS unit, circled the area until they hit another road, only to run into me at the road junction again. I redirected the men into the divisional area, rather amused at the merry-go-round.

When anti-tank guns were needed, an officer with a few prime-movers at hand would set up shop at a road crossing and wait for passing guns, the crews of which were not quite certain about their destination or attachment. The horses would be unhitched, the crews piled into the waiting prime-movers, and the caravan then proceeded into the re-forming area.

Chapter Three

TOPOGRAPHY, WEATHER AND CIVILIANS

In all armies commanders have to issue orders to their subordinates. The word 'subordinate' may include not only those over whom the commander has direct authority, but also those who are going to be affected by or have an effect on the execution of those orders. This could include other services, such as the navy or the air force, or other arms of the same service, such as Royal Engineers used to construct a bridge for the passage of tanks.

The process of giving orders is obviously different in detail and emphasis for a major military operation and the actions of an infantry platoon or a troop of tanks. However, the British Army, in common with all other armies, has developed a format for issuing orders. The format ensures that all 'factors affecting the situation' are considered in the planning to undertake an operation to achieve an assigned mission, in the preparation of orders for that mission, and the delivery of those orders to subordinates.

The headings for the 'factors affecting' are: enemy, own troops, topography, weather and civilians. We described the situation of the enemy in Chapter Two, and will describe that of 'own troops' in later chapters. In this chapter we review the other three items, topography, weather and civilians, as they might affect a major operation in the area of Antwerp and the Scheldt estuary.

TOPOGRAPHY

One of the functions of Intelligence was to inform commanders and their subordinates of the sort of country they were likely to meet as they advanced. Sometimes the salient features of the terrain were either not known, or their effects on movement were underestimated. A case in point was the bocage country of Normandy.

In this country the fields were divided by great banks of earth surmounted by hedges. These proved very helpful to defenders, and daunting obstacles to attackers. It was especially dangerous for a tank to climb over one of these obstacles. It had to be done slowly, and as the tank arrived at the top of the bank its lightly armoured underbelly was exposed, a prime target for German anti-tank guns and Panzerfausts.

Had the difficulties of the bocage been fully appreciated, techniques might have been devised to overcome them. It would have been meat and drink to Gen Percy Hobart, Commander of the specialised armoured 79 Division, had he been given the task of developing a solution to the bocage. As it was, an American sergeant came up with the very simple and effective idea of welding metal blades on the front of tanks to cut through the base of the banks.

Russell Weigley comments on the difficulties experienced by the Allied troops in this country:

> The bocage aggravated some of the limitations of the Allied armies and their weapons, all the more because the planners had neglected tactical preparation for this obstacle behind the Normandy beaches. It was now, belatedly, that Montgomery's HQ conceded that 'experience gained to date in Normandy has shown that the bocage country is most unsuitable for large scale armoured action, and further, that it would offer the enemy limitless opportunities for delaying actions during a withdrawal'. Bradley's HQ also acknowledged that 'hedgerow fighting has been far more difficult than we anticipated'.
>
> It was too bad that these revelations had to wait upon experience. Tactics and weapons for coping with the bocage were only now being improvised; hammering them out by trial and error in combat cost time and lives.

TOPOGRAPHICAL REPORTS

Intelligence staff generally provided useful information on the topography immediately ahead of the leading troops, and two examples of Topographical Reports produced by XII Corps are demonstrated in the following extracts.

The first extracts are taken from Appendix D to XII Corps Intelligence Summary No. 50 of 29 August 1944. The leading division of XII Corps at the time of crossing the Seine was 15 (Scottish) Division, and it crossed on the same day at St Pierre du Vouvray. The Corps as a whole, led by 7 Armoured Division, was directed north-east towards the Somme.

The Topographical Report covered the area bounded on the south by the Seine, on the north by the Somme, and extending inland some 50 miles from the Channel coast. The report dealt with the topography under three headings: general, including relief; river lines; and road communications. The first extract is from the section headed 'General, including relief':

General, including relief
The area under consideration is part of a low chalk plateau which makes up
the whole of Northern France. It has very little relief, and the only two
major breaks in the uniformity of the landscape are the valleys of the
Somme and the Seine which are the area boundaries. A detailed survey will
thus fall into three natural divisions:
   a. The chalk plateau proper
   b. The right bank of the Seine valley
   c. The left bank of the Somme valley
   [This extract deals with item a only.]

The chalk plateau
This extensive area consists of a number of 'Pays', the ancient limits of
which have little topographical significance. The extreme western part
between the Seine below Rouen and the sea is known as the 'Pays de caux',
'caux' being patois for chalk which is such a predominant feature of this
district. South-east of the Caux is the area of the 'Norman Vexin'. The
country between Beauvais and Neufchatel is the 'Pays de Bray', and the
remainder of the area is the plain of Picardy.
   The chalk plain of Picardy is highest in the centre, where it reaches 790 ft;
most of it is 350 ft. It is divided into parallel segments by the straight valleys of
short rivers flowing north-west into the Channel. The surface is now undulating,
now quite flat, and large stretches are quite tree-less except for orchards and tree-
hedges. However, there are some forests, especially where chalk has given way to
clay. The Haute Foret d'Eu and the Basse Foret d'Eu extend over 29 square miles,
and consist of beech copses interspersed with ploughed fields.

Going
The report describes the detailed characteristics of the other 'pays', and
then deals with the all-important item of 'going', or the suitability of the
terrain for movement generally, and particularly that of tracked and
wheeled vehicles:

Cross-country movement for both infantry and motor transport is reported to be
easy all over the chalk country. Woodland is nowhere thick enough to be tank-
proof. The valleys of the rivers running north-west are natural barriers, but are
not considered tank obstacles in the dry season when the marshy banks are firm.
   The concentrated layout of villages in Caux and Picardy makes it easy for
them to be turned into strong-points which, thanks to long unrestricted
fields of fire, might hinder progress considerably.

Bottlenecks
A particularly interesting section of the Topographical Report of
29 August listed 'bottlenecks' in the terrain ahead that might cause

problems for the advancing troops. These bottlenecks could be used by the enemy as sites for ambushes, or they could simply cause difficulties in physical movement. The list contains twenty-three sites, each with its map reference. Here are some extracts from the list (map references have been omitted):

- Road runs for 4 miles between high ground and railway, with river immediately west of railway.
- Road descends escarpment by three hairpin bends of minimum external diameter 60 ft.
- Road in defile for 2 miles.
- Road runs up side of valley with numerous bends of minimum 45ft radius.
- Road cut into steep hillside for 1 mile.
- Road runs between river or railway and steep hillside for 2 miles.

The next Topographical Report issued by XII Corps Intelligence was Appendix A to Intelligence Summary No. 57 of 6 September. By this time XII Corps had reached Ghent, although the German commander there was yet to surrender. The area covered by the report had already been entered, extending as it did from the Belgian–French border to the Dutch–German border, covering the greater part of south Holland and all of Belgium except the Ardennes.

The areas that we are interested in are the polders of Zeeland and Flanders, and the district called the Campine. We start with an extract which describes a polder:

Definition
A polder is land lying below the level of the sea and surrounded by a dyke. Each polder is generally independent of its neighbours, and although itself absolutely flat, may differ in level from those adjoining it. As the subsoil is impermeable clay, all drainage is artificial – water is pumped up from the ditches to intermediate reservoirs whence it flows to the sea by canal or river. Windmills which were formerly used for pumping have been largely replaced by steam, electric, or motor pumps.

Zeeland
The polders of Zeeland include the large islands at the mouth of the Rhine, namely: Overflakee, Duiveland, North Beveland, Tholen, and Walcheren; also included in Zeeland, although not quite an island, is South Beveland. They are mostly five feet below sea level, and almost entirely devoid of woods. Owing to its good soil Zeeland is predominantly arable land, pasture being confined to the southern islands. The polders are well populated, with small towns of which Flushing is the best known.

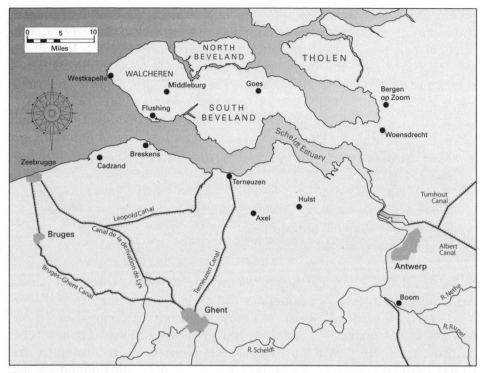

5. Antwerp waterways.

Belgian Flanders

Flat, low-lying drained clay fens extend inland from the southern shore of the West Scheldt and from the dune coast for about 10 miles. The land south of the Scheldt is mostly not more than three feet above sea level, while the rest is usually under ten feet. The region is covered by a close network of drainage runnels and dykes and there are extensive marshy areas south of Dixmude.

The region is divided between large farms, mostly interested in dairying and cattle-breeding. The population is relatively sparse. There are few towns and these are small.

In the area of Antwerp the waterways are extremely significant, and extracts from Intelligence Summary No. 57 give details of the waterways of Belgium and Holland generally; these are shown for the Antwerp area in Map 5:

Belgium

The waterways system of Belgium is based on the navigable rivers. These are interconnected by canals, especially close to the French frontier. They are connected to industrial centres which lie away from the main waterways by branch canals. The general direction of the waterways is north-east from the French frontier, Antwerp being the main focus of the waterways, and Ghent a secondary focus.

The principal navigable waterways converge on the Scheldt, except the Meuse which is linked with Antwerp by the Albert Canal. The Belgian and Dutch systems are only linked together by major canals on the extreme east and west.

Holland

The waterways are the most vital part of the communication system of Holland, although in recent times roads have been assuming greater importance. The Dutch waterways generally are deeper, wider and more important than those in Belgium, which are often secondary and supplementary to the railways.

Whereas the Belgian waterways serve heavily industrialised regions, both in Belgium and North France, the Dutch system has a great through trade and serves the industrial regions of Central Europe. The principal Dutch waterways normally have an east–west direction, linking the German waterways system and important commercial centres in Holland such as Rotterdam and Amsterdam.

COMMENTS ON TOPOGRAPHY

Much of the land in the area of Antwerp and the Scheldt estuary is very close to or below sea-level, and is protected from inundation by dykes. This gives a defender the opportunity to flood parts of the country, and thus once again to channel an enemy's attack on to a restricted axis, which could, if guns were available, become a daunting position to capture.

From the landing in Normandy until reaching the vicinity of Antwerp, the Allied armies had been operating mainly on firm ground, though there were some exceptions to this, notably the area inland from Utah Beach on the west flank of the Allied landing, and on the extreme right flank at the mouth of the River Dives. Fighting in Normandy was almost all on firm ground, and the advance of the British 2nd Army to the Seine and on to Antwerp was mainly on roads.

The nature of the topography in the Scheldt estuary was therefore something as yet little experienced by Allied commanders and formations. Lt Col T.A. Wysocki was on the staff of the Commander of the Polish Armoured Division during their advance to the Scheldt. The Poles were under the command of II Canadian Corps, and were thus on the left flank of the advance of 21 Army Group. He commented:

The terrain varied across Belgium. On the right was excellent tank-going country with only two rivers and no marshes, which was duly made use of by the Guards Armoured Division and 11 Armoured. Towards the left the numerous streams, rivers and canals running across our line of action made things more difficult. The Germans were not stupid. They were blowing bridges right before our very eyes, and slowed us up very effectively.

A few days later, when advancing north from St Niklaas towards the banks of the Scheldt, Lt Col Wysocki has further comments on the terrain over which the Poles were required to attack:

Now the division had the task of liquidating any enemy force still remaining on this side of the Scheldt estuary. This was Dutch territory; it was unknown to us that it was so, but we soon learnt. The terrain was ideal for the Germans and extremely difficult for us. Marshes, polders, canals and ditches made the operations most difficult. Making excellent use of the terrain's natural defences and improving them by flooding certain polders, the enemy was gaining time for securing the withdrawal across the Scheldt. Our units suffered heavy casualties in taking these German positions.

WEATHER

The weather is something notoriously hard to predict, but can have a very significant effect on military operations. Probably the best-known impact that weather had on Allied operations in Europe was the decision to launch the invasion. At 0430 hr on 4 June 1944 Eisenhower postponed the landings for twenty-four hours, to 6 June.

On 3 June the forecasts had predicted for 5 June weather which might permit landings from surface craft but would forbid air operations, including air landings. On the evening of 4 June the meteorological officers at SHAEF forecast a break in the weather that would last over the morning of 6 June, but not beyond. It would produce conditions that were 'barely tolerable' for the assault forces, but which would allow bombing of coastal defence batteries and air-spotting. Postponement would mean a very dangerous delay of a fortnight, while a decision to go might condemn Overlord to failure. Eisenhower decided for 6 June.

This decision caught the Germans by surprise. The bad weather of 5 June meant that there was little air reconnaissance by the Luftwaffe, and the commanders on land thought that landings from the sea were most unlikely. So much so that Rommel, Commander of Army Group B, had gone to Germany for a few days, and other senior commanders were also absent from their posts.

The achievement of tactical surprise was due to the adverse weather. But in its turn the adverse weather affected the ability of the Allies to exploit surprise or to use the offensive benefits of close-support aircraft. By creating confusion on the beaches, and delay in getting away from them, it hampered the Allied plans for rapid thrusts inland.

Intelligence on the movements of German formations, particularly Panzer units, was impaired by the fact that the poor weather almost eliminated the work of the Photo-Reconnaissance squadrons on D-Day. It was these two consequences of the unseasonable weather that prevented the Allies from reaching their D-Day objectives, in particular the rapid capture of Caen.

Considering the area and the period of the Great Mistake – the north European autumn – the factors that needed to be evaluated were rain, fog and cloud.

Under some circumstances rain can be of benefit, as for example it has a freshening effect on soldiers in the field. It may be helpful in dampening down dust that may betray a position to the enemy. But in the autumn in Belgium and Holland, on ground that was not far from being waterlogged for much of the time, it had a very negative effect. For successful attacking operations, the commanders needed to use every dry moment before the wet autumn weather began to make the ground and the operations sticky.

Cloud and fog also affected operations around Antwerp. Both, fog in particular, hampered the use of aircraft. The Allies had overwhelming air superiority, and made good use of it to eliminate heavy hostile weapons. The absence of air support caused many casualties in the capture of strongly held enemy localities. If airborne attack formed part of a plan, it was liable to be cancelled in the event of fog or heavy cloud cover.

The weather that was actually experienced in north-west Europe from the middle of September had a devastating effect on Operation Market Garden, the intended capture of a bridgehead over the Rhine at Arnhem. A number of factors were put forward to explain the failure of this operation, of which the three most important were the speed and strength of the German reaction; the breakdown of radio communication; and the weather.

Of these three factors, the most important by far was judged to be the weather. This was the opinion of Montgomery, commanding the Allied forces, and General Kurt Student in command of the German 1 Para Army, his principal opponent.

On D-Day of the operation, 17 September, the weather allowed the landings to proceed according to plan. On 18 September the lift for 1 British Airborne Division was five hours late taking off. On 19 September nothing was able to take to the air. The troops remaining on the ground in England were the Polish Airborne Brigade, which was to have helped capture the bridge at Arnhem; and three glider infantry battalions of the 82 US Airborne Division, without which the 82nd could not press home its attack on the Nijmegen bridge.

By the time this bridge was taken, the Germans had regained control of the Arnhem bridge, and were able to delay the Allied advance to the Rhine until the chance of making a successful crossing had gone.

On 20 September, the Poles and the glider battalions were still earthbound, and when they finally took off on 21 September only half of them found the Dropping Zone. On the 22nd the weather again prevented any airborne operations, and by the next day it was effectively too late to help 1 British Airborne Division at Arnhem.

We have to consider how much the factors of topography and weather affected the operations around Antwerp, and assess the degree to which those factors were taken into account when deciding not to advance north from the city immediately after it was reached on 4 September 1944. The Allied planners could obviously obtain all necessary information about the topography. And there must have been records of the local weather patterns and probabilities. Did the planners take this information into account in advising the commanders, and if so, did the commanders listen?

CIVILIANS AND RESISTANCE MOVEMENTS

Most military operations are likely to require an attacking force to advance through areas where there are civilians, local inhabitants who are not in the armed forces. The attitude of those civilians is an important factor in a military plan. If their country is being invaded they may be acquiescent, and require only their own police force to keep them in order. But if being invaded makes them hostile, they can become a military liability. How much of a liability depends on the temperament of the locals and the opportunities afforded by the physical features of their terrain. Two examples of highly antagonistic civilian populations are the Spaniards in the Peninsular War of 1808–14 and the Yugoslavs between 1941 and 1945. The combination of hatred, courage and inaccessible country allowed these two resistance movements to be very sharp thorns in the sides of the occupying armies. In the first case the French under Napoleon, and in the second the Germans under Hitler, had to commit substantial military forces to keeping those hostile civilians under control, and even then were only partially successful.

If a country is being liberated, however, the liberating forces are likely to get enthusiastic support from the people of the village, town, city or country they have reached. Sometimes, as accounts will show, the support or welcome can be completely overwhelming, to the extent that military operations cannot immediately be continued.

In Belgium and Holland after 1940, the resistance movements grew slowly. This was not due to any lack of patriotism or courage, but the terrain of both countries, as has been previously indicated, was not very suitable for covert operations, and both countries were heavily populated. As the Resistance developed, what were the resistance fighters trying to achieve?

The mission of any resistance movement was to do anything that would cause discomfort to the enemy and give aid to the potential liberators – for Belgium and Holland, the Allies – with the final objective of throwing the oppressor out of the country. Some of the activities that would help to achieve this objective were: sabotage, or the damaging of military installations or weapons of war, or infrastructure used by the occupying forces (bridges, railways, energy supplies, etc.); collection of information about enemy dispositions and intentions, and the transmission of that information to the Allies; the rescue and concealment of Allied airmen or escaped prisoners of war, and their restoration to Allied or neutral territory; and any other activity that would cause damage or inconvenience to the German occupiers, or give advantage to the Allies.

One somewhat unusual activity was described by M. Ugeux, who was in charge of the resistance 'Groupe Zéro', and who produced the underground paper *La Libre Belgique*:

In a little disused station in the centre of Brussels a transmitter gave the weather forecast five times a day. An extremely valuable factor, received only in London, and it looks as though the Germans never had anything similar. They started out on their operations without knowing what the weather was going to be like over England, while the English set out with at least a general idea, given by an expert who had been parachuted in especially for the purpose, and who had found a few accomplices with the same background.

Many Dutch people and Belgians wanted to take more direct action by developing paramilitary forces which could actually fight against their oppressors. Such a force would be of the greatest use when liberating forces appeared on the scene. The resistance fighters could then provide such support as: direct military action; providing local knowledge and directions; giving information on enemy whereabouts and strength; rounding up and guarding prisoners; and providing communication systems.

However, there were many obstacles, difficulties and dangers in executing the objectives of a resistance movement. The fundamental danger was the possibility of discovery by the Germans, resulting in retribution not only for the resistance fighters but also for the local population. As an example, a situation report from 2 Battalion, 723 German Regiment at midday on 5 September 1944 reads: 'Four Belgians were captured by 7 Company. They wore the uniform of the Armée Blanche and were in possession of weapons. After a brief interrogation the four terrorists were shot on the orders of the Battalion Commander.'

Two days later, German troops searched a farm near Middelburg on the island of Walcheren, where four British escaped prisoners of war had been in hiding for more than four months. Three of the British escapees managed to evade capture, but the Germans then took four Belgians who were living on the farm, and a fifth from a neighbouring farm, drove them to the nearby sand dunes, forced them to dig their own graves in the sand, tied them to stakes, and shot them. One of those shot was a teenage boy, Yvon Colvenaer. When offered his life if he would talk, he replied that he did not want to be a traitor; before he was shot he cried out: 'Long live Belgium!'

A second difficulty was the shortage of weapons; in addition, if there were weapons, how and where should they be kept? Until the Allies were getting close, the most common way of receiving weapons was by parachute drop. There was a reluctance on the part of some senior Allied airmen to divert planes from bombing Germany to dangerous operations which, they believed, had little real hope of delivering arms into the hands of those who had asked for them. The requesters, on the other hand, were upset when their very specific requests went unanswered.

M. Eugene Colson was the leader of armed resistance in the port area of Antwerp. In an analysis of resistance operations after the war, he was told that resistance requests for arms rarely if ever specified the place where they should be dropped. He strongly disagreed with this statement, and gave one example. He had asked for a drop at 51 degrees 10 minutes 45 seconds North, 4 degrees 42 minutes 45 seconds East at a specified time. At the nominated time and place a group of resistance fighters were there, but no arms came. As a result, he said, they had to start fighting in Antwerp with whatever weapons they could steal.

A third matter that caused frustration for resistance groups was the use made of intelligence they had gathered and transmitted to the Allies, often at great personal risk. This frustration is well illustrated by an incident involving Prince Bernhard of the Netherlands and Field Marshal Montgomery in early September 1944. The Prince was then thirty-three, and although named Commander-in-Chief of the Netherlands Armed Forces had little military knowledge and no battle experience. But he was patriotic, intelligent, and eager to serve the country he had adopted by marrying the monarch-in-waiting, Princess Juliana.

He had arranged to meet Monty in Brussels, and had taken with him a bulging briefcase containing Dutch underground reports. The interview started badly when Monty told him he could not visit the headquarters of the Dutch Princess Irene Brigade, then stationed at Diest, 10 miles behind the rather fluid front line. The Prince did not respond to this order, but went on to review the situation in Holland as reflected in the underground reports. He spoke of the disorganisation of the Germans, and of the composition of the resistance groups; knowing the people who had sent the information, he had every faith in its truth. Monty responded, as the Prince later recalled: 'I don't think your resistance people can be of much use to us. Therefore I believe all this is quite unnecessary.'

The Prince was naturally shattered by this attitude, and try as he would he was unable to make any impression on Monty. He acknowledged that earlier instances of unreliable information from resistance groups might have prejudiced Monty against ever using information from such sources; but the Prince was adamant that he could trust his sources. An attitude such as Monty's was likely to make the Prince feel that the effort and sacrifice of the resistance fighters was a complete waste of time.

Lack of knowledge about resistance movements is emphatically brought out by the comments of Maj Gen Pip Roberts, speaking at a postwar symposium on the liberation of Belgium and Holland. He was describing the situation when his 11 Armoured Division arrived in Antwerp on 4 September 1944:

I knew absolutely nothing about any resistance organization in Belgium or in Antwerp or anywhere, and I can't help thinking that we might have done better if we'd been informed what the general resistance situation was. A Belgian liaison officer arrived with us two days after we'd got there, but that was a bit late really to be of any value. I don't know whether there were any Government arrangements, but I was surprised that we didn't get any information about what resistance there was, what it could do, and how we could make contact with its people.

Chapter Four

ALLIED FORCES: COMMAND STRUCTURES AND COMMANDERS

One of the main items to be included in 'factors affecting the situation' is 'own troops'. The physical movements of Allied forces immediately prior to 4 September were described in Chapter One. This gave a picture of the size, strength and disposition of Allied troops in the 21 Army Group area over the period 26 August to 4 September. In the analysis of the Great Mistake, however, we need to include factors that have a more fundamental impact, and which would be taken for granted in the normal preparation and issuing of orders.

These additional factors are: the chain of command of the Allied Expeditionary Force (AEF), and the changes in that command structure from D-Day on 6 June 1944 up to 4 September; the philosophies of command in the United States Army, and the different philosophies that applied in the British Army; the personalities of the principal Allied commanders, and their applications of the philosophies of command to their own formations; the relationships between the commanders, and the effect those relationships had on the decisions they took and the plans they made; and, as a less important but still significant factor, the locations of their Headquarters as the campaign progressed, and the communication systems between those Headquarters and other formations.

We also need to amplify the factor of resistance forces, which was mentioned in Chapter Three. How they were organised, and how their activities were integrated with the more formally constituted armed forces of Canada, the United States and Great Britain.

CHAIN OF COMMAND, ALLIED EXPEDITIONARY FORCE (AEF)

When the Allied Expeditionary Force landed in Normandy on 6 June 1944, it consisted of a vanguard that was sufficiently small to land on the targeted beaches without overcrowding and confusion, but which was at the same time large enough to be able to seize and hold a viable bridgehead. The original planners had devised a three-division assault, but when Eisenhower was made Supreme Commander of the AEF and Montgomery his land force commander, they immediately insisted that such a bridgehead would be too small, and the assault force needed to be five divisions.

So five divisions it became – two American, one Canadian and two British. Each of these divisions was part of a Corps, the other divisions of which would pass through the beachhead established by the spearhead divisions and push forward and sideways to enlarge the bridgehead. Then, in turn, the Corps formed part of an army – US, Canadian or British – and in due course the follow-up Corps would move into the bridgehead and out into the Normandy hinterland.

Formations became progressively active in the bridgehead, and the speed of that build-up was influenced by the resistance of the Germans, the aggressive vigour of the Allies, and the weather. The resistance of the Germans was robust, the aggression of the Allies muted, and the weather dealt a bad hand with the Channel storm of 19–22 June. The weather changed, and for three days the breakers roared ceaselessly on the beaches; no such June storm had been known in the Channel for forty years.

Nonetheless, the build-up continued steadily, and the command structure expanded to incorporate the formations as they arrived.

Naval and air forces contributed enormously to the strength and success of the invasion, and they came under Eisenhower as the Supreme Commander. The navy, which included American, Commonwealth and British units, was designated the Allied Naval Expeditionary Force (ANXF). The air contribution consisted of the Allied Expeditionary Air Force (AEAF), which provided tactical support to the land forces, and the strategic air forces (heavy bombers) of the Eighth US Air Force and RAF Bomber Command. There was no single command for all the air forces. The strategic bombers were ultimately responsible to the Combined Chiefs of Staff, but for the Normandy invasion they were placed under Eisenhower's operational control. The coordination of all air operations, strategic and tactical, was entrusted by Eisenhower to his Deputy Supreme Commander, ACM Sir Arthur Tedder.

The diagrams that show the command structures are focused on land forces, and merely indicate the naval and air forces exist. This in no way suggests that their contributions were not of the greatest importance.

COMMAND STRUCTURE ON D-DAY, 6 JUNE 1944

The listing below shows the forces commanded by Eisenhower on D-Day. As the troops in the bridgehead built up in strength, Divisions, Corps, Armies and Army Groups became active under the overall command of the Supreme Headquarters Allied Expeditionary Force (SHAEF). All of these formations existed elsewhere before they landed in Normandy, most of them in the USA or the UK. The formations and the dates they became active in Normandy are listed below in chronological order.

Date	Formation
14 June	XIX US Corps
15 June	VIII US Corps
24 June	VIII British Corps
24 June	XV US Corps
13 July	II Canadian Corps
16 July	XII British Corps
23 July	1st Canadian Army (I British Corps and II Canadian Corps)
1 August	3 US Army
1 August	12 US Army Group (1st and 3rd US Armies)
1 August	XII US Corps (to 3rd US Army)
6 August	XX US Corps (to 3rd US Army)

It was necessary to introduce the senior Headquarters (1st Canadian Army, 3rd US Army, 12 US Army Group) as the number of formations increased, and an existing senior Headquarters staff began to lose effective control. It had been agreed that in the battle for Normandy there should be one commander in charge of all land forces of whatever nationality. It had also been agreed that when the AEF had broken out of its Normandy bridgehead, and the composition of the land force had become primarily American, that the 3rd US Army and 12 US Army Group, would become active. Gen Bradley would take over command of 12 Army Group which would comprise 1st and 3rd US Armies. Montgomery would continue to command 21 Army Group, and be responsible for the coordination of 12 and 21 Army Groups. The command structure at this point, 1 August, is shown in Figure 2.

At a later date, to be determined by the way operations were proceeding, Eisenhower was to take over direct command of all land forces, acting through his Army Group Commanders. It was anticipated that he would have a third Army Group, the 6th, after its landing in the south of France and its progress northwards to join up with 12 Army Group. That landing took place successfully on 15 August, the two armies of 6 Army Group being the 1st French Army and the 7th US Army.

During August, Gen George Marshall, Chairman of the US Joint Chiefs of Staff, strongly encouraged Eisenhower to take over as land force commander. The troops on the ground were now predominantly American, and newspapers in America were complaining that they were still commanded by a British general. Eisenhower decided that the change should take place on 1 September; as it turned out, this was during the

Figure 1: Allied Command Structure, 6 June 1944

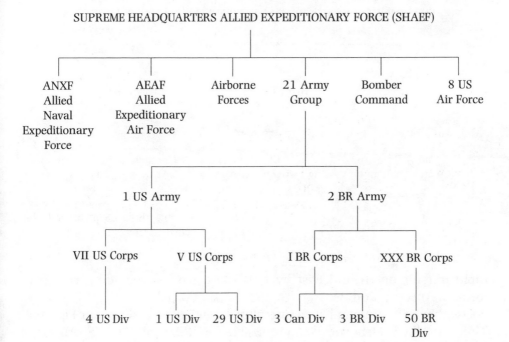

Figure 2: Allied Command Structure, 1 August 1944

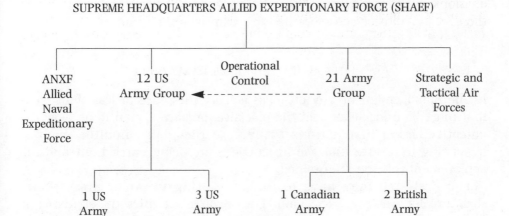

Figure 3: Allied Command Structure, 1 September 1944

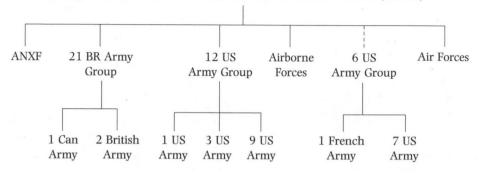

SUPREME HEADQUARTERS ALLIED EXPEDITIONARY FORCE (SHAEF)

| ANXF | 21 BR Army Group | 12 US Army Group | Airborne Forces | 6 US Army Group | Air Forces |

1 Can Army   2 British Army   1 US Army   3 US Army   9 US Army   1 French Army   7 US Army

6 US Army Group active 15 September 1944
9 US Army active 1 October

rapid pursuit north and east by the Allied armies, including the drive towards Antwerp and Brussels by XXX British Corps.

Eisenhower's command structure after 1 September is shown in Figure 3. The 1st Allied Airborne Army consisted of 82 and 101 US Airborne Divisions and 1 British Airborne Division. The 9th US Army was expected to become active at the beginning of October, thus further increasing the predominance of American troops. By now the British had almost exhausted their manpower reserves, and had had to break up one infantry division, the 59th, to provide reinforcements for the other infantry divisions. By contrast, new US divisions were still becoming available in the USA for transfer across to the European theatre of war.

PHILOSOPHIES OF COMMAND

In the management of any business activity there are at least four steps that must be undertaken: set the objective; prepare a plan to achieve the objective; issue instructions to execute the plan; monitor what is happening to ensure that the instructions are being carried out and the achievement is being maintained.

The first step may have to include setting up an organisational structure for executing the plan. For ongoing activities the structure is likely to remain the same, but for a one-off activity such as a project, a one-off structure may be needed. The final, 'monitor', step requires that there is good feedback to the manager from the people carrying out the instructions. In this way the manager is kept aware of how operations are going, and when difficulties are likely to arise or have arisen.

In the management of military operations the same steps apply. The objective, which in military terms may be called the mission, is transmitted from one level to the next level below, say from an Army Group commander to an Army commander. The Army commander makes his plan and then issues his instructions to his Corps commanders as *their* missions. The process is repeated all the way down the hierarchy.

In the planning stage, it can be useful for the senior commander to consult with his subordinates. The consultation should cover such matters as: resources required and available; suggestions for achieving the mission; and additional information about terrain, disposition of enemy forces, and anything else that might have a bearing on the achievement of the overall mission and the subordinate's part in it.

When the commander has gathered the information he needs, he alone makes the decision as to what has to be done. He listens to what his subordinates have to say, but the final responsibility lies with him as to what shall be done and who shall do it.

Command philosophies vary between countries, and within those countries between commanders. It is the national differences that are the most important, however, and these are especially significant when forces of different countries are fighting as allies, and even more significantly when a commander from one country is in command of forces from another. In the campaign in north-west Europe we need to look at the command philosophies of the Americans and the British, and in particular how those philosophies translated into action by Eisenhower and Montgomery respectively.

CONCENTRATION AND MOBILITY

The armies of European states such as Germany, France, Great Britain and Italy had been professional armies used as instruments of their countries' foreign policies, normally in a defensive or deterrent role. The American Army, on the other hand, had been nurtured as a constabulary force dealing with American Indians and Mexican rebels, and for most of its history had not been an instrument of the country's foreign policy. Some of the factors that shaped the American Army's combat and command philosophy in 1940 are described below.

A history of fighting small-scale campaigns across wide geographical areas had made mobility the essential characteristic of the American Army. The salient feature of the frontier experience of the Army that limited its fitness for orthodox European war was the frontier's elevation of mobility above the other military virtues, and particularly above the virtue of concentrated power.

The brief encounters with European-style battles interspersed among the Army's long history as a frontier constabulary – the Civil War of

1861–5, and the 1917–18 participation in the First World War – had convinced its leadership that victory in large-scale war depends on a strategy of direct confrontation with the enemy's main forces to destroy them. The method used by Gen Grant in the Civil War was to destroy the forces of the Confederacy through head-on assault with overwhelming strength. To the degree that US Gen Pershing had been able to affect the strategy of the First World War, he had applied Grant's methods.

The commitment to a strategy of head-on assault (which persisted in the US Army during the Second World War) in an army shaped for mobility undermined the possible uses of mobility itself. Mobility might have been exploited to achieve rapid offensive concentrations, as it was by Patton in his counterattack from the south in the battle of the Ardennes. More often, however, American generals preferred to advance on a broad front. The break-out from Normandy at the end of July 1944 was another exception, but when the front stabilised after the pursuit through France, the Americans reverted to assaults on a broad front, not only strategically but operationally, within a single army as well as across the theatre of war.

Russell Weigley comments in *Eisenhower's Lieutenants* on this internal contradiction in American military doctrine:

> The disjuncture between a power-drive strategy aimed at confronting the enemy's main forces to destroy them, and an army designed not to generate sustained combat power but for mobility, suggests a more basic flaw in the American army and its generalship. The American army lacked a clear conception of war. It had resolved neither upon a doctrine of winning the war by way of the direct application of superior power, in the manner of General Grant, nor upon a doctrine of winning by means of superior mobility and facility in manoeuvre, in the manner of the indirect approach of the British military thinker B.H. Liddell Hart. In the end the American army rumbled to victory because it had enough material resources to spare that it could exhaust the enemy's resources without adequately focussing its own power for a decisive, head-on battle of annihilation, or exploiting its mobility in a consistent strategy of indirect approach.

SINGLE COMMANDER

The British philosophy of command called for a separate commander for each aspect of the battle – on land, sea, and in the air. American doctrine, on the other hand, dictated a single commander for all forces in a theatre of war. In an unpublished manuscript Eisenhower records:

> Americans believed in one commander for one mission or theater, no matter what the composition of the forces. The British believed in a committee

comprising a Commander-in-Chief for each service (ground, navy, or air) represented in the region. They seemed to make the method work. I should here remark that so far as I know the two governments never exchanged philosophic views or arguments on the subject. I was at times the target of insistent advice, directly or indirectly given, but I was fully committed to the single commander theory.

PREPARATION AND MONITORING OF ORDERS

One of the major cultural differences between the USA and the UK is the strength of the class system. The class system in the UK has ensured that everybody knows his or her place in society, and changing that place has been a task of some difficulty. The upper classes have been accepted as innately superior, and instructions from them are obeyed without question. There have always been some who rebelled against this state of affairs, but for most the 'tugging the forelock' syndrome remained strong.

The origins of the USA have determined a very different culture in respect of class, and it could be summed up in the words of the Englishman William Morris: 'No man is good enough to be another man's master.' Once again, there are obviously many exceptions to this philosophy in the USA, particularly in relation to Afro-Americans and American Indians. But there is a much stronger feeling that in any superior–subordinate relationship it is the person that commands respect, not the position.

In the American services the effects of this were: first, more consultation in the preparation of plans; second, subordinates were issued with a mission – they were told what to do, not how to do it; and third, they were controlled on a loose rein, with a minimum of looking over the shoulder. Eisenhower gave his views on the American method of control: 'The American doctrine has always been to assign a Theatre Commander a mission, provide him with a definite amount of force and then to interfere as little as possible with the execution of his plans. In this way he is completely unfettered in achieving the general purpose of his superior.' Bradley carried this doctrine even further: 'You don't even tell a corps or division commander how to do his job when you have an army. You assign a mission and it's up to the fellow to carry it out. Of course, if you are in a position to have a look and talk it over with the guy you may make suggestions, but he doesn't have to take them.'

British command systems were much more rigid and centralised. Orders were more detailed and their execution more closely monitored. Eisenhower said he was shocked to find that the British Chiefs of Staff maintained the closest kind of contact with their commanders in the field, and insisted upon being constantly informed as to details. The insistence on frequent feedback extended all the way down the British command hierarchy. Montgomery used his small group of Liaison Officers as his eyes and ears to provide a very direct form of feedback. The Liaison Officers were all experienced and battle-hardened young officers who could quickly sum up the tactical position in a section of the battlefield. One of them, Johnny Henderson, records in his diary for 17 June 1944: 'Gen. Monty sent me off to see General Bucknall, commanding XXX Corps, to find out his plan for the part his Corps was going to play in the breakthrough. I then went on to visit 49 and 50 Divs. XXX Corps' plan was to strike south to Aunay with 49 Div and then do a wide right hook with the 7 Armoured directed on the same place.'

There was no problem in using the British methods of command and feedback within British formations, nor when American methods were used within American formations. It was when a commander from one nation commanded the formations and troops of another that problems could and did arise. Such problems were exacerbated by the attitudes and personalities of some, if not all, of the commanders.

THE COMMANDERS

Two of the commanders whose attitudes and actions had a bearing on the Great Mistake were the respective professional heads of their national armies, Gen George Marshall in Washington and Gen Sir Alan Brooke in London. The others were all in the field in north-west Europe. Of these, the two of greatest importance were Eisenhower and Montgomery, and they were supported by their subordinates Bradley, Dempsey, Patton, Crerar and Hodges. In this section we consider the salient features of all of these commanders except Hodges.

Gen George Marshall

Marshall fought in the US Army in the First World War, and afterwards acted as aide to Gen Pershing. He subsequently made a reputation as one of the most thoughtful, efficient and energetic officers in the US Army, and the possessor of a frightening degree of self-containment. He was appointed Chief of Staff in 1939, and held that post to the end of the Second World War. From the moment he was appointed, he maintained complete personal ascendancy over the officers of his own army, and won the confidence of everyone in the government in Washington from President Roosevelt down.

When the possibility of appointing Marshall to the Supreme Command of the Allied invasion of Europe was raised, Roosevelt is reputed to have told him that he (Roosevelt) would not sleep easy if Marshall was not in Washington. He was Roosevelt's chief strategic adviser, and acted as the chairman of the US Joint Chiefs of Staff, the body that had the overall responsibility for the employment of all of the armed services of the USA.

He strongly supported the concept of the invasion of Europe, and believed that the defeat of Germany should take precedence over the defeat of Japan. He was also attuned to the political implications of the conduct of the war, and the need to maintain popular support for the prosecution of the war and the employment of US armed forces. This meant that the Americans should receive appropriate recognition for their contribution, that recognition including allocation of senior command positions to Americans, and media publicity.

He viewed Churchill's motives with some suspicion, was a strong supporter of Eisenhower, and thought that Montgomery was an overrated general.

Gen Sir Alan Brooke

In 1941, Brooke succeeded Sir John Dill in the senior position in the British Army, Chief of the Imperial General Staff (CIGS). Brooke had had substantial fighting experience in the First World War and had held senior positions between the two wars, including command of the Mobile Division in 1937. During Dunkirk he handled II Corps with great skill in very difficult circumstances.

As CIGS he became Churchill's principal strategic adviser, a position which he held until the end of the war. His own description was that of turning Churchill's inspirations into military sense, and dissuading him from pursuing his numerous wild and ill-conceived ideas. He was a consummate professional soldier, and unfortunately viewed almost all Allied commanders as amateurs, with one or two British exceptions.

Gen Dwight Eisenhower

Eisenhower, known to millions as Ike, was born into a poor but religious and ambitious family in 1890. He secured a nomination to West Point, where he was an outstandingly successful sportsman and immensely popular, displaying the brilliant and invigorating charm that he retained throughout his life.

He saw no action during the First World War, but had a successful interwar career, largely through attracting the patronage first of MacArthur and then of Marshall, both of whom recognised his remarkable talents as a staff officer. Marshall appointed him to the war division in Washington at the outbreak of the Second World War, and then to head US forces in the European theatre of operations from London in June 1942.

In November 1942 he commanded the 'Torch' landings at Casablanca, Oran and Algiers, and the operations until the capitulation of the German forces in Tunisia. As Supreme Commander in North Africa, he directed the Allied landings in Sicily (June 1943) and Italy (September 1943). His success in commanding an Allied team in these operations resulted in him being appointed Supreme Commander of the Allied Expeditionary Force for the assault on north-west Europe.

Due to his lack of combat experience before 1942 and his extreme skill in welding together a team comprising soldiers from many different nations, containing people with prickly and egotistical personalities, he was viewed by some as a chairman of soldiers rather than as a soldier himself. But he had been a professional soldier of great experience all his adult life, and had every bit as much capability of understanding strategic problems as any other senior commander. His skills and personality enabled him to become a successful President of the United States, and it was in that role especially that he employed the 'hidden hand' method of influencing people. By this method he persuaded people to do what he wanted them to do – without them realising where the impetus for their actions came from.

Eisenhower's relationship with Montgomery was one of the major causes of the Great Mistake, and that relationship will be discussed in more detail in a later chapter.

Gen Miles Dempsey

Dempsey was one of the most self-effacing commanders in the British or any other army. He fought with distinction in the First World War, and then again distinguished himself as commander of 13 Infantry Brigade in the retreat to Dunkirk. In December 1942, he was appointed to command XIII Corps in North Africa. He took part in the early campaign in Italy, and became an expert on combined operations. Montgomery chose him to lead the British 2nd Army in Operation Overlord, the invasion of France.

As a Corps commander in North Africa and Italy, Dempsey was well aware of Monty's hands-on methods of commanding an army. In Normandy, Monty commanded 21 Army Group *and* was the Allied ground Commander-in-Chief. But as Monty's intelligence chief at 21 Army Group, Brigadier Edgar Williams, observed, Monty was acting more like an Army commander. He dictated what was to be done by the 2nd Army, and often bypassed Dempsey to give orders directly to Dempsey's Corps commanders. Monty would never have permitted his superior to bypass him.

Dempsey's freedom of action was thus limited, but he appeared to acquiesce in his role. This made him inconspicuous, which was not helped by his avoidance of publicity of any kind. And he has not written of his feelings about the situation in which Monty had placed him. For those who knew him well, however, he was a good commander. One of his senior staff officers, Selwyn Lloyd, later wrote of him: 'Wherever he went he inspired confidence and was a most welcome visitor to any harassed commander of a subordinate formation. Time and again he realised the tactical opportunity and saw it was exploited; I have never known anyone who got to the point quicker.' He was considered to be a 'thinker', and the most intellectual general then serving in the field.

Gen Omar Bradley

An obscure divisional commander in 1941, Bradley, who had graduated from West Point with Eisenhower in 1915, was selected by him to join the American forces in Tunisia in 1942 and was soon appointed by him to command II Corps. He handled II Corps with great success in the final battles for Tunisia under Patton, and added further to his reputation by his actions in Sicily.

Bradley was taken to Britain by Eisenhower to prepare for the Normandy landings, in which he had command of the 1st US Army. At the time of the invasion, his army was under the command of Monty as ground force Commander-in-Chief. After the arrival of Patton and his 3rd US Army on 1 August, Bradley was appointed commander of 12 US Army Group, with the 1st and 3rd US Armies as his subordinate formations.

Unremarkable in appearance and unflamboyant in manner, Bradley was known as 'The GI's General'. His reputation soared in Normandy, where he proved his worth as a very successful battlefield strategist. Towards the end of the war, Eisenhower said of him: 'Bradley's brains, selflessness, and outstanding ability as a battlefield commander are unexcelled anywhere in the world today.' It was of great benefit to Eisenhower and Bradley that they had trained together, had many shared experiences, and were friends. They could discuss matters constructively and harmoniously, taking pleasure in each other's company as they did so.

Gen George Patton

Patton served as a tank officer in the First World War, during which he fought in the Argonne in 1918 and was wounded. After the war he returned to the cavalry, but as the Second World War came closer he went back to tanks. In the 'Torch' landing in North Africa in 1942 he commanded II US Corps, and went on to command the 7th US Army in the invasion of Sicily. His command of the 7th Army was very successful, but was completely nullified by his angry slapping of a battle-fatigued soldier. He was removed from his command, and temporarily put into cold storage. Eisenhower appreciated his drive and vigour as a commander, and did not want to be permanently deprived of his services for future battles.

Patton was appointed Commander of 1 US Army Group, a fictitious formation that was part of the massive deception operation 'Fortitude'. The purpose of the operation was to persuade the Germans that the Normandy landings were only a feint, and that the real invasion would be launched across the Channel against the Pas de Calais. The fact that Patton was in charge made the plan much more convincing, and the

Germans retained a large part of their 15th Army in the Pas de Calais for at least two months after D-Day.

The deception plan involved the demotion of Patton, and his reassignment to command of the 3rd US Army. He was reassigned in late July, and arrived in Normandy in real command of the 3rd Army in time for the break-out from the bridgehead. It was marvellous timing for him to be able to demonstrate his exceptional skills as a leader of mobile forces.

In his *History of the Second World War*, Liddell Hart has this to say about Patton:

> Patton had a keener sense than anyone else on the Allied side of the key importance of persistent pace in pursuit. He was ready to exploit in any direction – indeed, on 23 August he had proposed that his army should drive north instead of east. There was much point in his subsequent comment: 'One does not plan and then try to make circumstances fit those plans. One tries to make plans to fit the circumstances. I think the difference between success and failure in high command depends upon its ability, or lack of ability, to do just that.'

Gen Harry Crerar

Crerar was a Canadian general who arrived in Britain in 1940 to organise the training of some 100,000 Canadian soldiers who were by that time stationed there. In 1943 he resigned to take up a command in I Canadian Corps, with whom he saw action in Sicily and Italy. He returned to Britain to form the 1st Canadian Army, which he commanded throughout the campaign in north-west Europe.

He was considered by Brooke and Montgomery to be less competent than was required to command an army in the field. Crerar was not given much opportunity to overcome this view. The Canadian Army was always on the left flank of the Allied advance, and after the break-out from the bridgehead had the tasks of clearing the Channel ports and the Scheldt estuary. The resources allocated by Montgomery for these tasks were invariably insufficient.

Gen Sir Bernard Montgomery

Montgomery served in the First World War with distinction, and as commander of 3 British Infantry Division in 1940 conducted an extremely skilful withdrawal to Dunkirk. He then held senior positions in the Army in Britain, until in 1942 a change in command in the Middle East took place. Gen Sir Harold Alexander was appointed Commander-in-Chief Middle East, with Montgomery appointed as his subordinate in command of the British 8th Army.

In all accounts of the campaign in North Africa from August 1942 Alexander is very seldom mentioned, and the glory of the victories is all accorded to Monty. The relationship between them appeared to be quite satisfactory, in that Alexander gave general directions – missions, in the American term – and did all he could to ensure that Monty had the resources he needed. Monty was in his element on a loose rein, and the campaign proceeded successfully.

In his position as Monty's superior, Alexander was able to observe him closely, and in his *Memoirs* written in 1961 he has some shrewd comments:

> I can't disguise that he was not an easy man to deal with; for example, administrative orders issued by my staff were sometimes objected to – in other words Monty wanted to have complete independence of command and to do what he liked. Eisenhower told me something about Monty that puts the thing in a nutshell. Ike's staff had issued some order that Monty ignored, or refused to carry out, and Ike said to him, 'But don't you ever obey orders?' Monty replied, 'If I don't like them I'll go as far as I can in disobedience and try to bluff my way through. But, of course, if I can't get what I want, then I must submit in the end.' In other words, he is one of those people who will always try it on.
>
> Monty is a first-class trainer and leader of troops on the battlefield, with a fine tactical sense. He knows how to win the loyalty of his men and has a great flair for raising morale. He rightly boasted that, after the battle of Alamein, he never suffered a defeat; and the truth is that he never intended to run the risk of a defeat; that is one reason why he was cautious and reluctant to take chances.
>
> Monty has a lot of personal charm – I always like him best when I am with him. Yet he is unwise, I think, to take all the credit for his great success as a commander entirely to himself; his prestige, which is very high, could be higher still if he had given a little to those who had made his victories possible, and there are those besides his own fighting men to whom he owes something. He was probably always rather a lone wolf, opinionated, ambitious, difficult and not a good mixer. As far as I know, he has few intimate friends; that is probably why, being still full of restless energy, he travels round the world on missions which are bound to have political implications – a role for which he is not suited at all.

RELATIONSHIPS BETWEEN COMMANDERS

Marshall–Eisenhower, Brooke–Montgomery
We have looked at some of the personal and professional features of eight of the senior commanders whose actions had some bearing on the Great Mistake. We have to consider next the relationships between these commanders, and to assess the effect these might have had on the operational decisions they made.

Marshall and Brooke were the professional heads of their national armies, to whom Eisenhower and Montgomery reported respectively. Marshall was greatly respected by Eisenhower, and Brooke by Montgomery; it was said, indeed, that 'Brookie' was the only person whose advice Monty was prepared to listen to or take.

Marshall had been Eisenhower's patron and, as we have seen, he had enormous presence and authority throughout the armed forces and the Government of the USA. Whatever he suggested – and he never suggested anything lightly – was almost always accepted by Eisenhower. One particular matter that concerned Marshall during August 1944 was the need to give due credit to the Americans for their contribution to the European campaign. That contribution was increasing all the time, whereas the British contribution was decreasing. Marshall was also aware of the political and public relations aspect of this imbalance, and knew that military operations are in part sustained by political will. It would be disastrous, as he saw it, if there was any substantial transfer of support from the European to the Pacific theatre of war.

In addition, Marshall had no high opinion of Montgomery as a general. He saw the battle of Alamein as an important victory, certainly, but against a smaller Axis force, its supply chain stretched to the limit, and its commander Rommel battling against illness. The follow-up from Alamein was slow, and Monty's performance in Sicily and Italy was not outstanding, and once again characterised by caution and slow movement.

Brooke was a strong supporter of Monty, advised him occasionally, stood by him in adversity or against hostile criticism, and rejoiced with him in success. This is entirely as a superior–subordinate relationship should work. The most pernicious thing in their relationship, however, was the way in which Brooke encouraged and shared Monty's contempt for Eisenhower, the man who was Monty's operational superior in Tunisia and in Europe. Several extracts from Brooke's diaries confirm this contempt:

24 January 1944: Had a long Chiefs of Staff meeting at which Eisenhower turned up to discuss his paper proposing increase of cross-Channel operations at expense of South France operations. I entirely agree with the proposal, but it is certainly not his idea and is one of Monty's. Eisenhower has got absolutely no strategical outlook. He makes up, however, by the way he works for good cooperation between Allies. [*Note*: In Eisenhower's account this proposal originated as much from him as it did from Monty.]

15 May 1944: Went straight from home to St Paul's School to attend Eisenhower's final run-over plans for cross-Channel operations. The main impression I gathered was that Eisenhower was no real director of thought, plans, energy, or direction. Just a coordinator, a good mixer, a champion of inter-Allied cooperation, and in those respects few can hold a candle to him.

But is that enough? Or can we not find all qualities of a commander in one man? [*Note*: This view of Eisenhower's military, as opposed to administrative, capacities ran directly counter to that held by nearly all American and many British officers at the time.]

27 July 1944: There is no doubt that Ike is all out to do all he can to maintain the best relations between British and Americans. But it is equally clear that Ike knows nothing about strategy. Bedell Smith, on the other hand, has brains, but no military education in its true sense. He is certainly one of the best American officers, but still falls far short when it comes to strategic outlook. With that Supreme Command set-up it is no wonder that Monty's real high ability is not always realised. Especially so when 'national' spectacles pervert the perspective of the strategic landscape.

In Brooke's diaries there never seems to be any record of a suggestion to Monty that he might support and help Ike in a tactful manner. Monty's contemptuous attitude and lack of tact might have made that impossible, but evidently Monty had been able in Normandy to give Bradley advice in a helpful and non-didactic tone.

Eisenhower–Montgomery

The central relationship affecting the Great Mistake is that between Eisenhower and Montgomery. As we have seen, they were two men of different backgrounds, experience and personality. But they were both professional soldiers, dedicated to the service of their countries, intelligent, courageous, and immensely hard-working.

Their backgrounds, up to the time that Eisenhower entered West Point and Montgomery entered Sandhurst, were different in status and in family environment. Eisenhower's father, although trained as an engineer at university, had, through no fault of his own, fallen on hard times. Home for Ike as a child was a one-storey shack in a run-down section of the small town of Abilene, Kansas. But he was part of a tightly knit and loving family in which his mother Ida was central.

Monty, on the other hand, was the son of a clergyman who became Bishop of Tasmania. His mother was also the central figure in his young life but, unlike Ida Eisenhower, Maud Montgomery was a strong-willed and domineering woman whose only method of bringing up a family was by rigid discipline. Monty had inherited many features of her temperament, and this made for an unhappy childhood; so much so that he emerged into adolescence convinced that life was a personal, perpetual struggle against unreasonable, unworthy authority.

The experiences of the two men as professional soldiers differed principally in the fact that Monty had fought on the field of battle. As a regimental officer in the First World War he was wounded and decorated, and after recovering from his wounds he served on the staff of a front-line division in France. He had thus seen war at first hand, but only as a platoon commander and only for a short while. Between 1919 and 1939 Monty served extensively overseas, and had staff and command experience of progressively larger formations. It was not until 1940, however, that he was once again in combat, and then as the general officer commanding 3 British Infantry Division. The days of combat were from 10 to 30 May, during which he commanded his division with great skill in its retreat to Dunkirk.

After returning to Britain, Monty retained command of 3 Division, and was then promoted to command V Corps and XII Corps successively. In August 1942 he was appointed to the command of the 8th British Army in North Africa, and from there on was in action across Libya, into Tunisia, and then into Sicily and Italy. One of the criticisms that Brooke and Monty had about Eisenhower was that he had had no combat experience in his military career until he was made Supreme Commander in North Africa. But an analysis of Monty's command experience in battle up to the time that he joined the 8th Army shows that it was not more than a few days altogether, some as a platoon commander and some as a divisional commander.

Eisenhower had no experience of command in action until the troops of Operation Torch landed in Tunisia on 8 November 1942. From then on he commanded the operations in Tunisia, Sicily and Italy until he was appointed Supreme Commander for the invasion of France. Thus, while Monty had certainly seen more action at a junior level than Ike, it was completely inappropriate to consider that Ike, as Supreme Commander of the Allied Expeditionary Force, had no experience or understanding of military command at a high level. It was mischievous of Brooke and Monty to keep maintaining that fiction.

One aspect of this difference in experience, however, was that Eisenhower *perceived* that Monty had more experience, had won what seemed to be a notable victory at Alamein, plus several more victories since, and was viewed by the British public as a hero, and the greatest British general since Wellington. Taking into account this reputation, deserved or not, and Eisenhower's overriding intention of maintaining Allied harmony, Eisenhower was prepared to bend somewhat in Montgomery's direction.

The personalities of the two men were very different. Eisenhower was gregarious, and was both liked and respected by almost everyone who came into contact with him. He could discuss matters with anyone whose opinion he needed and thought well of, but would, in the end, make his own decisions. However, he was accused by some of vagueness, including Stephen Ambrose in *The Supreme Commander*: 'Even two and a half decades later [when Ambrose was writing his book] it is impossible to read

Eisenhower's letters and telegrams to Monty without a feeling of frustration because of their vagueness. Any one taken by itself seems clear enough, but following a rejoinder by Monty the next message from Ike changed the priority again. The simple question as to whether Ike wanted Arnhem or Antwerp most cannot be answered.'

One difficulty in this situation was that Ike and Monty tried to communicate with each other via the written word. Ike had no trouble understanding Bradley and vice versa, in large part because they were together much of the time and could talk everything out. This in turn came about because they had trained together, served together, and enjoyed each other's company. But it is not at all certain that if Ike and Monty had spent more time together they would have reconciled their differences, or at least understood each other. The basis for mutual respect and understanding, so prominent in the Ike–Bradley relationship, was simply not present.

LOCATIONS OF HEADQUARTERS

The fundamental barriers to effective communication between Ike and Monty were made worse by the geographical locations of their Headquarters (Map 8), and the bad communication systems between them. Monty established his personal forward Headquarters (TAC HQ) in Normandy two days after D-Day on 8 June. The first location was at Creully near Bayeux. From there he moved a couple of miles west to Blay, which remained the site of TAC HQ during the battle of Normandy. After the break-out, TAC HQ moved south-east and then north-east towards the Seine. After 21 Army Group had crossed the Seine, TAC HQ followed closely in its path, and by 8 September was located at Everberg, half-way between Brussels and Louvain. From then until February 1945, TAC HQ was at various places close to the Belgium–Holland border.

Ike's Forward HQ was at Portsmouth during of the battle of Normandy. He made frequent visits to France to see his troops and their commanders, but it was not until 7 August that his Forward HQ moved to Tournières just outside Bayeux, close to where Monty had been six weeks earlier. The next move of Ike's Forward HQ was almost incomprehensible. When all the Allied armies in northern France were streaming north-east, Forward HQ moved *west*, and on 31 August settled into its new quarters in the little seaside village of Jullouville on the shores of the bay of Le Mont St Michel.

The distance between Ike and his forward troops was now something of the order of 400 miles, which meant long and tedious plane trips to visit his troops and their commanders. The communication systems were extremely erratic during the vital period of the first days of September, and by a great misfortune Ike damaged his knee when helping to move his plane after it had landed on the sandy beach near Jullouville. He was sufficiently

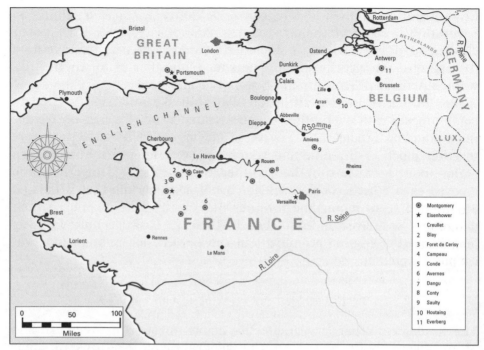

6. Locations of Forward HQs, June–September 1944.

incapacitated that he could not leave his HQ for a few days, and was thus out of touch with his troops at a critical moment in the campaign.

In his memoirs Monty describes how ineffective the communication system was: 'I sent Ike a message on 4 September, the day we captured Antwerp and Louvain. He received my message on 5 September. At 1945 hrs on that day he sent me his reply. The signal communications at his Forward HQ were so inadequate that his reply reached me in two parts. Paragraphs 3 and 4 came first and arrived at 0900 on 7 September; paragraphs 1 and 2 reached me at 1015 on 9 September.'

It is possible that had Ike been closer to the spearhead formations and had a better relationship with Monty, they might have jointly decided that the immediate course of action had to be the clearing of the Scheldt estuary. Ike had several times emphasised the importance of opening up the port of Antwerp, including access from the North Sea. Two points must be put forward.

First, would Monty have accepted Ike's instruction that priority should be given to the Scheldt estuary, or would he have argued with all the strength and bombast of which he was capable that a push to the Rhine was the only acceptable action?

Second, was it not the type of situation that a vigorous and thrusting commander would have seen as the moment to seize the opportunity while it lasted? That is, should Monty, as the commander on the spot, have seen the opportunity that existed while the Germans were unusually disorganised, and thrown his full weight at their positions surrounding Antwerp and up the Scheldt estuary?

We will look at these questions later when we analyse in more detail the reasons for the Great Mistake.

Bradley–Patton–Montgomery

The relationships between the senior generals were never easy. The easiest by far was that between Eisenhower and Bradley, and in his account of the campaign Bradley said: 'Quite frequently our long-range plans evolved during late night conversations at Ike's command post or mine. Sometimes we would sit until two or three in the morning, swapping opinions and discussing plans for successive phases of the campaign.' As we have seen, they had many shared experiences, and were good friends.

Bradley's relations with Patton in north-west Europe were initially not so easy. Patton was six years senior to Bradley, and he had commanded the 7th US Army in Sicily with Bradley as one of his Corps commanders. The soldier-slapping incident had resulted in Patton's suspension from duty, and when restored to active service he was now, as Commander 3rd US Army, serving under Bradley as Commander 12 US Army Group. Bradley says of this reversal in roles: 'I was apprehensive when George joined my command, because I was worried that I would have to spend too much of my time curbing his impetuosity. But I did know that George would keep his army on the move, and all we had to do was to point him in the right direction.'

Not long after Patton had joined 12 Army Group, Bradley repented of any reservations he might have had, and said: 'We formed as amiable and contented a team as existed in the senior command, and George trooped for 12 Army Group with unbounded loyalty and eagerness.'

The relationship between Monty and George Patton was never friendly, mainly because they had several personality similarities, the principal of which was vanity. Patton triumphed quite openly when he outdid Monty, as for example when the 3rd Army crossed the Rhine before 21 Army Group. He was not impressed by Monty's generalship, and at one point designated him 'a tired little fart'. Monty's views on Patton's qualities were not clearly expressed, but he often complained to Eisenhower about what he saw as an unfair distribution of supplies between himself and Patton – and Patton, not unsurprisingly, thought the same.

The qualities of the two generals were in fact complementary. Monty was rock-solid in defence, and deliberate and efficient in a planned set-piece attack. Patton was brilliant in fast-moving operations, and had a cavalryman's eye for seizing the moment; he could spot the opportunity *and* take the action to make the most of it. In addition, his military intuition was acute.

In November 1944 Patton's 3rd Army had as its northern neighbour VIII Corps of the 1st US Army. VIII Corps was strung out over a front some 90 miles long. Whenever Patton halted he ordered vigorous local attacks to make the enemy think that something larger was coming, and to detect any enemy build-up for an offensive. He was concerned that Gen Middleton in command of VIII Corps was not taking such action, and commented: '1 Army is making a terrible mistake in leaving VIII Corps static, as it is highly probable that the Germans are building up east of them.' He was sufficiently worried that on 12 December he had his staff carry out a study as to what the 3rd Army would do in the event of a German breakthrough on the VIII Corps front.

Subsequent contingent plans made by the staff of the 3rd Army included suspending the Army's drive east, and instead turning north with an initial force of three divisions. The Germans attacked VIII Corps on 16 December, and on 19 December Eisenhower called a meeting of his senior commanders to deal with the situation. They agreed that the shoulders of the German breakthrough should be held, and the gap closed by pincers moving from north and south. Eisenhower turned to Patton and asked him when he could move and with what force. To the surprise and disbelief of the other commanders Patton replied: 'In three days with three divisions.' This he did, and in a few days had relieved the Americans holding out in Bastogne.

Patton was a much more accomplished general than his 'blood and guts' reputation has suggested. He was not directly involved in the events surrounding the Great Mistake, but his personality and achievements were a constant spur, urging Monty to similar brilliant advances. Monty had indeed moved with great dash from the Seine to Antwerp and Brussels. Could he do more?

Montgomery–Crerar

The Canadian general Harry Crerar was very directly involved in the Great Mistake, and his relationship with Monty was not good. We have seen that Crerar resigned his appointment in England in 1943 to gain battle experience with the Canadian troops in the Mediterranean. Monty conducted a study week for senior commanders in Tripoli, attended by Crerar as Commander of I Canadian Corps. Monty's comment was: 'I don't think he has any idea of how to command a corps in battle.'

After being appointed to command 21 Army Group in Overlord, Monty gave his views on who should command the British 2nd Army and the 1st Canadian Army. In his evaluation of candidates he wrote: 'The more I think of Harry Crerar the more I am convinced he is quite unfit to command an army in the field at present. He has much to learn, and he will have many shocks before he has learnt it properly. He has already started to have rows with Canadian generals under me; he wants a lot of teaching.'

On 24 June 1944 Monty wrote from Normandy to his successor in command of the 8th Army, Oliver Leese: 'I have grave fears that Harry Crerar will not be too good; however, I am keeping him out of it as long as possible.' Monty managed to postpone the activation of the 1st Canadian Army (with Crerar in charge) until 23 July. Crerar's two subordinate formations were II Canadian Corps under Guy Simonds and I British Corps under John Crocker. On the day his army became operational, Crerar had a stand-up row with Crocker, whom he attempted to sack immediately. Monty wrote to Brooke on 26 July: 'Crerar had a row with Crocker the first day and asked me to remove Crocker. I have spent two days restoring peace, investigating the quarrel and so on. As always there are faults on both sides, but the basic cause was Harry. I fear he thinks he is a great soldier, and he was determined to show it as soon as he took over command at 1200 hrs on 23 July. He made his first mistake at 1205 hrs, and his second after lunch.'

The advance from the Seine in the last days of August gave rise to arguments between Crerar and Monty. On 2 September Monty signalled Crerar expressing dissatisfaction with Canadian efforts, on the grounds that Canadian divisions had halted for maintenance rather than kept pressing on. Crerar responded angrily.

This exchange preceded and may well have provoked an angry row between Crerar and Monty, ostensibly over Crerar's absence from Monty's conference on the next day. Crerar had gone to Dieppe to take part in ceremonies there and missed the meeting. Arriving after it was over, Crerar was subjected to a blistering attack which included Monty's assertion that 'our ways must part'. Crerar stood his ground and replied that 'he could not accept this attitude and judgement, and would never consent to being pushed about by anyone'. Monty quickly calmed down when Crerar spoke of dealing with the issue through official channels. Monty would have been happy to replace Crerar, whom he had never wanted as one of his Army commanders, but he was not prepared to risk a political row.

Chapter Five

THE PAINTED VEIL

'This painted veil that those who live call life.'

Percy Byshe Shelley

In every aspect of life we may be able to see as far as the veil, and sometimes we attempt to see beyond it. There are always limits to the amount and accuracy of what we perceive, and many distortions in how we interpret what we see. All too often we see only what we want to see, and bend our imperfect observations to meet our desires; we work on the basis of perceptions.

In military operations the commanders need accurate, immediate, objective and comprehensive information so that they can make the best decisions to further the attainment of their missions. This information is designated 'intelligence', and much effort is expended to ensure that it is as correct as possible. In the first four chapters we described the 'facts' applicable to the Great Mistake under the headings: enemy (the Germans), own troops (the Allied forces), and three of the other factors affecting the situation – topography, weather and civilians.

In the next three chapters we will see how the situation during the days around 4 September was *perceived* by the Allied commanders and their troops. It was on these perceptions, or this intelligence, that the Allied commanders made their decisions and their troops reacted.

The gathering, analysis and presentation of military information is the role of Intelligence services and personnel. In the broadest terms, intelligence information can be divided into sigint (information obtained from signals) and humint (information obtained from people).

SIGINT

Sigint is information obtained from the interception of messages sent by radio, telephone line or other communication media; these messages are almost always coded. It is only when in direct contact with the enemy that the sender can (and should) send messages *en clair*.

The coding systems range from the simple substitution cipher of 'Slidex' to the very complex system of Enigma. The intelligence that came from the Enigma code-breakers at Bletchley Park was given the codename Ultra, and was termed 'high grade' sigint. It was so high grade that its existence and effect were not made public until 1974, with the publication of *The Ultra Secret* by F.W. Winterbotham. Distribution of Ultra intelligence was restricted to the highest levels of government and the armed forces. In relation to the situation on 4 September 1944, Ultra would have been known to Eisenhower, Bradley, Montgomery, Patton, Crerar and Dempsey. Each commander authorised to receive Ultra intercepts had an 'Ultra-reading' officer at his Headquarters, the sole channel through which those intercepts were relayed to the commander.

Sir Harry Hinsley, the official historian of British Intelligence during the Second World War, wrote about the effect of Ultra in the months leading up to D-Day:

> As Ultra accumulated, it administered some unpleasant shocks. In particular, it revealed in the second half of May that the Germans were sending reinforcements to Normandy and the Cherbourg peninsula. But this evidence arrived in time to enable the Allies to modify the plans for the landings on and behind the Utah beach; and it is a singular fact that before the expedition sailed the Allied estimate of the number, identification, and location of the enemy's divisions in the west, fifty-eight in all, was accurate in all but two items that were to be of operational importance.

Low-grade sigint included information from the interception of signals between field units, Allied as well as German, and the location of enemy forces using direction-finding equipment. Coding of these signals normally used simple methods that could be decoded by field intelligence staff. The British system was called the 'Y' service, and is defined by Hinsley as follows: 'The interception, analysis, and decryption of wireless traffic in low and medium codes and ciphers. The term "low-grade" refers to the degree of security provided by a code or cipher, and does not imply that the traffic in it was either unimportant or easy to break and interpret.'

HUMINT

Humint (human intelligence) is obtained by direct personal actions, including at least: personal observation, interrogation or discussion, and analysis and interpretation of written, graphic and recorded information.

Observation
A particularly good example of personal observation is where the commander himself observes what is happening, or looks at the area where he intends to operate. Wellington would often get on his horse and

ride to see 'what was on the other side of the hill'. Eisenhower (*Crusade in Europe*), when the battle in Normandy was being fought, says: 'Our vision was so limited that I called upon the air forces to take me in a fighter plane along the battle front to gain a clear impression of what we were up against.' All troops in contact with the enemy will also make continuous observations, either from the ground or from the air.

Monty copied one of the methods of Wellington, the use of young battle-experienced Liaison Officers to observe and bring back information from the front line; their role was discussed in Chapter Four. Although it is extremely difficult to work out exactly what is happening on any battlefield, the Liaison Officers provided immediate and objective, even if incomplete, intelligence on the progress of operations. That intelligence was based on direct observation of the action and on face-to-face discussion with commanders at all levels.

Observations from behind enemy lines can provide extremely valuable information. The observers may be spies or special agents, resistance groups or local civilians. Two problems with this type of information are its reliability (how trustworthy is the source?) and its transmission. If a source of information is discovered by the enemy it can be used to transmit disinformation; operations using this may result in disaster, and a commander who has suffered in this way is likely to be very wary of information the provenance of which is not completely known and trusted.

Interview/interrogation
Questioning of or discussions with individuals or groups of people is another source. The interrogation of prisoners is a skilled task, normally performed by intelligence staff who are fluent in the language of the prisoner. The value of the interrogation will depend on what the prisoner knows; for example, a tank driver is unlikely to know much about the composition of the force of which he forms a part. It will also depend on his willingness to talk, and on whether he wants to be helpful or to mislead.

The same factors must be taken into account when obtaining information from civilians or resistance groups. Do they understand what they have seen, and what impact do they want to make on the questioner?

Analysis of documents, etc.
Analysis of documents and air photographs can once again provide useful information, with some caveats; the documents may be deliberately false (going map at Alam Halfa), or air photos may be misinterpreted (9 and 10 SS Panzer Divisions at Arnhem). Much of the time, however, the intelligence provided to the field forces is valuable. An example of such intelligence is given in Stephen Ambrose's *Pegasus Bridge*.

British Intelligence was collecting and analysing information on the bridges over the River Orne and the adjacent canal; these two bridges were the objectives of a paratroop force led by Maj John Howard. Thanks to the French Resistance and photo reconnaissance by the RAF, Intelligence was able to provide a wealth of information to Howard. He knew which of the inhabitants of the local village of Benouville were collaborators, and which were in the Resistance. His team made a detailed three-dimensional image of the surrounding countryside, so that the attacking force became very familiar with the terrain with its possible hazards and its areas for concealment. Howard was able not only to see the German defences, but also he was kept up to date on any changes to those defences.

Analysis of documents, coupled with information from or observations by individuals, can give guidance on the topography of the proposed operational area. The same procedure may also help to predict the weather and its effect over the operational time-frame, alerting commanders to factors that may be helpful or obstructive.

ESTIMATES OF WHEN THE WAR WOULD END

Although it seems to be tempting fate, it is important for the government of a country at war to make ongoing estimates of the probable date that war will end. It is a matter for delicate judgement. The two items of primary concern are the provision of war material, and the provision and training of manpower for the services and for industry. As a war appears to be coming to an end, there is also the need to switch from wartime to peacetime production. Output from the armament and munitions factories declines, and the materials, machines and manpower they absorbed are diverted to produce goods for a civilian population.

The balance that has to be achieved is between producing large quantities of military hardware that has to be scrapped – as happened with the sudden end of the First World War in 1918 – and the need to keep the forces up to fighting strength in military equipment and trained men. The estimates of the date when the Second World War was going to end reflected the views of the commanders in the field and the politicians at home; those estimates act as a barometer of optimism, and unwarranted optimism was a contributor to the Great Mistake.

In *Grand Strategy*, Ehrman writes: 'All estimates produced in the Spring and early Summer of 1944 for the forces which would be needed one year after the defeat of Germany were based on the assumption that the war in Europe would be over by the end of 1944.'

As the fortunes of war fluctuated, in the sense that operations were more or less successful than had been expected, so did optimism about the date for the end of the war. The table below shows the date the estimate was made, the estimator, and the estimate; all estimates were made in 1944.

Date Made	Estimator	Estimate
5 June	JIC	end of 1944
12 June	CIC	end of 1944
15 June	Churchill	first half of 1945
12 July	JIC	end of 1944
14 August	War Cabinet	30 June 1945
4 September	War Cabinet	31 December 1944
6 September	DMO	Berlin by 28 September, then guerrilla fighting
8 September	Churchill	some time into 1945

CIC: Combined Intelligence Committee (Anglo–US)

JIC: Joint Intelligence Sub-committee of the UK Chiefs of Staff

DMO: Director of Military Operations, UK War Office; this position was held for most of the war by Maj Gen Sir John Kennedy.

As the German resistance hardened from mid-September on, optimism died, and the general opinion settled on the middle of 1945 as the best estimate. It can be seen that with the benefit of hindsight Churchill gave the most realistic dates. He gave these dates, as he explained, on the feeling that the Germans had always been resilient, and there was no reason to expect them to change, especially when their enemies were attacking the Fatherland. We will see later how optimism and pessimism at the top were reflected in the views of subordinate commanders and their troops.

MAPS, TROOPS FOR THE USE OF

Before considering the perceptions of enemy strength and intentions contained in the intelligence summaries, war diaries, and unit and personal histories, we should take a look at the practical matter of maps. Map-reading is a very important element of military operations, and good map-reading can often result in a large reduction in casualties and a much better use of time. Map-reading obviously depends on having intelligible maps at an appropriate scale of the area you are moving or fighting in. One of the functions of the Intelligence Corps was to obtain sufficient maps of the required scale and geographical coverage, and then distribute them to relevant formations.

In Normandy the maps were excellent, and because of the slow rate of advance for the first months in the bridgehead the right maps were always available. They were also enhanced by defence overprints, which gave up-to-date information about enemy strengths and dispositions – units, gun positions, trenches, tank obstacles, etc. The defence overprints for Le Havre made that city look almost unassailable, although it was in fact captured in three days' fighting from 10 to 12 September.

However, after the Allies crossed the Seine at the end of August they advanced so fast that it became impossible, at least for a few days, to keep the forward units supplied with the maps they needed. So they had to make do as best they could; some of their improvisations left a lot to be desired.

11 Armoured Division was the spearhead of the advance on Antwerp. Divisional HQ and the constituent units of the division had many comments to make about the map problem: 'The confusion [in the advance] was made worse by the fact that the maps ran out somewhere north of Beauvais, and a school atlas was a valuable capture.'

After leaving Amiens, the 23rd Hussars crossed the River Authie, and then moved on: 'On we went, the pace growing faster as we realised that nothing was going to show fight. We rolled off our one-inch maps and had to use quarter-inch. Frantic officers from Brigade Headquarters rushed up the column, presenting us with little pieces of paper showing us the continuation of our route.'

It was the same for the infantry units: 'By now they [4th King's Shropshire Light Infantry, one of the motorised infantry battalions of 11 Armoured] were working on the 1/250,000 map, on which Antwerp was about the size of a thumb-nail, the pursuit having run off the edge of the last of the larger scale maps so far issued.'

The *History of 21 Army Group* records the same difficulty: '11 Armoured in Antwerp and the Guards Armoured in Brussels had to work off 1/250,000 maps to guide them through their respective cities.'

It is easy for those who know a city to be immensely surprised when a stranger has great difficulty in navigating his way through to a particular spot. The author was lucky to avoid this sort of problem in Liège on 26 December 1944, when his regiment was moving south to back up the Americans in the Ardennes. His troop of Churchill tanks was delayed in starting from the previous night's stopping place, and left Bilzen two hours after the rest of the squadron. On arriving at the outskirts of Liège, the route down through the city and across the River Meuse was meticulously signed by the Military Police. On the far side of the bridge, he met the Squadron Reconnaissance Officer, John Brecknell.

'Good to see you, Peter, rest of the squadron behind you?'

'Good God, no; they left two hours before us. Aren't they here?'

What had happened, of course, was that the rest of the squadron had reached Liège before the Military Police had put up their signs, and had to thrash their way through an unknown and quite complicated city – also, unfortunately, shrouded in thick fog – to reach an unspecified destination as best they could.

The situation in Antwerp on 4 September was similar, the major difference being that there were a lot of hostile Germans still in the city, and none in Liège.

The commander of 11 Armoured, Pip Roberts, says of this episode:

I made mistakes at Antwerp because I was not briefed that the Albert Canal was one of the most formidable obstacles in Europe. We only had small-scale maps, and I saw the canal as only a thin blue line on my map. The maps were so poor that it seemed that the canal went through the centre of the city. In fact it was at the city's northern edge, and beyond the canal was the suburb of Merxem. In hindsight it was Merxem that we needed to capture, together with the bridges leading to it.

I heard the population of Antwerp were mobbing my troops, and tempting the officers into the best hotels. I decided not to go into the city because with my divisional flag on my tank I would have been drowned in champagne. During the celebrations in the city there was a considerable battle on the Albert Canal inside Antwerp, and we failed to capture the northern suburbs over the canal.

Unfortunately, I did not appreciate the significance of the fighting on the Albert Canal, and the Germans did not blow the crucial bridge for another twelve hours. If briefed before, I would have crossed the Canal with tanks to the east of Antwerp and closed the Germans' route into Beveland and Walcheren.

Availability of informative maps may appear a trivial matter. On 4 September in Antwerp, however, their unavailability undoubtedly contributed to the Great Mistake. The Intelligence services cannot really be blamed for this deficiency, because the speed of the advance was so much greater than had ever been thought possible. How could this problem have been overcome?

The disappointing thing is that this problem *had* been anticipated, and action had been taken to solve it. A seminar was held in Belgium in 1984 to review and discuss the events of September 1944. It was attended by representatives of the Belgian Government, ex-members of the resistance movements, military historians, and a number of Allied servicemen who had taken part in the operations in Belgium at that time. One of these was Gen Roberts, who attended as a speaker and as a participant. The following exchange took place between M. Fayat, who had been chief assistant to the Belgian Minister of the Interior in exile in London, and Gen Roberts:

M. Fayat: I wanted to make a few remarks about the sudden advance of the British troops and what the General said: 'We didn't know what the Kruisschans was.' [*Note*: the Kruisschans Lock was the vital mechanism by which the level of water in all the Antwerp docks was controlled. It is shown on Map 13 in Chapter 10.]

Now, all this is due to the unexpected swiftness of the advance. It doesn't mean that preparations hadn't been made to avoid such difficulties. My Minister and I in London had cooperated for months with the British Intelligence Service under Cecil de Saumarez to compile a fantastic basic handbook about Belgium, complete with detailed maps and plans.

The idea was that the handbook and maps should be available to the units that were leading the liberation of our country. As soon as we knew which those units were, we were to arrange for Belgian Liaison Officers to accompany them and provide them with a copy of the handbook. It explained in detail the function and importance of the Kruisschans, and all other details of the port, the canals, the bridges, and everything that might be important in a military operation to capture the city and open up the port.

So the information had been prepared for you, there was no lack of preparation. It was simply that your advance went too quickly.

General Roberts: I quite appreciate that. I'm not sure that our side was so very helpful about it, because they knew exactly how we were going, and I think they could have warned you of the rather earlier arrival than you expected.

M. Fayat: You should have had these Liaison Officers with you the moment you started. You said you had no maps, you said you didn't know. But that was in the basic handbook; and you should have had Liaison Officers.

General Roberts: Yes, well, the map situation is to some extent similar. Why weren't the maps available?

M. Fayat: I don't know. They certainly should have been. It was quite clear you were going in that direction. It was not your fault. I'm sure it was our fault. I wouldn't blame anybody. I just know that there was good cooperation, that the British Intelligence Service worked full steam ahead to have that basic handbook ready. It was ready. It could have been given to Civil Affairs Officers, to Liaison Officers. But which were the units, where to send them? You were fortunate to have done as well as you did with so little information.

Thus the problem had been solved, but the solution had not been communicated to those who could have used it to very great advantage.

Chapter Six

PERCEPTION:
POLITICIANS AND COMMANDERS

The leaders of a nation at war define the missions they intend to undertake. These are normally: the defeat of their enemy's armed forces; the elimination of the enemy nation's will or ability to fight; the occupation of geographical objectives; or some combination of the three. In making plans to achieve these missions, the leaders must take into account the strength and morale of their own forces, and the strength and morale of the enemy forces. The strength of one's own forces is easy enough to compute, but morale and willingness to fight are more difficult to assess. However, both of these tasks are easier than the assessment of the enemy's strength and morale, and it is here that Intelligence fulfils its vital role.

Intelligence data can only be a best estimate, based on the analysis and compilation of information from the sigint and humint sources we have identified. The decisions that resulted in the Great Mistake were based on the perceptions of the leaders in the days around 4 September. We need to say who the leaders were, and what their perceptions were at that time. Later recollections have the benefit of hindsight, and it is the contemporary perceptions that reflect the mindset of the leaders making the decisions or of the people carrying them out.

The levels of command in the two nations most closely concerned with the events at Antwerp on 4 September start with the countries' leaders, Roosevelt and Churchill. This should in no way downplay the importance of Canadian, Polish, Belgian and Dutch forces in the operations, but their leaders did not have the same weight or participation in international councils.

The next level of command relating to the conduct of the war against the Axis powers was the Allied Supreme Command. This comprised the US Joint Chiefs of Staff and the British Chiefs of Staff Committee. Their intelligence bodies, mentioned in Chapter Five, were:

The Combined Intelligence Committee (Anglo–US): CIC

The Joint Intelligence Sub-committee of the UK Chiefs of Staff: JIC

Figure 4: Allied Supreme Command

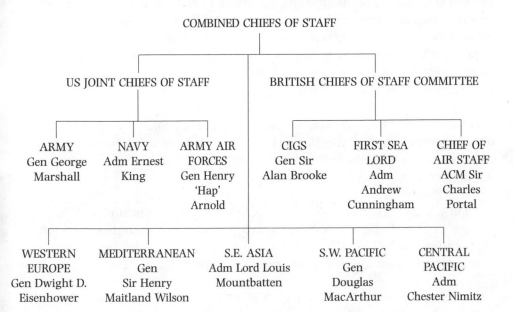

Figure 4 shows western Europe (the Allied Expeditionary Force under its HQ SHAEF) as one of the subordinate bodies reporting to the Allied Supreme Command. Eisenhower and his staff had their intelligence apparatus, which was used for their own purposes and for contributing information to the JIC and the CIC. Then, working down the chain of command and focusing progressively more closely on Antwerp and 4 September, we have: 21 Army Group, Montgomery; British 2nd Army, Dempsey; 1st Canadian Army, Crerar; XXX Corps, Horrocks; XII Corps, Ritchie; and 11 Armoured Division, Roberts.

We now review a sample of the perceptions of these levels of command in the early days of September regarding the relative strength of the Allies and the Germans, concentrating on apparent German strength and morale.

ALLIED SUPREME COMMAND: SELECTED INTELLIGENCE
SUMMARIES, JUNE–SEPTEMBER

CIC, 12 June (CAB 88/59): It is apparent that Germany cannot long maintain her land and air forces in the face of further heavy attrition. If the cross-Channel attack succeeds, and the Russians pierce the Niemen–Bug–Carpathians–Danube delta line, it is quite possible that high German military authorities will seek to end the conflict before the then inevitable collapse of military resistance occurs.

JIC, 14 July (CAB 121/413) [*Note*: by now the Germans had failed to prevent the Russian breakthrough, the Allies were established in Normandy, and the Germans were withdrawing in Italy]: All the elements for a collapse already exist; when it comes it is likely to develop with startling rapidity. It is impossible to predict how long this unprecedented state of affairs can last, since ordinary standards cannot be applied. It is difficult, however, to see how Germany can prolong the struggle beyond December.

2 August: Gen Brooke, CIGS, to C-in-C Mediterranean: It becomes more obvious every day that the Boche is beat on all fronts. It is only a matter now of how many more months he can last. I don't see him lasting another winter.

3 August: Quote from The Times*:* Mr Churchill, in a long and heartening review in the House of Commons today of the war situation, declared that, although he greatly feared to raise false hopes, he no longer felt bound to deny that victory would perhaps come soon.

CIC, 5 September (CAB 121/413): The further catastrophic disasters the German Army has suffered on every front convince us that the process of final military defeat leading to the cessation of organised resistance has begun. The task of forecasting is complicated by the fact that Hitler is increasingly out of touch with all reality. His only hope of prolonging the war is to withdraw his troops from outlying areas. Even if he has so changed his strategy, however, he has left it too late.

6 September: Sir John Kennedy, Director of Military Operations, UK War Office: If we go at the same pace as of late, we should be in Berlin by the 28 September. The Germans have only ten to twenty divisions to man their frontier, as against a requirement of seventy or eighty. We should therefore go into Germany quickly. Then we may be faced with guerrilla fights.

SHAEF INTELLIGENCE SUMMARIES

19 August (WO 219/1922): Two things are certain. The enemy has lost the war and the defeat of 7 Army and Panzer Gruppe West [5 Panzer Army] will hasten the end. One thing is uncertain. Would it have been more profitable for the Allies if Hitler's bomb [used on 20 July by German generals in an attempt to kill Hitler] had been a better and bigger one? Or ought the Allies to feel grateful that he has lived to continue his strategic blunders?

26 August (WO 219/1922): Two and a half months of bitter fighting, culminating for the Germans in a blood-bath big enough for their extravagant tastes, have brought the end of the war in Europe in sight, almost within reach. The strength of the German Armies in the West has been shattered, Paris belongs to France again, and the Allied armies are streaming towards the frontiers of the Reich.

An operational order issued by SHAEF shortly afterwards began: Enemy resistance on the entire front shows signs of collapse. The bulk of the remaining enemy forces, estimated as the equivalent of two weak panzer and nine infantry divisions, are north-west of the Ardennes but they are disorganised, in full retreat, and unlikely to offer any appreciable resistance if given no respite. South of the Ardennes the enemy forces are estimated as the equivalent of two panzer grenadier and four poor infantry divisions. A heterogeneous force withdrawing from south-west France may number some one hundred thousand men, but its fighting value is estimated as the equivalent of about one division. The equivalent of one-half panzer and two infantry divisions are being driven northwards up the Rhone valley. The only way the enemy can prevent our advance into Germany will be by reinforcing his retreating forces by divisions from Germany and other fronts, and manning the more important sectors of the Siegfried Line with these forces. It is doubtful whether he can do this in time and in sufficient strength.

2 September (WO 219/1923): The enemy has no coherent order of battle and no strategy outside the West Wall. His armies have been reduced to a number of fugitive battle groups, disorganised and demoralised, short of equipment and arms. Organised resistance under the control of the German High Command is unlikely to continue beyond 1 December 1944, and it may end even sooner.

4 September: Eisenhower, in a directive to his Army Group Commanders: Enemy resistance on the entire front is showing signs of collapse.

9 September: Maj Gen K.W.D. Strong, Chief Intelligence Officer, SHAEF: Hitler has very few reserves to call on from any theatre. The whole wreck of the Balkans and Finland may yield up perhaps half a dozen divisions. These will go no way to meet the crying need for more divisions to man the West Wall; moreover, a line in Transylvania will need to be manned. Where, then, are more divisions to be found? Not in Norway, withdrawal would take too long. Denmark might supply one division, and a dozen or more may yet be formed in Germany, given time, from training units, remnants and so forth. The Italian and Russian fronts risk collapse if anything more is withdrawn from them. In short, OB West may expect not more than a dozen divisions within the next two months to come from outside to the rescue.

OB West will soon have the true equivalent of about fifteen divisions, including four panzer divisions, for the defence of the West Wall. A further five or six divisions may straggle up in the course of the month, making a total of about twenty. The West Wall cannot be held with this amount, even when supplemented by many oddments and large amounts of flak.

Two observations should be made about these intelligence summaries at the highest level. First, the German forces were very disorganised, certainly; but as Chapter Two has shown, they still had a coherent command structure, and the troops themselves automatically rallied and regrouped under the encouragement and coercion of their leaders at all levels. The Allied high-level intelligence summaries have become very optimistic, and the writers of the summaries appear to have lost sight of the immensely resilient character of the Wehrmacht, as evidenced in all the campaigns it had fought since late 1942.

Second, Winston Churchill, in spite of what he said in the House of Commons on 3 August, was by no means convinced that a German collapse was imminent. On 8 September he argued that: 'It is at least as likely that Hitler will be fighting on 1 January 1945 as it is that he will collapse before then. If he does collapse before then the reasons will be political rather than military.'

21 ARMY GROUP

At Montgomery's Headquarters the staff were very optimistic:

> At the end of August the situation was developing even beyond our expectations. The Allies were up to the Seine from Paris to the sea, while to the south 12 US Army Group was driving forward on a broad front. The American and French forces which had landed on the Riviera coast were achieving spectacular success. The enemy front was broken almost everywhere; his chain of command had gone and his forces fought as a series of independent units. Some were half-hearted, others offered stiff resistance. But whatever their performance they could do no more than delay us; it was always possible to by-pass opposition.

This optimism was high on 11 September in some sections of 21 Army Group. In *Montgomery in Europe* Richard Lamb says:

> There was by now considerable euphoria in the Allied camp. On 11 September the Chief Planning Officer at Army Group, Brigadier Charles Richardson, sent this signal to Monty at his Tactical HQ: 'If Germany should

not surrender when Second Army reaches Osnabruck I suggest Arnhem is the most suitable location for our HQ after Brussels provided not destroyed in battle. If damaged I recommend we should move to either Munster or Bonn.' General Richardson agrees that this was typical of the 'super-optimism' prevailing among senior officers in those few days after the giddy successes. After all, it was reasoned, the Kaiser had been overthrown in 1918, and the German armies had surrendered when they had suffered nothing to equal the defeat in the West of 1944. Most people could not believe that the evil of Hitlerism had so entered the minds of the German people that they would fight until the bitter end, nor that the Führer would sacrifice his country in a vain effort to remain in power, with all his hopes pinned on his secret weapons being able to wipe out London and thus destroy the British ability to fight him.

Optimism still reigned up until the commencement of Operation Market Garden on 17 September. During the planning for this operation, intelligence officers at SHAEF and at HQ I Airborne Corps provided a warning, based on information from Dutch resistance forces, that German armour was stationed near Arnhem – as indeed it was. II SS Panzer Corps under General Willi Bittrich, with 9 SS Panzer (Hohenstaufen) Division and 10 SS Panzer (Frundsberg) Division, had been sent to Arnhem to refit after the battering they had received during the fighting in the Normandy bridgehead. The intelligence officers recommended photo reconnaissance to confirm the presence and strength of the German tanks. Air Ministry documents record that only eight planes were used for photo reconnaissance flights between 12 and 16 September, and nothing significant was detected. Hinsley's *British Intelligence in World War II* comments: 'The fact that the photo reconnaissance was so limited provides further testimony to the euphoria with which 21 Army Group and I Airborne Corps responded to the warnings. They clearly felt that these warnings added nothing to their existing intelligence, and called for no revision of their latest estimate of the strength of the German opposition.'

BRITISH 2ND ARMY

Intelligence summary to 2400 hr 4 September: Enemy situation: Yesterday morning British troops crossed the Belgian frontier; this evening they are reported in Antwerp, and the Dutch frontier is less than 10 miles beyond. East of Brussels we have captured Louvain. Thus in two days an advance of more than 100 miles has been made, and the coastal defences of Belgium and the remainder of North East France have been cut off. This magnificent achievement represents the final blow to the West Wall of Europe, and leaves the enemy forces who are still sheltering behind it with little to do except demolish their handiwork and await their captivity or, if they prefer to fight, their death. The number of enemy troops thus roped off is estimated to be between fifty and sixty thousand.

In contrast to the victorious progress made on our right flank to Antwerp and Louvain, the left sector of Second Army has been held up by persistent and reasonably well-organised resistance. In this area we have identified two divisions, 59 and 712. Both are fresh for battle, and although they are not regarded as capable of sustained resistance, their freshness may account for their continuing to fight in a situation which is in fact hopeless. Another reason may be that these formations are responsible for holding open the door to allow the forces on the coast to withdraw northward, ignorant of the fact that at the end of the garden the gate has now been barred.

If enemy broadcasts for home consumption are any guide to his intentions, he will not delay for long his move back to German soil. The advantages of a shortened line and the dubious value of occupied territory are now being presented to the German public as an explanation of what can no longer be concealed, and the arrival of Allied forces on the German doorstep is the signal for a renewed urge to keep the German war machine in motion. So far as the Germans' Western Army is concerned, there is as yet no sign that it will be better able to cope with Allied pressure on its own ground than it has been elsewhere, and the control of so rapid a withdrawal over so great a distance must be taxing the powers and resources of the German High Command beyond their most elastic limits.

Intelligence summary to 2400 hr 5 September: Enemy situation: News received today from Antwerp is indeed satisfactory, since it appears that owing to the speed of our advance and possibly owing to the incompleteness of enemy preparations, the extent of enemy demolitions has been much less than was anticipated. One bridge was found to be blown, and mines are reported in one of the docks, but generally speaking the dock area is undamaged.

Now that the way of escape from the coastal corridor is firmly barred, the process of cleaning up is going on, and at both ends a further advance is reported. Ghent is now in the hands of 2 Army, and the obstacles of rivers Authie and Canche have been surmounted. St Omer and Guines, lying inland from Calais, have been reached, if not entirely cleared of enemy, and although the ports of Boulogne, Calais, Dunkirk, and Ostend may need something more than an ultimatum to surrender, their capture cannot be long delayed.

There is not yet sufficient information to form any useful conclusion about the strength of the Siegfried line or the troops available to man it. One thing is tolerably certain, however, and that is that the enemy has not kept at home a reserve which is either well enough trained or well enough equipped to hold an invading force at bay for long. This would be particularly so if the invading force had tanks, against which the enemy is becoming increasingly short of anti-tank weapons. Artillery is also said to be very short, and without an abundance of these essential weapons the inferior troops that must man Germany's defences cannot hold out for long.

Intelligence summary to 2400 hr 6 September: Enemy situation: While Second Army was cutting through the ill-organised enemy defence in the centre of Belgium, American armour achieved an outstanding success in the area of Mons. In a three-day battle they encircled and destroyed an enemy force and caused 30,000 casualties, mainly prisoners-of-war.

Another prisoner, although from a different battle, was the Commander of 136 Division, the defenders of Antwerp. Maj General Graf von Stolberg-Stolberg attributed his failure to save Antwerp to two main factors: first, strong activity by the Belgian Resistance which prevented his plan from ever taking shape; and second, the lack of time, during which he could make only very hurried preparations.

His allusions to the orders he received from higher formations indicated that he had no great respect for their general policy. In his view German strategy in France was misconceived, and it would have been better to give ground rather than sacrifice troops in tasks which were too much for them.

He had been told that every effort would be made to defend the frontiers of Germany, and that this was a matter in which bluff could play no part. He was not aware of the exact defence lines, but in his opinion the Meuse/Maas was the only possible line.

Today carried Second Army's advance a further stage. Civilian sources have reported several large enemy movements, the most important being six thousand men moving north-east from Ghent. In mere numbers this force is capable of forcing its way through our link between Brussels and Antwerp. But they are hopelessly lacking in mechanical transport, and although supplies behind coastal areas are believed to be reasonably good, there is no prospect of anything further reaching them.

It is probable that the enemy realises only too well that the climax of five years of war is here. Last minute preparations are being made for an event which all the offensive ridicule of former years has not been able to prevent. As the invasion of Germany appears over the horizon, there are many regrets for divisions squandered in France and other battlefields. A prisoner taken yesterday said that Party officials in Germany were being mobilised, and it is only to be expected that the last available man will be forced to bear arms in an effort to bolster the West Wall defences. But there is nothing in the way of a field formation of which notice has not been given, and those that exist will be no better than those which we have met already.

Reports are in today that all the bridges on the Albert Canal between Antwerp and Hasselt are gone, demonstrating that the enemy has given up trying to extract forces that way. Prisoners are talking of Panzer formations resting and refitting. This is wishful thinking. There can either be rest and refit, or defence of the West Wall in Holland. There cannot be both.

The enemy's main concerns now are: the defence of Holland and Germany; evacuation behind this defence line of his five armies in France (I, V, VII, XV, and XIX), and prevention of a large part of these armies falling into our hands. In neither can he succeed, but by fanatical last stands he may delay the capture of good ports by us long enough to be an embarrassment.

The Albert Canal and 15 Army are our immediate concern. We may expect 15 Army, having failed to break out to the east, to turn back and attempt to cross the Scheldt at Flushing or by other ferries.

Intelligence Summary to 2400 hr 7 September: Enemy situation: As a result of today's progress the amount of Belgian territory still in enemy possession has been further reduced. They hold two separate pockets, divided by our solid block connecting Antwerp with Brussels. They have made one or two half-hearted attempts to break out from the Western part, but these have been unsuccessful.

In the Western part five enemy infantry divisions have been identified: 59, 64, 70, 712, and 182, a training division). As well as these there are the remnants of LXVII Corps with its Normandy divisions and a mixed collection of other formations in tow. Other troops include Coastal Artillery units, Flak units, and a number of administrative personnel.

In the Eastern part the furthest point we have reached is over the Albert Canal at Beeringen, where we have established a firm bridgehead. For the moment this is the only point east of Antwerp where we are up to the canal. The main line of our forward positions runs south-east from Antwerp to Aerschot, and thence north-east to the canal. Opposition here consists of 719 Division, brought down from Holland, 347 Division, and troops from other assorted units.

The enemy seems to have realised that 15 Army has no hope of escape, at any rate by land, and shipping from Dunkirk and other coastal ports may be used to evacuate some of the troops in the corridor. Others will no doubt be ferried across the Scheldt; but speaking generally, the doom of 15 Army is already sealed.

The other point which the enemy may now be grasping somewhat late is the peril in which his defences of Germany will be placed if our bridgehead across the Albert Canal becomes the springboard for another thrust. The troops now manning the canal are hardly competent to hold their positions for long, and the enemy is likely to pledge some of his few remaining assets in a desperate attempt to maintain this line. A prisoner taken today, for example, said that he belonged to 176 Division. This is not included in the Order of Battle lists, and may have been either created ad hoc, or have escaped notice until now.

We shall run into more of these newly fledged formations, but none of them is of vintage quality, and their title to divisional status is by courtesy of the OKW and not by their deserts. 176 Division probably has ten battalions, and is unlikely to have any artillery or heavy anti-tank weapons.

A week ago the enemy was not, if his dispositions and actions are any guide, unduly concerned by a move north to the Albert Canal. But now, with three divisions identified in the canal area, bridges blown, and counterattacks at Antwerp, it seems the enemy is aware of the danger and is doing something about it.

The 2nd Army intelligence summaries exude the strong sense of the war ending before the end of 1944. There is also the conviction that the German 15th Army was being pushed back against the line of the Scheldt estuary, which would form a barrier it could not cross. The conclusion is also drawn that there were few reserves left for Germany to call on. We will see that the Germans surmounted the barrier of the Scheldt with relative ease, and we have already seen that there were substantial reserves at the disposal of the German High Command.

It is interesting to read the more realistic warning given on 28 August by Colonel Oscar Koch, Intelligence Chief (G2-I) of Patton's 3rd US Army:

> Despite the crippling factors of shattered communications, disorganization and tremendous losses in personnel and equipment, the enemy has never-theless been able to maintain a sufficiently cohesive front to exercise overall control of his tactical situation. His withdrawal, though continuing, has not been a rout or mass collapse. Numerous new identifications in contact in recent days have demonstrated clearly that although he is operating under enormous difficulties, the enemy is still capable of bringing new elements into the battle area and transferring some from other fronts.
>
> Barring internal upheaval in the homeland, and the remoter possibility of insurrection within the Wehrmacht, it can be expected that the German armies will continue to fight until destroyed or captured.

Patton was not interested in such talk.

In the other major formation of 12 US Army Group, 1st US Army, optimism remained high. Hubert Essame was at this time commanding a brigade in the British 43 Division, and in his book *The Battle for Germany* he writes:

> This overweening optimism infected even the unemotional, dependable Commander of 1 US Army, Lt Gen Courtney Hodges. On crossing the

German border on 16 September he ordered a reconnaissance in force of the Western Wall about Aachen. On the 15th he hoped for an enemy collapse in the Rhineland, and the 'enormous' strategic advantage of seizing the Rhine bridges intact. As late as the last week of September he believed that, given two weeks of good weather, Allied air and ground forces could 'bring the enemy to their knees'.

XII CORPS INTELLIGENCE SUMMARIES (WO 171/310)

XII Corps, under the command of Gen Neil Ritchie, consisted at this time of 7 Armoured Division, 15 and 53 Infantry Divisions and 4 Armoured Brigade. The centre-line of its advance after crossing the Seine at St Pierre du Vouvray led through Gournay, Arras, Lille, and then Ghent as its immediate objective. The Corps would then presumably close to the banks of the Scheldt. Corps intelligence summaries were produced daily, and were based on information gathered up to midnight on the previous day. The extracts from the summaries that follow concentrate on enemy dispositions, intentions, and capabilities.

No. 56: to midnight 5 September: With the capture of Antwerp yesterday another large body of German troops ceases to have more than an outside chance of playing much part in the battle for Germany which is to come. For the moment it is unprofitable to speculate on what this new 'bag' contains, but 712, 59, at least a battlegroup of 64, 245 and elements of 226 Divisions are there, with groups and stragglers from at least another twenty divisions, coastal defence troops, flak units and other headquarters troops. There is also the possibility that 182 Training Division, last reported in the area of St Omer, and 70 Division, last reported in Antwerp, should be included. However, the latter may have made its getaway in time, to judge from yesterday's Tac R [tactical reconnaissance] reports. Meanwhile the area of the bag continues to diminish as our advance from the south forces the enemy back, and as he himself releases the waters over the area immediately north of Bruges and including Ostend, Blankenberge, and Het Zoute.

On our XII Corps front La Basse was taken without much resistance, and our troops reached the area Merville–Estaires. In so far as any coherent enemy front has existed it has been here in the area between Lille and Aire, though it would appear that both flanks of this force are now completely exposed. 64 Division, which was operating north of St Pol, appears to have withdrawn to the north-east, while 712 Division seems also to have fallen back at least as far as the line Estaires–Armentières. Thus we have most of four divisions compressed into the general area Hazebrouck–Poperinghe–Ypres–Armentieres–Forêt de Nieppe. The future intention of this force is obscure, but it may be that it will

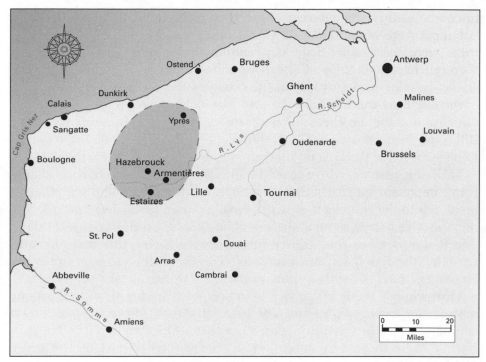

7. German concentration, 5 September 1944.

attempt to withdraw to the north-east as far as the area Roulers, and then turn east and endeavour to break out. It is however doubtful whether the German Command is still sufficiently in control to stage-manage a manoeuvre of this kind.

To the east little coordinated resistance has been encountered. Our right-hand neighbours, XXX Corps, found Antwerp held by 136 ZBV Division staff controlling a nondescript assortment of units made up of stragglers and invalids suffering from gastric complaints.

Thus so far as the Army Group front is concerned the story is one of increasing disorganisation and a growing tendency to turn eastward and make a getaway. The High Command has no thought save to salvage as much as possible from the wreck and get it back to the West Wall as quickly as they can; but at the moment the thoughts of the High Command have not the smallest effect on the course of events in the field. Units and formations must take what care of themselves they can until they reach the shelter of the Siegfried line, and are organised for what may prove to be the farewell appearance of the Armies of the Third Reich.

No. 58: to midnight 7 September: Little fresh information has been received today, but further light has been thrown on yesterday's fighting. Several uncoordinated efforts appear to have been made to break out to the east. Attempts were made north of Ghent and between Ghent and Courtrai; these were successfully dealt with, although doubtless small parties got through here and there. Considerable casualties were inflicted on the enemy by our covering troops in the course of these abortive efforts.

On our own front Zonnebeke and Menin have been captured. Round Courtrai and the north-east of it resistance of a sort continues. There are still some enemy troops in Ghent, although part of this group are reported to have moved to the area of Lokeren, which our patrols entered yesterday.

Thus the position with regard to the bag is as follows: it is gradually being impressed on the enemy that there is little future in attempting to break out to the east, such attempts having proved costly and fruitless. The only possible escape route is therefore the Scheldt ferries. From yesterday's Tac R it was clear that the enemy proposed to try this method, and doubtless he has taken advantage of today's weather to accelerate the crossing of such elements as have managed to withdraw far enough north.

Meanwhile if the ferry service is to operate at all he must hold up our advance for as long as he can. The Fifteenth Army is in fact conducting a 'Dunkirk' of its own, with the difference that Walcheren and Beveland are hardly likely to prove a secure refuge for whatever part of the army survive the passage of the Scheldt. With regard to the ports of Boulogne, Calais and Dunkirk, the enemy may well appreciate that he can best gain time to improvise the defences of Germany by denying us the use of these ports for as long as possible.

Fresh evidence of the enemy's intention to hold the line of the Albert Canal has been provided by a reliable civilian from Bruges, while the heavy resistance met with by our troops on the canal north-east of Antwerp proves that such was in fact the plan. Unfortunately for him, however, our troops have secured a bridgehead on the canal at Beeringen, where the bridge was captured intact.

From the identification of 743 Grenadier Regiment today in the area north of Antwerp, it would appear that 719 Division, or at any rate part of it, has been brought from Holland to assist in the defence of the canal line. This move indicates the importance attached by the enemy to this line, because it will leave Holland's garrison pitifully weak unless 15 Army has a better Dunkirk than can be reasonably expected.

The XII Corps intelligence officer writing these summaries gives his readers a touch of melodrama: 'the farewell appearance of the Armies of the Third Reich'. Unfortunately his assessment was wrong, as was his belief that the Beveland peninsula would be 'hardly likely to prove a secure refuge for whatever part of the army survive the passage of the Scheldt'. As it turned out, that passage was successfully completed by the best part of six German divisions, and they escaped down the Beveland peninsula to become a considerable thorn in the side of the British 2nd Army's north-western flank after the defeat at Arnhem.

XII Corps intelligence reports were grossly misleading and subjective, presenting assumptions as facts and ignoring all that was known of the recuperative powers of the German Army. The reports were wrong about the 15th Army being unable to cross the Scheldt, wrong about the loss of control by the German higher command, and wrong about the ability of the German soldiers to regroup and counterattack. This type of intelligence report was one of the major reasons for the Great Mistake.

XXX CORPS INTELLIGENCE SUMMARIES (WO 171/341)

XXX Corps, under the command of Gen Brian Horrocks, consisted at this time of the Guards Armoured Division, 11 Armoured Division, 43 and 50 Infantry Divisions and 8 Armoured Brigade. After crossing the Seine at Vernon the leading formations followed the general line Beauvais, Amiens, Arras and Douai. The Guards on the right axis took Brussels on 3 September and Louvain on 4 September, and 11 Armoured Division on the left took Antwerp on 4 September. Intelligence summaries that related to enemy capabilities were based on information gathered up to midnight on the previous day.

Summary 494: to midnight 7 September: Although the enemy's main line of defence at this moment is supposed to be the Albert Canal, they have surely envisaged the possibility of having to withdraw even further back. The Rhine (called the Waal along its lowlands stretch) is obviously the most important obstacle, since it is at once the largest and the last between us and Germany. Evidence of the enemy interest in it is shown by digging on the north bank on air photos dated 5 September.

In addition the Wolfsberg–Muntberg feature south of Nijmegen is the highest hill in Holland, and it is a bastion which guards a vulnerable part of the German frontier at the end of the Siegfried line. It seems obvious that such a feature should be made into a hedgehog defensive position by the Germans. This is borne out by bridge defences and weapon pits along the canal, both of which are visible in air photos as well as being reported by Dutch sources.

There is considerable railway activity at Arnhem and Nijmegen, and the placement of heavy and light antiaircraft guns is increasing noticeably. This is hardly surprising, because both towns are the main centres of communication for movement in any direction in Holland, and contain the crossings most important to the Germans.

It is therefore apparent that whatever his present intentions as regards defence of the Albert Canal, a pretty desperate resistance will be attempted later along the line of the Waal.

The principal force available for defence consists of the heavy antiaircraft guns mentioned above, their strength being some fourteen battalions armed with a total of two hundred 88 mm guns. In this country of a multiplicity of rivers and canals these guns could and will be deployed very effectively, and we are likely to meet them in every village and at every water-crossing.

Dutch resistance sources report that battered panzer formations have been sent up to Holland to refit, and mention Eindhoven and Nijmegen as possible reception areas. This is quite plausible, because there was no panzer formation in Holland, and any one of the 2 Panzer, 116 Panzer, 9 SS Panzer, or 10 SS Panzer may have been sent up.

This force, if it ever arrives, is not likely to be worth more than one motor brigade and one armoured regiment in strength. After its refit its task will probably be to lend support to the defence of the Albert Canal. Its non-appearance in our bridgehead within the next 24 hours will show that either these reports have no foundation, or that the panzer divisions are not fit to fight.

Summary 496: to midnight 8 September: There was no lessening of enemy resistance on the Corps front today. The expansion of our existing bridgehead at Beeringen was as stubbornly contested as the establishment of a new one south-west of Gheel. Hechtel is still not clear of the enemy. There has been heavy fighting today both here and at Beverloo. The latter was eventually mopped up, and our troops are now just short of Bourg Leopold.

Two of our infantry battalions are now across the canal at the bridgehead south-west of Gheel. They met fairly strong enemy opposition, and were counterattacked four times during the day. Two armoured regiments were sent across the Beeringen bridge with the object of striking north-west to join up with the infantry near Gheel. They too met considerable opposition; by last night they had advanced about 4 miles.

The resistance was provided by the three weakened battalions of 723 Regiment and by a motley collection of parachutists and German Air Force (GAF) troops estimated to be about six battalions strong. Including those portions of ex-7 Army divisions opposite the Corps front, the total enemy strength opposite the two bridgeheads is estimated to be about ten battalions. In support were some 50 Armoured Fighting Vehicles, mainly self-propelled anti-tank guns.

The sudden appearance of parachutists on our front suggests that our bridgeheads on the canal have caused the enemy some concern. From statements by prisoners-of-war it appears that more of these units are likely to arrive shortly. It is doubtful whether all of these will be parachutists; GAF units are apparently being used to made good the gaps. Documents captured today suggest however that part of 6 Para Div is already here, and 3 Para Div may well follow.

From the statements of a Dutch SS soldier captured today, it looks too as though the SS Training units in the north of Holland may be diverted from their task of guarding the coast and be sent to the Albert Canal instead.

In view of the serious enemy situation at Antwerp and to the west of it, it is unlikely that troops escaping from Flanders (the Breskens–Terneuzen area) will be sent opposite XXX Corps. Nor can much armour be spared from the south. In yesterday's summary it was suggested that up to four weak armoured divisions might be moving north. However, today 116 and 2 Panzer Divisions were identified near Liège, and 10 SS Panzer is reported to have been so badly mauled near Mons a few days ago as to be virtually written off. 9 SS Panzer is admittedly unlocated, and might be able to get to Holland in time.

Likely enemy reinforcements therefore amount to about five more parachute-cum-GAF battalions from Germany, five SS training battalions from the north of Holland, and possibly one weak armoured division in reserve. The enemy's decision to commit the gathered fragments of his parachutists to containing a bridgehead which he cannot hope to eliminate is in part dictated by what is going on in Flanders. The remnants of 15 Army are still queuing up for ferries across the Scheldt. However, we shall have soon amassed enough forces in the bridgehead to make further resistance along an undefended line impracticable. In that case the enemy will fall back to the nearest rather than the best line of defence. This will be the Meuse–Escaut canal.

The writer of the XXX Corps intelligence summaries adopts a drier and more objective tone than his XII Corps counterpart. His analysis of the probable situation along the Waal and the information from the Dutch about the Panzer formations was spot-on. It was unfortunate that his opinions were not given greater weight by the commanders in charge of the joint ground–airborne operation Market Garden.

General comments on Intelligence presented to senior commanders
Intelligence presented to senior commanders at the end of August and the beginning of September was incomplete, inaccurate and incautious. The impression given was that the Germans were in a state of complete chaos, and would be able to offer little systematic resistance before they collapsed entirely. As this Intelligence reinforced the mindset of the commanders, they were persuaded to make unbalanced and uninformed decisions. The Intelligence services have to take significant responsibility for the Great Mistake.

Chapter Seven

PERCEPTION AT THE SHARP END: EUPHORIA

Up to the crossing of the Seine during the last days of August the going was still slow, hampered by damaged roads, bridges and villages, and the debris of fierce resistance by the Germans. The crossing was also hotly contested at most points, the one at Vernon being well remembered by 43 Division.

Once on the other side of the river the opposition became much less, and determined leadership encouraged all units to 'bounce' the Germans still resisting. The Allies went either through or round the enemy, and the speed of their advance allowed them to capture many bridges intact, resulting in a great saving in time.

The speed of the advance meant several things. First, there was little damage to the countryside and the towns and villages the Allied troops traversed. Second, they had little time for rest or maintenance. Third, their unexpected appearance in many parts of France and Belgium produced an immediate outpouring of joy, thanks and welcome. The combination of the first and the third gave the soldiers that experienced it a feeling that not only were they doing something rather special, but also that their efforts were very much appreciated. The word that comes through strongly in all accounts of those few days is 'euphoria' – sometimes explicit, sometimes implicit in the accounts.

This sense of euphoria was a factor that contributed to the Great Mistake in several ways. The soldiers themselves, particularly after the severe struggles in Normandy during the first two and a half months after the invasion, felt that opposition was almost at an end, and all that would have to be done was to brush aside some more light opposition while motoring to Berlin.

When a unit reached a village, town or city there was a tumultuous welcome involving a great deal of drink and a good deal of kissing – the due reward of the weary, bruised and battered soldier. Nobody, then or now, would begrudge them their rewards and their opportunity to relax. But as we shall see, the euphoria led to delay, and the delay led to ferocious fighting, much of it at least as bad as that experienced in Normandy.

It was the responsibility of the commanders to continue urging the soldiers on, understanding but ignoring the euphoria and the complacency. However painful it might be to keep going so as to seize the opportunity, it is often even more painful to reap the harvest of not doing so. The unforgiving minute does not allow replays.

At the battle of Vittoria in north-east Spain in 1813, Wellington inflicted a substantial defeat on the French. But his victory was not followed up by pursuit for two reasons. The first was the lack of a determined leader for the British cavalry. The second reason is described by Arthur Bryant in *The Age of Elegance*:

> To Wellington's rage the King of Spain's baggage train proved too much for his men's discipline. Around it gathered the soldiers of three nations (England, Portugal and Spain) with powder-blackened faces, fighting one another for boxes of dollars, fine clothes, and feasting on the wines and foods of a luxurious court. 'Come, boys,' shouted an Irish grenadier, 'help your-selves wid anything yez like best, free gratis and for nothing at all! The King left all behind him for our day's trouble. Who'll have a dhrink o' wine?'

The scenes in Belgium in September 1944 were not so bacchanalian. But there was no doubt that delays resulting from celebration meant that military opportunities were lost.

The euphoria was even more evident in the liberated Belgians and the soon-to-be-liberated Dutch. Seeing such a sudden and unexpected change in their German oppressors, their views about the Germans changed from fear and submission to contempt. Their reports on the enemy were thus conditioned by this changed attitude, and much of what was reported by resistance fighters and civilians was – understandably – grossly optimistic or inaccurate.

In reviewing the progressive euphoria that peaked for most people a few days after 4 September, we will first see how it affected the soldiers, and then the liberated civilians.

MILITARY EUPHORIA

The soldiers of 21 Army Group had crossed the Seine at five places, and as they drove north and north-east along their separate axes they had somewhat similar experiences and feelings. An officer of the 1st Canadian Army wrote graphically to his family after he had driven through Rouen and continued northwards on 2 September:

I cannot possibly convey the cumulative effect of passing for hours through a liberated countryside, with the wreckage of the beaten enemy – his tanks and vehicles, his dead horses and the graves of his dead men – littering the roadside ditches, and the population, free once more, welcoming the oncoming troops with smiles and flowers and the V-sign.

The scene in a liberated town is quite extraordinary. The place, of course, is festooned with flags. They always have plenty of tricolours; but the Union Jack and the Stars and Stripes are in short supply, and had to be homemade for the occasion. I saw some versions of the Canadian Red Ensign which would scarcely have pleased the College of Heralds, but must have pleased a good many Canadians. Everyone seems to be in the street, and no one ever seems to tire of waving to the troops passing in their vehicles, who likewise never tire of waving back – particularly at the female population. The young people wave and laugh and shout; the children yell and wave flags; the mothers hold up their babies to see the troops, and they wave their little paws too; the old people stand by the roadside and look happy.

The Canadians were on the left flank of 21 Army Group, and the Guards Armoured Division were on the right. Two of the units with the Guards Division were the 2nd Household Cavalry Regiment (2 HCR) and the 2nd (Armoured) Battalion of the Irish Guards (2 IG). Here are some comments from their unit histories as they approached and then entered Brussels.

Before they started on their final leg on 2 September, Col J.O.E. (Joe) Vandeleur, senior Commanding Officer of the Irish group, gave his orders: 'Enemy information: one word, chaos; our intention, the Irish group will dine in Brussels tomorrow night.'

On their way to Brussels the Irish Guards received a very warm welcome. Through the Belgian villages roared the tanks – St Patrick, Leinster, Connaught, Achill, and sixty-nine other Irish place-names. The noise of the tracks on the cobbled streets brought the inhabitants out of their houses to cheer and wave. The Guardsmen had become used to enthusiastic receptions as they passed through France, but those given by the Belgians were both warmer and wilder than they had imagined possible.

In the small villages the inhabitants showed their practicality over their French counterparts. Instead of *throwing* all the fruit they had, they established plum, pear and apple points, and threw only bottles of Lion d'Or beer into the passing vehicles. This sense of organisation, however, had long been abandoned by the time the leading groups of the 2nd Household Cavalry reached Brussels. Here enthusiasm took the place of practicality! It was difficult to remain calm and unaffected in this atmosphere; it was such a tonic after the grim days of Normandy, with its fierce battles. This was a complete change, a rapid advance and little opposition.

All competed to welcome the liberators with embraces in which one felt were pent up all the sufferings and emotions of the past four years. It was as un-English a scene as could be imagined, comparable perhaps to Armistice Day in 1918, and yet so natural and touching did it seem at the time that scarcely one of us could feel shy or embarrassed at the enforced attention of the occasional bearded old gentleman.

Were Col Joe's orders followed in all respects? Yes! Officers of the Irish Guards did indeed dine in Brussels that night, in the largest café in the square at Audeghem. During the meal a report came in of some Germans holding out in a nearby house. Col Joe recalled: 'Everybody was having far too much of a good time to be disturbed, so a combined mess party went off to deal with the matter. We found some miserable little Huns in full marching order, fixed them up quickly and returned to dinner. The night was uproarious, and we could not get any work done on the tanks or vehicles.'

The celebrations went on well into the night, and dawn was just as uproarious as the enthusiasm continued. One of the Irish Guards was forced to breakfast on whisky, not because he liked it, but because a kindly Belgian had kept a bottle for 'the day'. As the Guardsman said, it would have been churlish to refuse!

The Irish Guards stayed in Brussels a little longer, but after two nights even they were too exhausted to stand the noise any more, and so moved into the grounds of the Château Dietrich and shut the gates behind them. Col Joe called it 'protective leaguer against Belgian girls'.

Robert Boscawen was a troop leader in the 1st (Armoured) Battalion Coldstream Guards, also part of the Guards Armoured Division. On the evening of 3 September his tanks arrived in Brussels:

The lights went on in the city and all windows and doors were flung open. To describe the welcome would only be to repeat what had happened all the way across France and Belgium. Here it was magnified to cheering thousands. My tank halted behind the one in front in the centre of the city at the Bourse. Immediately I was smothered with kisses, flowers and wine. The smaller scout-cars completely disappeared from view. Soon we were dragged away from our tanks into houses. Forcibly, with two or three girls round my neck, I was taken into a house and given a royal feast. George was already there guzzling. We drank glass after glass, bottle after bottle appeared and we had to be self-controlled not to be laid out.

A shout of 'the tanks are moving' eventually got us back into our tanks again, and finally, tanks covered with dozens of Belgians, we managed to move, and in the end find a place to harbour for the night. The next morning, 4 September, we stayed in the square where we had harboured, and the locals came to see us eating breakfast and washing, rather like animals at the Zoo. After lunch we moved to a better place for the tanks, and our move was a triumphant drive round Brussels. We drove slowly round sitting on the top of the turrets. All my four tanks had reached Brussels and I led them round flying our troop flag on the aerial with a Belgian and French flag on either side of the turret. Down the colourful avenues every window had its allied flags, and the girls were clothed in their national colours.

That evening was a free night for the British, but most were exhausted; for those who could, the chief of the Underground movement held a tremendous party at the Koekelberg Brewery.

The next morning, 5 September, everybody was recovering from the night before, and I went into a café with Henry and John Sutton to have a glass of iced beer. Then an extraordinary thing happened. The rumour went round that the Germans had capitulated, and 'La guerre est fini'. In a few minutes it had spread over the whole of Brussels, and the Belgians went completely mad, dancing about shouting 'il est fini, the war is over'. We did our best to tell them it was only a rumour, but they all believed it.

It was not only the Belgians who believed the war was over. The transmission from Brussels Radio was heard in Britain, and the rumour spread throughout the country. The *Daily Herald* reported that: 'People left their suburban homes and came to town to join in the celebrations. There were taxis full of singing soldiers.'

Antwerp was the objective of 11 Armoured Division. On the morning of 4 September, 29 Armoured Brigade began its final approach, and encountered little opposition until it reached the outskirts of the city. The inhabitants seemed far more concerned that their liberators receive a warm welcome than for their own personal safety. One member of the leading unit recorded his impressions:

Civilians were all over the vehicles, and numbers were killed or wounded by the remaining German snipers or machine-gun posts that one was quite likely to meet round any corner. No heed was taken of any warnings, and it was quite impossible to keep our vehicles clear of civilians and at the same time be alert ourselves.

When we reached the centre of the city we were given a welcome none of us had ever dreamed was possible. Our vehicles were unable to move, and progress was made extremely difficult owing to the great joy and enthusiasm of the enormous crowds who came out into the streets to greet their liberators.

As soon as any vehicle stopped for whatever reason it was swamped by excited citizens. Glasses of cognac and bottles of champagne were thrust on tank commanders. Drivers and co-drivers with their heads exposed were pelted with fruit and flowers. Cigars were stuck in their mouths. It was like a floral procession. I drove up a boulevard with six tanks in line and saw a column of German lorries trundling slowly down the other side of the road. The leading Sherman tried to engage, but was unable to traverse its gun because of the mass of humanity on the turret. I sent two tanks, which were relatively unencumbered, down a side-street with the idea of doubling back and cutting off the enemy. But he had the same idea, and a farcical game of hide-and-seek developed, ending with us in a single column, British and German vehicles alternating. The enemy gave up under sheer pressure from the crowd.

I parked outside a café overflowing with people shouting about the German HQ which was just round the corner, and full of German officers. I had a look and saw a big building flying a swastika flag. Snipers were shooting from the upper storeys, and spectators insisted that I should use the 'beeg cannon' – they had spotted the 17-pounder on the nearest Firefly tank. The tank commander backed down the street to get enough elevation, and told the crowd briefly about the effects of blast in built-up areas before ordering his gunner to fire. There was an appalling crack, and every window within 75 yards disintegrated. The glass was still tinkling to the ground when all the crowd roared out 'Encore!'

There were still Germans in the city, and many more on the northern bank of the Scheldt. Maj John Dunlop was a squadron leader with the 3rd Royal Tank Regiment, and one of his last memories before the regiment moved out of Antwerp was '. . . of sitting in a comfortable office chair on the top floor of a sky-scraper block with a gunner major bringing down fire on a concentration of enemy we could see across the Scheldt. Meanwhile a trim little Anversoise office girl was bringing in relays of café-cognac and playing us American blues on the office record player. Now that was the right way to fight a war.'

The axis of advance of XII Corps led to Ghent, and its spearhead was 7 Armoured Division. The 'War Diary' of the 13th Royal Horse Artillery, one of the artillery units of the division, reads:

Great as the reception had been in France it was exceeded when the troops crossed the frontier into Belgium. There were even more flowers and larger and better fruit. There were flags on every church and banners strung across the roads that read 'Welcome' and 'Vive les Anglais'. Everyone it seemed had kept a bottle or two of either brandy or wine which they insisted the nearest British soldier should have. To those who were beginning to feel the strain it was a great encouragement, and to all it was an unforgettable and cherished memory.

CIVILIAN EUPHORIA, HELP AND HINDRANCE: BELGIUM

The liberated civilian population was understandably ecstatic at the arrival of Allied troops in Brussels, Antwerp, Ghent and all the other towns and villages. They had been under the German jackboot for four years and more, and presumably the more observant of them had watched what the Germans were doing, where they were, what strength, what units, what equipment, and so on. There was obviously a wealth of information available somewhere, but who had it, who could be trusted, how accurate was the information anyway? The 23rd Hussars – for this final advance on Antwerp the reserve regiment of 29 Armoured Brigade – had these sorts of problems on reaching the suburbs of Antwerp on 4 September:

As we entered the suburbs, crowds of people rushed to greet us. Amongst them were innumerable secret agents, each with a more important plan of Antwerp than the last. As they closed in upon us we heard over our regimental wireless set the news that 3 RTR [Royal Tank Regiment] were in the city itself. We were able to inform the agents, to their incredulous dismay, that their plans were already out of date. They nevertheless persisted in pressing pieces of paper upon us, and they all talked loudly, at great length, and simultaneously. One of them assured us that he was in direct touch with Mr Churchill, and although this might have been true, it had little bearing on the battle which was developing.

C Squadron had done considerable execution on some staff cars containing German officers, and were about to leave the suburbs to cross the open space in front of the city wall. Suddenly a Belgian boy scout rushed up and stopped the leading tank. He jumped up beside the commander and said that there were guns covering the road and mines across it. With great clearness, and what later proved to be most accurate detail, he outlined the defences in front of us. Of all the wildly enthusiastic Belgians in the street at that moment he was the only one who really was quietly and materially helpful.

The White Brigade dashed about offering advice. One of them insisted that it was safe to go round the corner in front of us. Our boy scout said emphatically 'No, there is a machine-gun trained on it.' Eventually stung by the White Brigade man's insistence that it was safe, Captain Bishop walked round the corner. A machine-gun bullet ripped through his breast pocket, and he darted back, unhurt but wiser.

From the window of a luxury flat the vanguard commanders surveyed the defences through their binoculars, while their hostess pressed them to take cocktails with her.

CIVILIAN EUPHORIA: HOLLAND

Rejoicing among the civilians was not confined to Belgium. In the Dutch villages and towns north of the Dutch–Belgian border a few miles outside Antwerp, the people watched in disbelief as the shattered remnants of Hitler's armies streamed through their streets, all, so it seemed, headed for the Fatherland. The soldiers were accompanied by civilians, almost all of them German sympathisers or active members of the Dutch Nazi Party.

The retreat appeared to begin on 2 September, and gathered a momentum that reached its peak on Tuesday 5 September, a day that became known in Holland as Dolle Dinsdag, or Mad Tuesday. The German flight was disorganised and panic-ridden, and among the more normal forms of motorised transport there were bicycles, scooters, farm-wagons, and even a black and silver hearse drawn by two slowly plodding farm horses.

Dutch people along the roads leading north and east observed that the soldiers came from many different arms and divisions, those without transport marching doggedly on. Some of them had their own personal weapons, but no tanks, guns or other heavy equipment. Many appeared dishevelled and directionless, and gave some amusement to the watchers by asking for directions to the German frontier.

The observers could not help but see the destruction of equipment, supplies, and infrastructure, and the removal of weapons such as antiaircraft guns from their emplacements. As yet, however, they had no confirmation that the flight of the Germans would be followed by the arrival of the Allies. They heard a message from Gen Eisenhower, saying that 'the hour of liberation the Netherlands have awaited so long is now very near'. The Prime Minister of the Dutch government in exile, Pieter Gerbrandy, was even more optimistic when he told his listeners: 'Now that the Allied armies in their irresistible advance have crossed the Netherlands frontier, I want all of you to bid our Allies a hearty welcome to our native soil.'

On the nights of 3 and 4 September, some German soldiers were so desperate to flee that they ignored the dangers from Allied aircraft and drove with their headlights on. The officers seemed to have lost control, and soldiers threw away their rifles – in some cases offering to sell them to the Dutch. Besides throwing away their equipment, many tried to desert. Some begged the Dutch for civilian clothes, some demanded it at gunpoint. Dutch observers sensed that the Germans were totally fed up with the war, and all they wanted to do was to evade their officers and the military police, change into civilian clothes, and leg it back to Germany.

The German historian Walter Goerlitz wrote that: 'Naval troops marched north without weapons, selling their spare uniforms. They told people that the war was over and they were going home. Lorries loaded with officers, their mistresses, and large quantities of champagne and brandy managed to get back to the Fatherland.' The Dutch were ecstatic at the scenes, and began to prepare Dutch flags, as well as buttons and ribbons of orange – the Dutch national colour – and some even displayed or wore these symbols of a liberated nation.

It was very unfortunate for many Dutch people that they saw only a small and unrepresentative sample of the German Wehrmacht. In any army there are always those who would prefer not to fight, and who would take any opportunity to leave the battlefield if it could be done without too great dishonour. It is often said that in a section of ten soldiers there is one leader, perhaps two, seven or eight who will stay there and do their duty without showing any particular initiative, and one who actively does not want to be there.

In a time when the structure of command and discipline is in disarray,
that one soldier in ten will behave as the servicemen in the fleeing columns
observed by the Dutch. The observation is quite correct – *those* soldiers
were fleeing. But the implication of many of the statements is that *all*
soldiers were fleeing, which was untrue. And there was another factor
relating to the German Army of 1944. Many of its soldiers were from
countries that the Germans had conquered, and those nationals had been
given the opportunity to fight in a German uniform. Until the Normandy
landings these foreigners, or auxiliaries, to use a Roman term, had as
comfortable a life as anyone could expect in 1944. It was unlikely, however,
that many would want to sacrifice themselves for the honour of Germany.

The above observations, coupled with other information both factual
and conjectural, presented the Intelligence services with a very tricky
piece of analysis. They had to get the information through whatever
channels were open; the reliability of the source had to be established; the
validity of the information had to be tested; for example, could you
estimate a soldier's morale by his outward appearance and actions? And
what proportion of the whole did the observed sample represent?

It was then necessary to consider whether the summation of the available observed behaviour reflected a fundamental change in the German
soldier's attitude to war. As we have seen, the majority of the soldiers in
the formations around Antwerp were still prepared to fight defiantly,
courageously and with their usual skill.

The intelligence analyst cannot penetrate the painted veil to see the
truth, and may be influenced by the atmosphere in which he is living. He
might, in some cases, be swayed by what he thinks his commander wants
to hear. He or his commander might also take note of the hopes of their
countrymen, their politicians and their war correspondents.

Capt Harry Butcher of the US Navy had the title of 'Naval Aide' to
Eisenhower. His job involved many duties, one of which was to help with
the flow of information to war correspondents. He wrote in his diary for
7 September 1944:

> In an effort to sober the flow of news, I arranged for General Betts to talk to
> the correspondents, and first briefed him on our need. I wanted him to tell
> them how difficult it will be to get through the Siegfried Line. My reasoning
> is that if we should get through easily, the public will appreciate their victory.
> If we get stuck in front of it and have a hell of a fight to get through, then
> the public won't be surprised, and the soldiers will get deserved credit.
> Otherwise they fight their hearts out and the public will regard the feat as
> another easy victory.
>
> General Betts quickly saw my point, and said his story should dampen
> some of the ardour of those who think the war will soon be over. He gave a
> fine talk; in fact, it was so good that when he finished the correspondents

rose and applauded. Then someone asked: 'General Betts, sir, do you think we will get the Siegfried Line?'

'Why, of course,' replied the General, 'We'll go right through it!'

COMMENTS ON EUPHORIA

In the early days of September most Allied soldiers lived in an atmosphere of movement, exhilaration, overwhelming welcome and appreciation, and invincibility. Naturally enough, they paused to gather the fruits of liberation, and in both Brussels and Antwerp the memories of front-line soldiers are of drinking, relaxation and the opportunity to sleep comfortably.

There is no sense of urgency to move on in any of the memories, although, as both Horrocks and Roberts acknowledged, there was no urgent need to halt. The tanks could have moved with no more than routine maintenance, and there was enough petrol immediately available to allow an advance of 100 miles or more. While the troops were tired, they were not too tired to enjoy themselves. They had been given the chance to relax, and they did so.

The responsibility for this unnecessary, and as it turned out, tragic, pause for relaxation and refit was entirely in the hands of the senior commanders. Had they ordered their troops to continue to advance without delay, the troops would have obeyed – although with the grumbling natural to front-line soldiers. Horrocks and Roberts subsequently agreed that they were at fault in halting at Antwerp, but Montgomery made no such acknowledgement. It was basically Montgomery who was responsible for not ordering the immediate continuation of the advance after Antwerp was captured.

He was fully aware of the situation, and had the authority to take whatever action he thought appropriate. He would have needed no more resources than those he actually had, and the advance north from Antwerp would have helped rather than hindered his future plans for an advance to the east. Montgomery was the man who could have ordered and followed through on an advance north from Antwerp on 4 September. He did not.

Chapter Eight

ALLIED STRATEGIES

In the weeks immediately after the landing on 6 June 1944, the predominant objective in the minds of the Allied commanders – and their troops also, for that matter – was to cement and reinforce a bridgehead that the Germans could not dislodge. The general strategy was next to break out of the bridgehead, and then go – where? Because the conflicting strategies were so hotly debated and supported in the days following the break-out, it is important to see if there was a clear objective that the chosen strategy should have been aiming to achieve. This lack of an agreed strategy was certainly one of the contributors to the Great Mistake.

The person charged with drafting the plans for the assault on German-held France had the lengthy and imposing title Chief of Staff to the Supreme Allied Commander (Designate). He was Lt Gen F.E. Morgan, and he shortened the title to COSSAC. Gen Morgan's orders were to set up an Anglo-American Headquarters for the eventual Supreme Commander, and to prepare an outline plan for the invasion of north-west Europe from the United Kingdom.

Morgan reported to the Combined Chiefs of Staff (CCS), and he was charged by them to draw up a plan of assault and, in addition, to prepare for a campaign which would deliver a vital blow at the heart of Germany with a force of one hundred divisions. In more detail, the CCS Directive declared that the objective of the assault and follow-up, codenamed 'Overlord', was:

> To mount and carry out an operation, with forces and equipment established in the United Kingdom and with target date 1 May 1944, to secure a lodgement on the Continent from which further offensive operations could be developed. The lodgement area must contain sufficient port facilities to maintain a force of some twenty-six to thirty divisions, and enable that force to be augmented by follow-up shipments from the United States or elsewhere of additional divisions and supporting units at the rate of three to five divisions per month.

When Eisenhower was appointed Supreme Commander, he was given *his* directive by the CCS. He was told that he was to land on the coast of

France and thereafter to destroy the German ground forces. The significant paragraph read: 'You will enter the Continent of Europe, and, in conjunction with the other Allied nations, undertake operations aimed at the heart of Germany and the destruction of her armed forces.'

The 'destruction of Germany's armed forces' is spelt out clearly enough, but 'the vital blow at the heart of Germany' is less precise. Should it be a blow with political implications, such as the capture of Berlin, or an economic blow, such as the encirclement and destruction of the industrial complex of the Ruhr? Could it be the capture or assassination of Hitler, or the destruction of German morale by the annihilation of her major cities?

It is difficult to find a consistent definition of the vital blow in the contemporary documents, and in the early days of September there were several alternative strategies that could have been followed to meet the requirements of the imprecise directive. Four of these were:

1. To close up to the Rhine along its entire length, and then make a set-piece assault at one or more crossings. After the crossings, the objectives could be one of the following three (any one of which could be done without closing up to the Rhine along its entire length).
2. To thrust all the way to Berlin with a large armoured and motorised force.
3. To encircle the Ruhr from the north.
4. To encircle the Ruhr from the south.

Two other important objectives – although neither could be called a blow that was vital – were: to free North Holland and capture the sites that were launching V2 rockets on London; and to capture the supposed 'German National Redoubt' in the mountains of southern Germany.

Eisenhower's strategy was to advance on a broad front to the Rhine, and then plan an assault on the German heartland. If the German resistance was as weak as the intelligence summaries suggested, then the Rhine might be reached in no more than a few days. This would allow time to cross the Rhine and tear out the heart of Germany before the winter set in to reduce the mobility of his troops. The war could be over by Christmas 1944.

Montgomery's strategy, supported at least by Brooke, was to leave all troops stationary except for one main assault with a very large mobile force. This, Monty advised, should be in the north, with the Ruhr as one objective and Berlin as another. Bradley and Patton also thought that there should be one main thrust, but from further to the south.

Monty put his views on the correct strategy to Eisenhower in a concise message sent on 4 September:

I would like to put before you certain aspects of future operations and give you my views.

1. I consider we have now reached a stage where one really powerful and full-blooded thrust towards Berlin is likely to get there and thus end the German war.
2. We have not enough maintenance resources for two full-blooded thrusts.
3. The selected thrust must have all the maintenance resources it needs without any qualification, and any other operation must do the best it can with what is left over.
4. There are only two possible thrusts: one via the Ruhr and the other via Metz and the Saar.
5. In my opinion the thrust likely to give the best and quickest results is the northern one via the Ruhr.
6. Time is vital and the decision regarding the selected thrust must be made at once, and paragraph 3 above will then apply.
7. If we attempt a compromise solution and split our maintenance resources so that neither thrust is full-blooded we will prolong the war.
8. I consider the problem viewed as above is very simple and clear cut.
9. The matter is of such vital importance that I feel sure you will agree a decision on the above lines is required at once. If you are coming this way perhaps you would look in and discuss it. If so delighted to see you lunch tomorrow. Do not feel I can leave this battle just at present.

As a passing observation, this was not a message that many superiors would be happy to receive from a subordinate, and a further pinprick to increase Ike's irritation with Monty.

After some more correspondence between them, Eisenhower wrote on 15 September, two days before the start of Market Garden, and in one paragraph he says: 'Clearly, Berlin is the main prize, and the prize in defence of which the enemy is likely to concentrate the bulk of his forces. There is no doubt whatever in my mind that we should concentrate all our energies and resources on a rapid thrust to Berlin.'

LOGISTICS

In almost all of their messages, Monty and Ike and the other commanders are concerned about supply. While some extremely resourceful innovations were used in Overlord, there appears to be some lack of logical coordination between supply needs and the operations undertaken to satisfy those needs. All supplies had to be brought from the UK, and the only two methods of so doing were by air or by sea. Air was used, but it was expensive in its use of man and machine power. It also diverted planes from the much more aggressive task of ferrying airborne troops.

Sea was the only practical way of bringing the supplies needed by the forces of SHAEF. One of the methods of bringing supplies was landing over

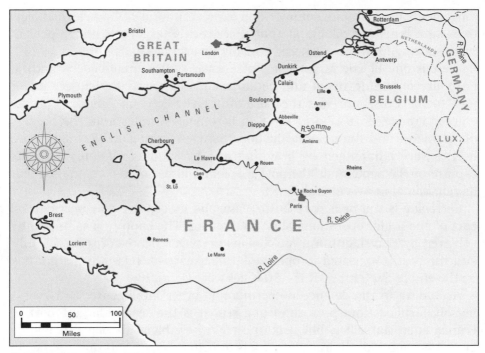

8. Ports of North-West Europe.

the beaches using the Mulberry harbours. By far the most efficient method was to capture an existing port in working order; or one capable of being restored to reasonable capacity in a short time.

The ports that could be considered to have a worthwhile capacity were, starting from the western end of France's northern coastline and travelling east to Holland: Brest, Cherbourg, Le Havre, Dieppe, Boulogne, Calais, Dunkirk, Ostend, Antwerp and Rotterdam.

Because the missions of Overlord were the destruction of the German Army and the striking of a vital blow at the heart of Germany, the Allies needed supply close to the borders of Germany. That is the area from where they could lunge for the heart, and where the strength of the German Army would be assembled. Therefore, those planning the operations to establish supply needed to evaluate each of the ports listed above against the factors: distance from the borders of Germany; transport systems in place from the port to the borders of Germany; probable realistic capacity of the port facilities after capture; ease of capture, as far as could be judged.

We can now evaluate each port with the benefit of hindsight, and we can say that the operational effort should have been directed on this or that port to the exclusion of the rest. But it would seem that some of the judgements made in late summer and early autumn 1944 overlooked facts that were readily available at that time. Let us take each major port in turn, starting from the west, and conduct an evaluation as if it was 1944.*

Brest is one of the larger ports of France, with a magnificent natural harbour containing naval and commercial docks. It is the closest major port to the USA, and was the port through which the American forces entered France in 1917 and 1918. It is some 450 miles from the borders of Germany, and the communications between Brest and Germany have been severely damaged by bombing and by sabotage. (Note: After its capture on 19 September, the port was found to be so badly damaged that its rehabilitation was abandoned.)

Cherbourg is the next port to the east, and its capture was an essential part of the initial operations after the landing. The capture was brilliantly achieved by Gen 'Lightning Joe' Collins and his VII US Corps on 15 July, and the port is expected to operate at a capacity of 10,000 tons per day by the end of September. It is 350 miles from Germany.

According to the defence overprints and other intelligence, *Le Havre* is heavily fortified from both land and sea. It is the second-largest port in France after Marseilles, but it is uncertain how badly damaged it will be after it is captured; the rail network is in better shape than that further to the west, and the distance to Germany is 280 miles.

The next major port is *Antwerp*, about 75 miles from Germany, with a capacity of 80–100,000 tons per day if it is captured undamaged. The rail network in Belgium is very little damaged, and the inland location (50 miles from the North Sea) means that transport systems radiate from it in all directions.

The last major port is *Rotterdam*, close to the mouth of the Lower Rhine. This is the closest port to Germany, and is one of the largest in Europe. Its capture will require the crossing of several rivers, and we can expect to find it heavily defended.

In making the evaluation of the actions to be taken to ensure that appropriate supply facilities were captured or established with minimum loss of fighting soldiers, the August 1944 planners were to some degree blinkered by the brief given to the COSSAC planners. Those original planners had been preoccupied with the amphibious assault and with keeping it ashore. They had been obsessed with the need for ports, and the residue of this obsession remained to stifle the flexibility of the August 1944 planners, and to distract their attention from more immediate and much larger opportunities.

---

* The ports between Le Havre and Antwerp, namely Dieppe, Boulogne, Calais, Dunkirk and Ostend, were classed as secondary ports. Their capture would have been useful, but the effort needed to capture them would have been a complete waste of resource that could much better have been directed on Antwerp.

There were two occasions on which the planners at Allied Supreme Headquarters appeared to be constrained by the original Overlord brief. The first was the capture of Avranches at the base of the Cotentin peninsula. From that road junction, a west turn led to Brittany and its ports, particularly Brest; east led to Germany. The second occasion was the crossing of the Seine in the last days of August, and the apparent collapse of the German armies between there and the Reich. The second occasion is the more important in respect of the Great Mistake, but we will look at each and review its significance in the achievement of the Overlord mission.

DECISION AT AVRANCHES

The original Overlord plan included the overrunning of Brittany and the capture of the Brittany ports to be used for supply. The plan predicted that the advance from the bridgehead would gradually move east, south and west, and by D + 90 the lodgement area would have expanded to form a rough rectangle bordered by the English Channel on the north, the Atlantic on the west, the River Loire on the south, and the River Seine on the east. The only substantial ports in this rectangle were Cherbourg in Normandy, and Brest, Lorient, St Nazaire and St Malo in Brittany.

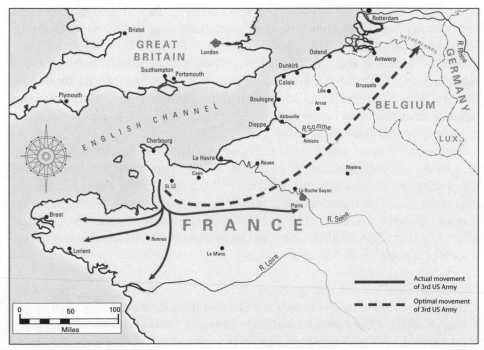

9. Decision at Avranches.

The Allied operations in Normandy created a different situation when the American armies punched a massive gap in the German line in the last days of July, and the spearhead of the breakthrough reached Avranches on 1 August. It was on this day that the 3rd US Army was activated, with Patton in command.

The 1st US Army continued to thrust south, but some of its units were able to turn east, and thus outflank the German line. The 3rd US Army, emerging from the corner at Avranches, could have moved east, south-east, south-west, and west. They could have gone in all these directions – and they did – and at the same time as capturing the Brittany ports, carry out a very wide flanking movement to reach the Seine on either side of Paris.

There was a decision to be made at Avranches. Given the sudden crumbling of the German line, was there any point in going in any direction but east? The Brittany ports could be left to wither on the vine, and the garrison forces in those ports were so short on mobility that they would pose no threat to the Allied forces in the field.

One of the leading divisions in the American break-out, starting on 25 July, was Maj Gen John Wood's 4 Armoured. When his division reached Avranches on 1 August he came under the command of Patton's 3rd US Army. Patton ordered him to advance south-west through Brittany with the small and relatively useless port of Vannes as his objective. At the same time Patton ordered Gen Grow's 6 US Armoured Division to move rapidly west and capture Brest. Wood protested to his Corps Commander Middleton that he was being ordered to advance in the wrong direction, west; Wood saw that from where he was Paris was the same distance to the east as Brest was to the west, and it was towards Germany that they should be going. It was ten days before Wood was allowed to turn east. He later recalled: 'I could have been there in the enemy's vitals in two days. But no! We were forced to adhere to the original plan – with the only armour available, and ready to cut the enemy to pieces. It was one of the colossally stupid decisions of the war.'

The reduction of Brest took the combined efforts of three American divisions, large quantities of ammunition, and was not complete until 19 September. When finally taken, the port was so badly damaged that it was abandoned by the Allies as a possible source of supply. A comment by Russell Weigley suggests that part of the responsibility for this wasted effort lay with Gen Bradley, who had been elevated to the command of 12 US Army Group on 1 August:

Up to a point, Bradley had displayed admirable flexibility in leaving open his course of action after the breakout, Operation Cobra. When Cobra shattered the left wing of the German position in Normandy more completely than he had dared to hope, he did not stop his troops when they reached the Coutances–Caumont line that was their objective. Instead, they capitalised on the mobility of the American army to keep them moving onward at a pace that strained supply lines. Nevertheless, perhaps in part under the weight of his new responsibilities as operational commander of an Army Group, Bradley was inflexible about Brittany. The Overlord plan called for the thrust into Brittany, and amid the bewildering rush of events at the end of July and the beginning of August Bradley evidently found an anchor of security in the plan.

Montgomery, still in operational command of all Allied ground forces, appears not to have considered or realised the possibility of ignoring Brittany and concentrating everything on a push to the east. In *Normandy to the Baltic*, he records: 'On 1 August HQ 3 US Army became operational, taking command of VIII US Corps; this included 4 and 6 US Armoured Divisions. This Corps moved south and west into Brittany with the task of cleaning up the peninsula and capturing its ports.' There is no suggestion that they could have been employed in any other way.

The conclusion to be drawn from 'decision at Avranches' is that a commander must be flexible enough to depart from previously laid-down plans if the change appears to promise greater benefit. The commander takes a risk, certainly; but there is the opposing risk – as occurred in the decision at Avranches – that slavishly following the original plans will waste material resources and the irreplaceable resource of time.

DECISION AT THE SEINE

We saw in Chapter One that the crossings of the Seine took place in the 21 Army Group sector between 25 and 31 August. It appeared that German resistance had been substantially broken, and there was an opportunity for determined and rapid pursuit. What precisely should the aim of that pursuit be? There were several alternatives, and each of these should be evaluated against the two principal missions of Overlord – the destruction of the German forces and a vital blow against the heart of Germany.

The two main strategies were the broad front and the narrow front. The broad front entailed attacking all along the front, with the first principal objective being the Rhine. The narrow front envisaged a strong push on a limited section of the front, the objective being to close up to a sector of the Rhine and then to force a bridgehead over it. Speed was important in both cases, but particularly in the second. If the bridgehead could be established well before the onset of winter, then it might be possible to exploit opportunities for deeper penetrations into Germany. The northern push, strongly advocated by Montgomery, proposed that the first objective after the Rhine should be the Ruhr, and the second Berlin.

To sustain either strategy, adequate supplies were essential. As the Allies advanced away from the beaches and Cherbourg, the supply lines were

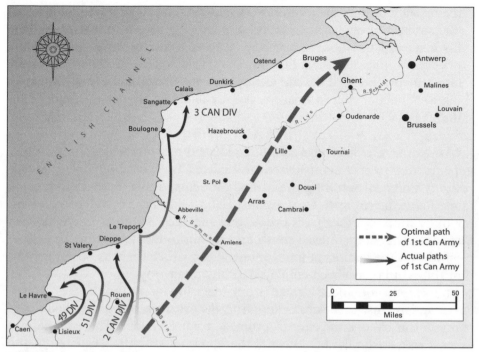

10. Decision at the Seine.

becoming more and more stretched. The obvious solution was to capture one or more of the Channel ports and put it into working order as quickly as possible. The bigger the potential capacity of the port the better, and the closer to Germany the better. We have seen that the major ports to be evaluated after crossing the Seine were Le Havre, Antwerp and Rotterdam, with Dieppe, Boulogne, Calais, Dunkirk and Ostend as secondary opportunities.

The Allied High Command had to make decisions to balance the need for establishing supply against the desire to obtain a bridgehead over the Rhine in time to exploit that bridgehead before winter. The need for a port could be satisfied most economically, both in time and in manpower, by concentrating on a large port rather than a number of smaller ports. After the Seine crossings the two ports that could be considered as objectives were Le Havre and Antwerp. Rotterdam was a third possibility, but in view of the greater distance and the number of very wide waterways to cross, it was less preferable to the other two. For this brief analysis the choice would then be between Le Havre and Antwerp. Le Havre would take forces westward, Antwerp eastward towards Germany; Antwerp would have to be the choice.

On 1 September 1944 the options facing the local commander, Montgomery, included:

1. Capture all ports between Le Havre and Antwerp inclusive.
2. Leave out some of the smaller ports, say Dunkirk and Ostend.
3. Leave out Le Havre as being in the wrong direction, and capture the rest.
4. Capture Antwerp, leaving all other ports until later.

Another factor to be taken into account was the presence in the Pas-de-Calais of the German 15th Army. It was known that it had shed divisions to the battle for Normandy, but it still had at least six divisions, plus perhaps the remnants of several others. Most of them were static or reserve divisions, not strong on mobility. However, if they had only to retreat slowly, and with the benefit of many defensible waterways, they might be able to inflict substantial delays unless they were hustled along quickly to the banks of the Scheldt estuary and there destroyed.

The Allied troops along the Channel coast were under the command of Gen Harry Crerar and his 1st Canadian Army. His two Corps Commanders were John Crocker, I British Corps, and Guy Simonds, II Canadian Corps. Simonds was an exceptional commander, and he had been designated as Crerar's replacement should that become necessary. Because of his role as Army Commander Designate, he was one of the very few people to whom the decrypts from Ultra, the intercepts of signals made between the German High Command, were made available. Jeffery Williams records Simonds' thoughts:

In the welter of situation reports by retreating German formations and orders from Hitler's headquarters, Simonds saw two related facts which offered both an opportunity for encircling a retreating army and a compelling reason for doing so. The first was that six divisions, nearly one hundred thousand men of 15 German Army, were falling back on the Scheldt where they intended to cross to Walcheren Island and then eastward, north of Antwerp. The second fact was that Hitler had ordered them to block the seaward approaches to Antwerp, to defend Walcheren, the banks of the Scheldt, the northern outskirts of Antwerp, and the Albert Canal as far as Maastricht.

The bulk of 15 Army was still south of the Scheldt. To Simonds the opportunity was obvious. Ignoring the channel ports for the moment, his corps should drive with all possible speed to Breskens, the port on the Scheldt opposite Walcheren, then turn to sweep along the south bank to Antwerp. The garrisons of the channel ports would be masked until they could be dealt with later. Only a few days would be involved in opening them, a small price to pay for destroying six undefeated enemy divisions.

Simonds urged his plan on Crerar, but Crerar declined either to seek Montgomery's approval or to change his own plan to capture the Channel ports. On the face of it, Crerar's reaction indicated a lack of imagination, a lack of that instinct to go for the enemy's jugular which is characteristic of a great field commander. It may have been quite true that Crerar was not an imaginative commander, but at that time he had been criticised by Monty in such a way that he was not going to risk any further actions that might give rise to complaint. And he knew that Monty at that time was little interested in Antwerp.

Monty was passionate about a deep thrust into Germany, and calculated that with the four smaller Channel ports he could support a push to the Ruhr and even to Berlin without the use of Antwerp. A note on his intentions recorded by his operations staff on 9 September show his calculations which gave the task of clearing the islands blocking the access to Antwerp 'last priority' among the tasks of the 1st Canadian Army.

Crerar's unwillingness to put forward Simonds' plan to Monty showed not a reluctance to argue, but rather an awareness of what was in Monty's mind, and Crerar's intention to follow the spirit of his superior's orders.

Monty always maintained that 'everything was proceeding according to plan'. In fact, he changed his plans very intelligently to meet changing circumstances such as weather, new German formations, unexpectedly difficult terrain such as the bocage, and under-performing Allied formations. However, he reported to the world at large that he had no need to make any changes, and this mindset may have influenced his subordinates' thinking and actions. They may have felt that the plan, especially the Overlord plan, should be carried through without modification. So Bradley had to liberate Brittany and capture Brest, and Crerar had to free all the Channel ports, rolling them up from the west.

This was a stultifying mindset.

Senior British commanders and staff officers in 21 Army Group put forward other variations on the appropriate strategy for the first weeks of September. The two of the greatest interest are those of generals de Guingand and Dempsey.

Maj Gen Freddie de Guingand was Monty's Chief of Staff at 21 Army Group Main HQ. Because Monty operated mainly from his TAC HQ, most of the communication between them was in writing rather than face to face. On 7 September, de Guingand wrote to Monty (this correspondence is in WO 205/5D):

Jock Whiteley came to lunch and we discussed various matters. [Major-General J.F.M. (Jock) Whiteley was a British officer on the operations staff of SHAEF. He was a strong supporter of Ike, and less than enthusiastic about Monty.] Ike still gives first priority to the northern thrust. 5 US Corps has not been withdrawn and is in line today on right of First Army. One division of 19 Corps has been withdrawn and sent to Third Army owing to lack of space north of the Ardennes. Other US divisions will be available if you require them and they can be maintained. Air supply: northern thrust will have priority. Whiteley's opinion is that we could have two US airborne divisions in accordance with Ike's directive allotting airborne army to 21 AG. These might be employed for the capture of Walcheren Island; this might be the right answer to speed the use of Antwerp, and should not affect air supply greatly, because after the capture these divisions could be immediately withdrawn. Project is being examined.

On 8 September, de Guingand wrote again to Monty:

The more I consider the use of the American airborne divisions for the capture of Walcheren Island the more I like it. It would perform the twofold object of clearing the way for the opening of Antwerp, and will block the German escape route from the Pas de Calais.

I have told Charles Richardson [Brigadier-General Staff (Plans) 21 Army Group] to get on to the Airborne Army about it, and when we receive your decision we will take the necessary action. I understand the air are keen on doing it because the air commitment for neutralising the island will be a big one.

Gen Miles Dempsey commanded the British 2nd Army. He kept a brief diary (WO 285/9) and his entry for 9 September reads:

Saturday 9 September 1944: D + 95
1000: Saw C-in-C at TAC HQ 21 AG with Crerar and Hodges. We discussed future operations. Canadian Army will clear Le Havre, Boulogne, Calais, and Dunkirk as soon as possible, and will clear the area north of Ghent as a second priority. They will take over the Ghent area from me at once.

1300: Saw Commander XXX Corps [General Horrocks] at his HQ at Diest. His operations in the Albert Canal bridgehead continue to be strongly opposed and I told him to postpone the airborne landing until the night 11/12 September at the earliest. [*Note*: This was Operation Comet, the cancelled predecessor to Market Garden.]

1530: Saw Commander XII Corps [General Ritchie] at my HQ. The transfer of his corps to the Antwerp area is proceeding satisfactorily, and he is planning an operation with 53 Division to strike north from Antwerp. He may be able to carry this out on 11 September.

It is clear that the enemy is bringing up all the reinforcements he can lay hands on for the defence of the Albert Canal, and that he appreciates the importance of the area Arnhem–Nijmegen. It looks as though he is going to do all he can to hold it. This being the case, any question of a rapid advance to the north-east seems unlikely. Owing to our maintenance situation, we will not be in a position to fight a real battle for perhaps ten days or a fortnight. Are we right to direct Second Army to Arnhem, or would it be better to hold a left flank along the Albert Canal and strike due east towards Cologne in conjunction with 1 US Army?

REVIEW OF ALLIED STRATEGY

The Overlord mission issued to Eisenhower was to 'enter the Continent of Europe and . . . undertake operations aimed at the heart of Germany and the destruction of her armed forces'. This mission was presumably to be achieved with the minimum of Allied casualties, although no overt statement was made about this. However, the need to conserve manpower would have been in the minds of all the Allied commanders, particularly the British. They had been at war for exactly five years on 3 September 1944, and their reserves of manpower were fast running out. The women of Britain were already making an enormous contribution to the workforce so that men could be released for military service.

In the first weeks of the Normandy battles the losses, especially in infantry, were much higher than expected. On 14 August Monty cabled Brooke (CAB 106/1066):

Regret time has now come when I must break up one infantry division. My infantry divisions are so low in effective rifle strength that they can no – repeat NO – longer fight effectively in major operations. The need for this action has been present for some time but the urgency of the present battle operations forced me to delay decision. Can now do so no longer. Request permission to break up at once 59 Division. Its 56 Infantry Brigade will be retained as an independent brigade for the present. Request matter be treated as urgent, repeat urgent, and authority sent tomorrow.

Permission was granted immediately, and 59 Division was disbanded before the end of August, as were other units. 56 Brigade became part of 49 Division when its 70 Infantry Brigade was disbanded; 33 Armoured Brigade lost two tank regiments, 8 and 34 Armoured Brigades each lost a tank regiment, and 27 Armoured Brigade was disbanded.

The British planners knew before D-Day that 21 Army Group would be limited by the number of reinforcements that could be made available. The greater-than-expected losses further reduced 21 Army Group's capabilities, while the US forces had many replacement divisions, as well as reinforcements for divisions, already in Normandy. The manpower status must be evaluated against the stages of the Overlord mission. There were in effect three stages:

1. Secure a firm lodgement in France.
2. Break out from the lodgement area to an intermediate objective; this might have been the line of the Seine or the line of the Rhine, depending on how decisively they could shatter the German opposition before it could regroup.

3. From the intermediate line, deliver a vital blow to the heart of Germany, two possibilities being the capture of Berlin or the annihilation of the industries of the Ruhr. In all of the stages there would be the progressive destruction of the Wehrmacht.

It was of course necessary to maintain adequate supply to allow the achievement of the three stages of the mission. The strategies had thus to encompass the optimum methods of achieving the operational objectives, and maintaining supply to allow their achievement.

In view of the known manpower problems, and as a matter of common sense, it would seem logical that there should be no dissipation of resources in operations that were not going to contribute positively to the mission. We have seen that the Brittany excursion achieved nothing positive. It removed VIII US Corps from the main attacking echelon, caused substantial casualties and expenditure of ammunition, and wasted time when every minute was precious if advantage was to be taken of the weather.

The capture of the Channel ports, although adding to the flow of supply, was again a time-wasting strategy in relation to the weather.

There are several lessons to be learnt from the post-break-out operations of SHAEF, and we will consider those later. For now we will restate the decisions that were made. In a subsequent chapter we will look at the results of the execution of those decisions. The decisions cover only the northern sector of Allied operations, essentially those made by Montgomery when he was Allied Ground Force Commander and C-in-C 21 Army Group at the same time; they were:

1. Overrun Brittany and capture its ports.
2. Capture all the Channel ports.
3. Advance to Brussels and Antwerp.
4. Establish a bridgehead over the Rhine and then advance to the Ruhr, Berlin, or both.

Montgomery's intentions on 3 September are made explicit in 21 Army Group Operational Situation and Directive of that date (WO 285/2), which reads in part:

General Situation
1. Second Army is advancing to secure the area Brussels–Ghent–Antwerp. Its left flank (XII Corps) is echeloned back to watch the left flank until the Canadian Army can get forward to the Bruges area.
2. Canadian Army is moving forward across the Somme at Abbeville to its task of clearing the coastal belt.

Intention
3. To advance eastward and destroy all enemy forces encountered.

4. To occupy the Ruhr, and get astride the communications leading from it into Germany and to the sea ports.

Canadian Army

5. Canadian Army will clear the coastal belt, and will then remain in the general area Bruges–Calais until the maintenance situation allows of its employment further forward.

Second Army

6. On 6 September the Army will advance eastwards with its main bodies from the general line Brussels–Antwerp. Before that date light forces will operate far afield as desired.

7. The western face of the Ruhr between Düsseldorf and Duisberg will be threatened frontally.

8. The main weight of the Army will be directed on the Rhine between Wesel and Arnhem. The Ruhr will be bypassed round its northern face, and cut off by a southward thrust through Hamm.

9. One division, or if necessary a corps, will be turned northwards towards Rotterdam and Amsterdam.

10. Having crossed the Rhine, the Army will deal with the Ruhr and will be directed on the general area Osnabrück–Hamm–Münster–Rheine.

No mention was made of freeing the waterway leading to the Antwerp docks, and nothing about the elimination or containment of the German 15th Army. This directive was issued to Dempsey and Crerar, and must have made it clear what was important as far as Montgomery was concerned. Even if Dempsey had suggested a strong thrust northwards immediately after the capture of Antwerp, such an operation would almost certainly have been turned down. The suggestion was not made.

The instructions to Crerar are devoid of any urgency, and allow a leisurely closing up to the south bank of the Scheldt. And Crerar, as we have seen, was unlikely to challenge these orders.

Chapter Nine

GERMAN STRATEGY AND ITS EXECUTION

After the disaster of the Falaise pocket, the Germans, personified by Hitler, realised that unless they took great care, aggressive action by the Allies could well breach the West Wall and lead on to the encirclement of the Ruhr and the capture of Berlin. Hitler did take prompt action. There were several things he could do, but first he had to define his intentions and the tasks needed to achieve them.

While it is not stated precisely, his objective in relation to his west front was to delay the invasion of Germany by the Allies. Among the tasks that he could authorise were:

1. Strengthening the West Wall.
2. Strangling Allied supply lines.
3. Calling up new formations.
4. Creating temporary defence lines to delay the Allied advance.
5. Transferring formations from other theatres of war.
6. Strengthening the command structure.

Hitler decided to take all of these actions, although the number of formations transferred was not significant. He was particularly concerned to block supply through the Channel ports and Antwerp. We look now at the War Directives and other instructions he issued to carry out these tasks.

SIEGFRIED LINE REBORN

The West Wall was the 1944 name for the Siegfried Line. Construction of the Siegfried Line fortifications began in 1936, immediately after the demilitarisation of the Rhineland. Work was pursued vigorously until 1940, when it was felt that it had become redundant. The Line extended from the Swiss border to the junction of the German, Dutch and Belgian borders. From there north to Cleve the strength of the Line tapered off into a series of isolated bunkers and tank obstacles. It was at its strongest

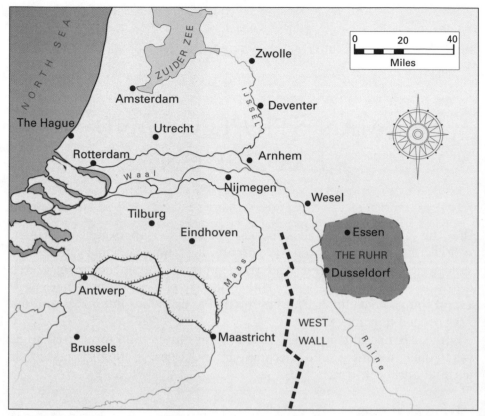

11. The West Wall.

in the Saar, where it was nearly 3 miles deep. For much of the rest of its length, the depth varied from a mile to a hundred yards. Typically, it was half a mile deep, and contained two rows of forts.

The forts were of different designs, but were usually manned by either machine-gun or anti-tank gun crews, and were sited to produce a closely interlocked zone of fire. The roofs and walls were built of concrete 5 feet thick, and their average size was 35 feet by 45 feet. The normal complement of soldiers for a fort was ten, and they had a cold and damp existence.

No new work had been done on the fortifications since May 1940, and much of the wire entanglements had been removed and many of the mines lifted since then. But the Line could still present a formidable barrier to attacking troops. On 24 August 1944 Hitler issued War Directive 61, 'Order for the construction of a defensive position in the West'. The part of it that relates to the northern end of the Line describes an extension of the fortifications in a north-westerly direction from the existing line, and reads: 'I order the construction of a defensive position in the West by means of a call-up of the civil population in sector "a" [the only sector relevant to the Great Mistake]. Gauleiter Grohe, Reich Commissioner in Belgium and Northern France, will be responsible for the line Scheldt–Albert Canal to the west of Aachen, where it will join the West Wall.'

On 1 September Hitler published his War Directive 63:

I issue the following orders for placing the West Wall in a state of defence.

a. The position (including those portions of the Maginot Line which are to be incorporated) will be strengthened by the construction of field works.
b. The extension of the West Wall, already announced, will be strengthened by field works and, where possible, by permanent structures extending as far as the Zuider Zee.
c. The whole construction will be carried out by a call-up of the civil population acting under the instructions of the local Gauleiters.

This directive was overtaken by events, specifically the advance to and capture of Brussels and Antwerp by the Allies. Hitler at once gave orders for the 'fortresses' of Boulogne and Dunkirk to be reinforced and held at all costs, and for the Albert Canal from Antwerp to Maastricht to be defended. His War Directive 64, dated 3 September, states:

Directive for further operations by Commander-in-Chief West:

1. Our own heavily tried forces, and the impossibility of bringing up adequate reinforcements quickly, do not allow us at the present moment to determine a line which must be held, and which certainly can be held. Therefore it is important to gain as much time as possible for raising and bringing up new formations, and for the development of the Western defences, and to destroy enemy forces by local attacks.
2. I therefore issue the following orders for the conduct of operations: the right flank and centre of the Army in the West will dispute every inch of ground with the enemy by stubborn delaying action. The likelihood of local penetrations must be accepted, but these must not lead to the encirclement of large German formations.

Further directives on 7 and 9 September (64a and 64b) gave plenary powers over all forces in the West (with some minor naval exceptions) to Field Marshal von Rundstedt, and confirmed that he would assume command of the German western defences on 11 September.

Rundstedt emphasised the importance of the Siegfried Line in an order he issued on 15 September to his formations: 'The Siegfried Line is of decisive importance in the battle for Germany. I order: that the Siegfried

Line and each of its defensive fortresses will be held to the last round and until completely destroyed. This order will be communicated forthwith to all headquarters, military formations, battle commanders and troops.'

CHOKING ALLIED SUPPLY

At some point during the twentieth century the supply of military necessities was dignified by renaming it 'logistics'. Whatever it is called, the steady provision of an adequate flow of ammunition, petrol, food, maintenance spares, clothing and thousands of other items, is essential if an army is to be able to fulfil its role in either attack or defence. Planning the logistics for the Normandy invasion was done with great skill by Allied staff officers who by this time had a wealth of experience to call on.

At the beginning of the invasion, supplies came over the beaches, and then the artificial Mulberry harbours were put in place. As long as the campaign did not move far away from the beaches, supplies came into the bridgehead in adequate quantities. Formations were able to access the supplies they needed by travelling short distances only, without tying up their transport resources to any abnormal extent.

As soon as the Seine had been crossed, however, and Allied movement north-east and east had become so rapid, the supply services became greatly overstretched. The original planning of Operation Overlord had envisaged that the Germans would retreat in an orderly fashion to the Seine. They would establish a defensive position on the river, and a formal, massive set-piece attack would be needed to force a crossing. By this time the logistics services would have been able to establish supply dumps close to the west bank of the Seine sufficiently large to maintain an advance to the borders of Germany, if not beyond.

As we have seen, the Allies, in spite of severe fighting at some crossings, were able to bounce the Seine and build bridges in three to five days, and then push on at a speed unthinkable to the planners. The supply chain lengthened dramatically, and this had several effects.

The logistics services were put under extreme pressure in terms of both men and machines. This was not helped by the unserviceability of 1,400 British-built trucks, the debris on the roads, the clogging of the roads by masses of traffic, civilian and military, and the innumerable detours in unknown country.

The normal establishment of trucks, which had proved quite adequate in Normandy, now became much too small to meet the tonnages and the distances. The solution to this problem was to ground complete divisions and use their trucks to meet the needs of the divisions leading the advance. However, the grounded divisions were then unavailable to reinforce and speed up the pursuit of the German troops retreating in disarray.

One way to increase the delivery of supplies to the forward troops was by air. This is obviously a slow and expensive method, and diverts the planes from other possible uses such as dropping airborne soldiers. But it was used, and certainly to some effect. During the four weeks 19 August to 16 September the average weekly delivery to 21 Army Group and 12 US Army Group combined was 5,000 tons.

Another method of speeding up supply was to capture ports along the Channel coast between Cherbourg and Antwerp. There were other large ports in Brittany, such as Brest, Lorient and St Nazaire, but they were in the wrong direction, and it was the Channel ports that mattered. And they mattered to Hitler just as much as they did to the Allies. The longer he could keep the ports unusable, the slower the Allies' advance would be, and it would be with a smaller quantity of tanks, guns, ammunition and weight of artillery fire. It would also give him more time to strengthen the defences along the western borders of Germany.

The significant ports along the Channel coast are listed below, together with the dates they were captured by the Allies and the dates they were able to discharge cargo. The table also shows the daily tonnage they could handle. In all cases, the ports were able to discharge some cargo before the dates shown, and in most they were able to increase their capacity after those dates.

Capacity of Channel Ports

Port	Captured	Open	Tons per day
Cherbourg	15 July	29 September	10,000
Le Havre	12 September	9 October	3,650
Dieppe	1 September	7 September	6,500
Boulogne	22 September	12 October	11,000
Calais	30 September	November	Personnel only
Dunkirk	Did not surrender until May 1945		
Ostend	9 September	28 September	5,000
Antwerp	5 September	26 November	*19,000

* Later increased to 80–100,000 tons per day.

There were two strategies that Hitler could pursue in respect of the Channel ports: evacuate, or hold for as long as possible.

Evacuation would have been preceded by complete destruction of all docking and unloading facilities in the port. All machinery and equipment would be destroyed, waterways blocked by sinking ships and creating other obstacles, and all would be garnished with multitudinous mines and booby traps. The troops could be progressively withdrawn, by land where there was still land access, and by sea where there was not. Evacuation by sea exposed the German troopships to Allied naval and air power, but it was probable that most of the troops would reach the shores of 'Greater Germany' in safety.

Had the garrisons of the ports been evacuated in this way, they could have been reconstituted into field formations. The morale of the troops would have been boosted by their rescue, and by the feeling that the German High Command still remembered them, and cared enough to make the rescue effort.

The alternative strategy was to hold the ports as long as possible. The factors to consider in this strategy were: if the garrisons remained, how long could they hold out; and what efforts would the Allies make to capture the ports? Obviously the Allies needed ports, but would they bypass the smaller ones and concentrate only on the two or three big ones? In that case the garrisons of the bypassed ports would represent a complete waste of manpower. Such garrisons would not constitute a thorn in the side of the Allied forces because they were essentially static troops, had little if any equipment to give them mobility, and were for the most part untried in battle.

The balance that Hitler and the German High Command had to strike could be evaluated thus:

Evacuation

Benefits: troops from the garrisons would be brought back to Germany where they could be trained as necessary for incorporation into field divisions. This would be a significant addition to the dwindling strength of the Wehrmacht; it was estimated that there were at least 120,000 soldiers in the fortresses.

Disadvantages: if the ports were abandoned they could be occupied by the Allies without incurring casualties – except those killed or wounded by mines, booby traps and other hazards in the process of repairing and restoring the port facilities. The Germans may also have been uncertain about the Allies' capabilities for this type of repair and restoration. If the Allies could just walk in, even with the obstacles of mines and so on, would they be able to get the ports operational in only a few days?

Retention

Benefits: if a port was vigorously defended it could deny additional supply to the Allies, could tie up Allied troops, and possibly cause substantial casualties. It might also cause political pressure, because the inhabitants of the ports, French or Belgian, could feel they had been abandoned by the Allies, and left to starve slowly or be killed by shelling and bombing that might be undertaken to make the Germans realise that their presence had not been forgotten.

Disadvantages: as stated earlier, garrison troops could not contribute directly to the defence of the borders of the Fatherland. If they had to receive any supplies by sea, such as ammunition or other military necessities, the supply ships and their escorts might well suffer loss.

In choosing between the alternative strategies, Hitler's mindset against giving up territory made the retention of the ports the only possible choice for him. The guarding of the Atlantic Wall, as the chain of fortresses set up around the coastline of France and Belgium was called, was the responsibility of the Commander-in-Chief West (OB West). The fortresses were subject to specific instructions from Hitler both as to their construction and their operation. On the north and west coasts they included Dunkirk, Calais, Boulogne, Le Havre, Cherbourg and Brest. They were to be defended 'to the last drop of blood', and the fortress commandant was to be personally responsible with his head if this was not carried out. The fortresses were to be given the biggest guns, the thickest concrete and the best troops.

These orders were executed in part. There was plenty of concrete in the shape of gun-emplacements, pillboxes and tank obstacles. There were big guns pointing seaward; but as with other strongholds of this type, of which Singapore is a prime example, the landward defences were distinctly flabby. And the garrisons, with one or two exceptions, were neither first-rate troops nor were they highly motivated.

A resolute garrison can cause very substantial casualties to its attackers, as well as delay to its enemy's operations or logistics. One of the most imposing examples of resolute defence was that provided by the Spaniard Mariano Alvarez de Castro in the antiquated fortress of Gerona in 1810. He was besieged by the French 7th Corps, and held out until half of the inhabitants and two-thirds of the garrison of 9,000 soldiers had died. He told those who urged surrender that when the last food was gone they could eat the cowards. When asked by his officers as to where they should retire, he replied 'to the cemetery'. His resistance cost him his life under appalling circumstances, but he had closed the principal road into eastern Spain for seven months, and had killed 14,000 of Napoleon's best soldiers.

The only German garrison commandant to come anywhere near emulating such a defence was the General of Parachute Troops Herman Ramcke at Brest. He had 30,000 tough soldiers under his command, and it took three American divisions three weeks of hard house-to-house fighting to gain possession of the port. But the harbour facilities had been so thoroughly destroyed that the Allied plans for its use as a major port had to be abandoned.

CREATION AND TRANSFER OF FORMATIONS

In Chapter Two we saw that there was potential for Hitler to transfer formations and create new formations. Transfers came initially from Holland, as for example 719 Division. Other areas from where formations could have been withdrawn included Norway, Denmark, Yugoslavia, Italy and the Eastern Front. II SS Panzer Corps had been transferred from Russia in June, but that front was under considerable pressure at the end of August. In balancing the threats between the Eastern and Western Fronts, it appears that Hitler decided he could not afford to move anything more from east to west.

He did authorise the transfer of 3 and 15 Panzergrenadier Divisions from Italy on 15 August (DEFE 3/122 and 3/123), the divisions being destined for use by OB West. These transfers and others, however, had no effect on the Scheldt–Albert Canal sector of the front. But what did have an effect on this part of the line was the calling-up of paratroop formations and Luftwaffe field divisions. Volksgrenadier (VG) divisions were also created as rapidly as possible and, while undertrained and not well equipped, they were able, under determined officers, to offer a static but resolute defence.

STRENGTHENING THE COMMAND STRUCTURE

Von Kluge replaced von Rundstedt as OB West on 4 July. Under his command were Army Group B under Rommel in the north, and Army Group G under Blaskowitz in the south. Rommel was badly wounded on 17 July, and was not replaced. Von Kluge, who was now simultaneously OB West and OB Army Group B, committed suicide on 17 August, and was replaced by Model.

As the break-out from Normandy became a progressively greater threat to the borders of Germany, Hitler had to decide whether his command structure in the west was appropriate to meet the threat. Between 1 and 11 September he modified the structure. The major change was to reappoint von Rundstedt as OB West, thus relieving Model from his dual responsibilities. This allowed Model to concentrate on the operations of his Army Group B, while von Rundstedt took responsibility for the allocation and operation of the Wehrmacht along the entire Western Front.

Figure 5: Oberbefehlshaber (OB) West 30 September 1944

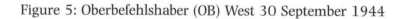
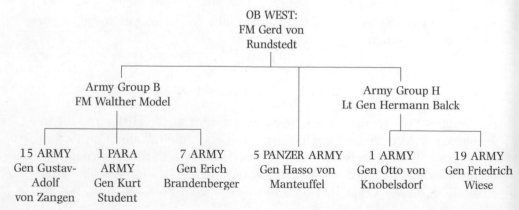

The assault on Le Havre by I British Corps on 10 September 1944 was preceded by very heavy bombing attacks by the RAF. (*IWM BU 1196*)

Operation Astonia (the assault on Le Havre) was made by 49 Infantry Division supported by 34 Armoured Brigade and 51 Infantry Division supported by 33 Armoured Brigade. These are some of 34 Brigade's Churchill tanks. (*IWM BU 1197*)

Lt Gen Brian Horrocks was one of the most successful British Corps commanders, and was well respected and liked by the troops he commanded. (*IWM B 7302*)

Field Marshal Gerd von Rundstedt was much respected in the German Army, both for his conduct in battle and for speaking his mind on contentious issues. (*IWM MH 10132*)

Field Marshal Walther Model was a strong supporter of Hitler, and showed his support by aggression in attack and resolution in defence at whatever level he commanded. (*IWM MH 12850*)

Army supplies are hoisted by crane from the hold of an Allied ship in Antwerp docks, and are loaded directly into railway wagons, December 1944. Belgian dock workers assist in the operation. The photograph clearly shows that the docks were undamaged by the bombing. (*CS (Cegesoma) 29996*)

Spectators on the upper deck of an Antwerp wharf watch the unloading of the first ship to enter the liberated harbour. (*CS 81375*)

Belgian Resistance fighters put their lives at risk in helping the Allies. Here the funeral of Francis Cogels, leader of the White Brigade in Herenhout, is shown. He was killed in a skirmish with the Germans. (*IWM B 10017*)

Gen Dwight D. Eisenhower commanded the Allied forces during the invasion of Europe. He was a very good leader and coordinator of the troops of several nations, but was continually denigrated by Brooke and Montgomery. (*IWM CH 12031*)

Gen Miles Dempsey (left) was the least flamboyant of generals, but one of the most effective. He deserves the title of 'the quiet achiever'. He is accompanied by Canadian Lt Gen Guy Simonds, one of the effective Corps Commanders in 21 Army Group. (*IWM B7268*)

Gen Harry Crerar (left), seen here with Monty, commanded the 1st Canadian Army. He was conservative and cautious, and was despised by Monty. This made for a lack of rapport between the two, and led to some lost opportunities. (*IWM BU 1733*)

A jeep of the 11th Armoured Division in the City Park, Antwerp. The 'Boom' chalked on the front may refer to the Antwerp suburb through which the Division entered. (*CS 28794*)

Welcome to Antwerp. No one would deny the soldier his reward from an attractive Belgian girl, but it would have been better for him and many other soldiers had he been commanded to move on without stopping, so that the Germans would not have had time to escape and regroup. (*IWM B 10021*)

'The beeg cannon.' Had the gun fired, the eardrums of most of the spectators would have been shattered. One 17-pounder that was fired broke all the windows in the street. (*IWM B 10020*)

A turretless Honey tank stands outside St Joseph's Church, Antwerp. It was a very swift and manoeuvrable tank, much used for reconnaissance. (*CS 28704*)

Lt Gen Guy Simonds, shown here with Monty, commanded II Canadian Corps. He was a brilliant and perceptive commander, but his suggestions were generally ignored by his superior, Harry Crerar. (*IWM B11552*)

Ferries carrying German troops being attacked by 2 Tactical Air Force at Breskens, 12 September 1944. Flying with 2 TAF was a squadron of the Royal Dutch Naval Air Service, the pilots of which recognised many landmarks over their home country. (*IWM CL 1091*)

Shermans of 11th Armoured Division in Antwerp after its liberation. (*CS 28389*)

In late October Clarkeforce, consisting of an infantry battalion and a regiment of Churchill tanks together with supporting arms, thrust north-west in the direction of Bergen op Zoom to relieve pressure on Canadian troops. (*IWM BU 1771*)

At the request of the Canadian Army, and with the acquiescence of the Zeelander population, bombing of the dykes by the RAF turned the centre of the island of Walcheren into a vast lake. (*IWM B 12451*)

Zeelanders enduring the floods and overcoming the difficulties of obtaining supplies, December 1944. They are reported to have said that the sea was better than the Germans. (*IWM B 12452*)

A bridge-laying Churchill puts a bridge across a canal in Roosendaal soon after the town was liberated by 49 Division and 9 RTR. (*IWM B11485*)

An Allied landing craft beaches during the assault on Flushing. A Weasel is approaching the exit ramp, and some of the devastation and defences can be seen in the background. (*IWM A 26868*)

An armoured bulldozer at work clearing a road through what was Westkapelle. (*IWM BU 1270*)

The coast of Walcheren Island was defended by heavy guns and blockhouses, which had to be put out of action to allow shipping to enter the Scheldt Estuary. (*IWM BU 1273*)

The result of land and air cooperation at Westkapelle. Before Allied troops landed at this point the RAF blasted a gap through for them. (*IWM BU 1271*)

Half-tracks of 11th Armoured Division roll down a sunny, leafy boulevard in Antwerp and are greeted by the Belgians they have liberated, September 1944. (*CS 28760*)

Members of the Antwerp Resistance who fought against the Germans and with the Allies in the liberation of the city. These Belgian patriots were of great assistance in guiding Allied soldiers through the city. (*CS 28972*)

taff of Headquarters at every level had to meet changes of plan all the time, and this meant working at all hours. (*IWM B 7408*)

A British Military Policeman surrounded by grateful townsfolk. MPs were not loved by all soldiers, ut they had an important and often dangerous role to play. (*CS 28766*)

Edouard Pilaet, codename François, was assistant to Lt Urbain Reniers and was responsible for the militia and partisans in the Antwerp area. (*CS 32500*)

Lt Urbain Reniers, codename Réaumur (centre), was placed in charge of the armed resistance groups in Antwerp. By September 1944 there were 3,500 people in these groups. (*CS 32677*)

REVIEW OF GERMAN STRATEGY

Hitler had a simple mission at the beginning of September 1944: to delay the assault on Germany from the west for as long as possible, and to put up maximum resistance if and when it came. The main elements of his strategy to achieve this mission were:

1. Strengthen the West Wall.
2. Set up defence lines to delay the Allies' approach to the West Wall.
3. Prevent supplies reaching the Allies by denying the use of the Channel ports, particularly the port of Antwerp.
4. Make total use of Germany's human resources in its defence.

In this analysis of the Great Mistake we are concerned only with German strategy in the Scheldt estuary–Albert Canal area. The strategy that was adopted in this area is contained within the entries in the War Diary of the German High Command – in German, Oberkommando der Wehrmacht (OKW). These entries record messages from field commanders, assessments of the situation and instructions issued by OKW.

Extracts from OKW war diary
4 September: An order was issued to the effect that the fortresses Boulogne and Dunkirk, the defence area Calais, the island of Walcheren with its harbour Flushing, the bridgehead at Antwerp, and the position along the Albert Canal as far as Maastricht were to be held.

15 Army was asked to prepare the fortresses and fortress areas for the defence. The defence of the Albert Canal was assigned to the newly created 1 Parachute Army (General Oberst Student). For this purpose all of his units in the Fatherland and 3, 5 and 6 Parachute Divisions were assigned to him. In addition he was assigned XLVIII Infantry Corps with two divisions, ten battalions and forty flak batteries, new activations of the replacement army, security units and combat groups from the north-west.

Work was to begin on a bridgehead south of the Scheldt estuary (the Breskens pocket), on defences on the island of Walcheren, and on the construction of a front line along the Albert Canal.

6 September: OB West was instructed that the 15th Army should refrain from penetrating in the direction of Louvain, the proposed break-out to the east (see Map 6), and instead that von Zangen should ferry his troops across to the islands of Walcheren and Beveland under the protection of the Ghent support line. In the case that the enemy would follow hesitantly in the Antwerp area, an attempt to slip through north of the city was held in abeyance. [Note: But not for long; much of the 15th Army did slip through north of Antwerp using the isthmus at Woensdrecht; the fact the Allies allowed this to happen is what constitutes the Great Mistake.]

The 15th Army was charged with the responsibility for the flooding which was to protect our forces.

7 September: Since the fortresses Le Havre, Boulogne and Calais tied down the Canadian Corps, and inundations as well as streams aided the 15th Army, the latter could continue its movements on this day according to schedule. The line Zeebrugge–Ghent was reached during the night 7/8 September. Up to noon 7 September 25,000 men were already ferried across to Walcheren. High seas, fog and attacks by enemy aircraft interfered with further ferrying; but despite these difficulties we succeeded in concluding this operation better than was originally expected.

The Führer again requested that a bridgehead opposite Flushing be held, and said that he attached great importance to additional inundations.

EXECUTION OF THE STRATEGY

The strategy for the Scheldt–Albert Canal area was executed by Model and his Army Group B. There were three operations of major importance in the initial stages of the execution; two were planned from above, and one was self-generated by the initiative of one man. The three operations were: ferrying units of the 15th Army across the Scheldt; activation and assignment of 1 Parachute Army; and the self-generated operation was the reconstitution of 85 Division by its commander, General Leutnant Kurt Chill under the name of Kampfgruppe (KG) Chill. We will look at each of these in turn.

The withdrawal of the 15th Army over the Scheldt
Report by General von Zangen
While the fighting for the Scheldt was still going on, the withdrawal began on the night of 6 September, first to take the line of the barricade Bruges–Ghent St Nicholas, under cover of which the crossing had then to be effected. The movement was started by 59 Division. The withdrawal of 59 and 345 Divisions was carried out under intense enemy action.

At the crossing places Breskens–Flushing and Terneuzen–Hoedekenskerke, there was unified control from 6 September. Both of the commanders in charge of the crossing places had complete authority over all branches of the armed forces. March routes were fixed and allocated to formations about to cross the river, along which they were to come up to when called for.

Enemy air activity was extremely harassing in its effects. Up to six air attacks were made per day. Even the fairly strong static antiaircraft artillery at Breskens and Flushing, and that mounted on barges, was not able to give adequate help. On and after 15 September the embarking, docking and the crossing of the river had to be carried out at night.

8 September: Ghent was lost after a heavy battle; the canal on its north-western edge was still held by us. LXVII Corps arrived on the line of the

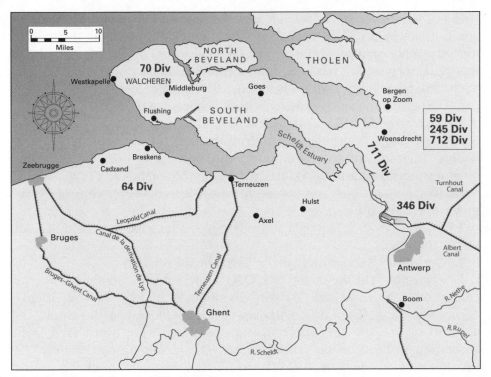

12. Relocation of German 15th Army.

barricade. Naval formations from the Ostend–Bruges area (200–300 men) were incorporated into the defence along the Bruges–Zeebrugge canal.

9 and 10 September: With the exception of Bruges, the enemy was feeling his way forward reluctantly, while he was more active north-east of Ghent. The enemy maintained a bridgehead near Moerbrugge and was building a bridge there; attempts to prevent the building by artillery fire failed. The Woensdrecht bridgehead north of Antwerp was further improved and reinforced considerably with artillery, antiaircraft and anti-tank equipment. [Note: The Woensdrecht bridgehead guarded the isthmus across which the 15th Army was escaping to the east.]

11 and 12 September: The enemy started to make powerful scouting raids on the whole extent of the front, with centres of gravity near Bruges and north of Ghent. Enemy troops undertook several assaults from the bridgehead at Moerbrugge to the north and north-west.

LXVII Corps staff was making preparations for crossing in order to be employed in the area of 1 Parachute Army. On 13 September LXVII Corps was transported over the river and started to take over one of the areas north of Antwerp.

Heavy air attacks on the Scheldt ferries, considerable bombing of Breskens and the railway installations on Walcheren and South Beveland; the bulk of the ferry boats were put out of action; the passage out of Terneuzen harbour was blocked by sunken boats. As soon as the Scheldt barricade line is further narrowed, 64 Infantry Division is to move to the region north of the Leopold Canal to occupy the newly ordered Scheldt Fortress South.

13 September: LXXXIX Corps, after several useless attempts to wipe out the Moerbrugge bridgehead, withdrew behind the Leopold Canal. The enemy pursued our troops closely, and soon started preparations for building a bridge north of Maldeghem. The 15th Army was preparing to move its command post to Doordrecht in order to take over control of the sector north of Antwerp.

15 September: 70 Infantry Division completed its crossing of the Scheldt to Walcheren.

18 September: 245 Division was relieved by 64 Division.

19 September: On the sector of LXXXIX Corps breaks were made by the enemy near Assende and Sas van Ghent on either side of the Ghent–Terneuzen canal. The Corps withdrew to positions east of the canal. On account of artillery fire, the crossing operations were transferred from Terneuzen to Breskens on 20 September. The remaining portions of 712 Division crossed the river at Breskens. LXVII Corps, now in charge north of Antwerp, took Wilmarsdonk and destroyed the railway bridge at Merxem. The remaining portion of 245 Division were being transported to the Tilburg area, sector of 1 Parachute Army.

Summary by von Zangen
Up to 29 September 82,000 men and 580 artillery guns were taken across the river, not including supply service vehicles, motor vehicles, antiguns and assault guns, nor the troops left in Scheldt Fortress South. The movement across the river, despite the extraordinary strain for the troops, was carried out without major losses. The performance of the troops and their ability to rebuild was of the highest order. By the heavy engagements south of the Scheldt, the troops had not been used up but on the contrary they had improved their combat spirit considerably.

The ferry-master at Breskens
Von Zangen delegated responsibility for the evacuation of the 15th Army through Breskens to General Leutnant Eugen-Felix Schwalbe, whose 346 Division had been destroyed on the Seine. He had been unemployed since then, and was now given a task which he recalled as one of the most satisfactory of his whole military career:

When I was told what my new job was to be I set up my HQ in Breskens. Gathering about me as many officers as I could find, I sent them along the roads leading to Breskens, where they set up collection posts for the assembling of the retreating units. They would telephone to tell me what formation had arrived and was ready to cross, and I would allot it a specific hour when it was to be evacuated. Until that hour it was to remain well-camouflaged and hidden along the roads.

For the task of crossing the Scheldt I had assembled two large Dutch civilian ships, three large rafts capable of holding eighteen vehicles each, and sixteen small Rhine boats each with a capacity of 250 men. The trips were made chiefly at night, although because time was pressing some had to be made during the day. Allied planes constantly harried the ships, and a number of them, laden with troops, received direct hits. However, in sixteen days we managed to evacuate the remnants of nine infantry divisions: 59, 70, 245, 331, 345, 17 Luftwaffe Field, 346, 711 and 712. By 21 September my task was completed and the bulk of the 15th Army had been rescued from encirclement.

The number of German troops evacuated over the Scheldt between 4 and 21 September cannot be stated precisely, but the best estimate is: 86,000 men, 616 guns, 6,200 horses and 6,200 vehicles. The 15th Army had no Panzer divisions, and we can assume that the category 'vehicles' did not include any tanks. However, the 86,000 men were already to some degree organised into divisions, and together with the various remnants could easily have been regrouped into seven or eight infantry divisions capable of providing stiff resistance. As we have seen, the Germans had the command structure and the expertise to carry out such a transformation.

The German divisions we are interested in are those shown in Map 12, and those listed by General Leutnant Schwalbe as having crossed the Scheldt. The records of their movements are far from complete, but we will follow them as best we can, and see the regrettable impact their escape had on the Allies' subsequent operations.

Map 12 shows that on 2 September the 15th Army consisted of LXVII Corps (which comprised 245, 70 and 226 Divisions) and LXXXIX Corps (which comprised 64, 59 and 712 Divisions). In the same coastal strip between the Somme and the Scheldt there were also the remnants of several other divisions escaping from the defeat in Normandy. They were trying to make their way back to Germany by whatever route they could, and the coast road was one of them.

Taking all the divisions in LXVII and LXXXIX Corps combined with those listed by General Leutnant Schwalbe, and dealing with them in numerical order, the first is 59 Division.

59 Division: In his report on the withdrawal of the 15th Army over the Scheldt, General von Zangen states:

When the fighting for the Scheldt bridgeheads was still going on, the withdrawal was begun on the night of 6 September, first of all to take the line of the barricade Bruges–Ghent St Nicholas, under cover of which the crossing had then to be effected.

The movement was started by 59 Division. The withdrawal of this division, as well as that of 345 Division, was carried out under intense enemy action. On 8 September the main body of the division was ready for defence of the barricade line on the right wing of LXXXVI Corps at Eecloo. The enemy, who obviously had made all preparations to ward off an attack east of the Scheldt, later pursued the withdrawing troops rather reluctantly.

59 Division crossed the Scheldt sometime around 12 September, and by 18 September was under the command of 1 Parachute Army. During the night crossing the divisional commander, General Major Walther Poppe, 'expected the convoy carrying my splintered division to be blown out of the water. The one-hour trip from Breskens to Flushing, in complete darkness and without any defences, was to me and all my men a most unpleasant experience.' But they reached Flushing in safety, marched down the Beveland peninsula and then north-east to Tilburg. They were there, with a considerable quantity of artillery, when 101 US Airborne Division landed 10 miles to the south-east.

64 Division was in the Pas-de-Calais as a 'rest division', composed largely of convalescent soldiers, many of whom had fought and been wounded in Russia. They were thus battle-experienced soldiers, and their commander, General Leutnant Kurt Eberding, was determined and resourceful. The division withdrew from the positions it occupied north-west of Lille on 2 September, and eventually became the garrison of Scheldt Fortress South. As such they held the ground between the Leopold Canal and the Scheldt, with their HQ at Breskens. The area they held was designated the 'Breskens Pocket'.

Fortress South held out until 3 October. The fighting was very much a hard, miserable infantry slog. It is described by one of 64 Division's opponents in this battle, a regimental historian of 3 Canadian Infantry Division:

The fighting in the Breskens Pocket was marked by the utter misery of the conditions and the great courage required to do the simplest things. Attacks had to go along dykes swept by enemy fire. To go through the polders meant wading, without possibility of concealment, in water that at times came up to the chest. Mortar fire, at which the Germans were masters, crashed into every rallying point. Spandaus sent their whining reverberations across the marshes.

Our own artillery was deprived of much of its effectiveness because of the great difficulty in reaching an enemy dug in on the reverse slope of a dyke. Even that most potent weapon, the flame-throwing Wasp, was denied both cover and room to manoeuvre. The conditions for heavier supporting vehicles were so bad that, at first, little use could be made of them. It was peculiarly a rifleman's fight in that there were no great decisive battles, just a steady continuous struggle.

A Canadian Army intelligence summary of 7 November called 64 Division 'the best infantry division we have met'. And the Canadians had met some tough opponents, including the fanatical 12 SS Panzer Division.

70 Division had the alternative title 'the White Bread Division'. Many of its soldiers suffered from stomach disorders, and it made for easier administration and supply to group all people needing special diets into one unit. But many of them were experienced soldiers, and in the event they put up a good fight.

On 2 September the division was a few miles south-east of Boulogne. They fell back towards the Scheldt, and then became part of the same defensive position as 59 Division, just north of Bruges, on 10 September. They were then ferried across to Walcheren, the transfer being complete on 15 September. There they became the garrison of Scheldt Fortress North under their commander, General Leutnant Wilhelm Daser. They held out stubbornly for two months, even though some of their sub-units were transferred to the east, and it was not until 7 November that General Daser finally surrendered.

226 Division, one of the divisions of LXVII Corps, was a Volksgrenadier division. It left LXVII Corps some time after 2 September and was directed to the Fortress Dunkirk, where it stayed until Dunkirk surrendered on 9 May 1945.

245 Division was in Dieppe on D-Day. The Canadians captured the port on 1 September. Presumably 245 Division had left earlier, because on 2 September they were with LXVII Corps south-east of Boulogne. They moved to Breskens, where they were relieved on 18 September. They were ferried across the Scheldt, and then transported rapidly to Tilburg. On 21 September they were identified as part of 1 Parachute Army on the eastern flank of XXX BR Corps' corridor to Arnhem.

331 Division was transferred in March 1944 to France after two years' service in Russia. It was below strength on arrival, but was reinforced and fought in Normandy under its commander, General Major Karl Rheim. Elements of the division were able to escape and make their way across the Seine and along the coast. These elements were evacuated to Flushing, and by about 13 September they had reached Maria ter Heide, a few miles north-east of Antwerp. There they, together with the remnants of 344 Division, were incorporated into 346 Division, whose story is told below.

345 Division and *17 Luftwaffe Division:* Other than that they were ferried across the Scheldt in General Schwalbe's evacuation operation, no further information has been discovered regarding these two divisions.

346 and *711 Divisions* were both in LXXXVI Corps for the battles in Normandy and the retreat up the coast after the Falaise pocket. Their Corps was part of Panzer Gruppe West, which was renamed 5 Panzer Army during this period.

On 25 July they were between the coast and the Caen–Mezidon railway, and the other formation in the Corps was 21 Panzer Division. By 11 August, 21 Panzer had been replaced by 272 Infantry Division, and by 23 August they had been joined by the remnants of 85 Division, which later formed the nucleus of Kampfgruppe Chill.

346 and 711 were evidently separated from the other two divisions, and found their way along the coast to Breskens, where they were evacuated over the Scheldt by the efficient and enthusiastic General Schwalbe. The pleasure felt by 346 divisional commander General Leutnant Erich Diestel on reaching the northern bank is evident in his interrogation report.

Having successfully escaped once more, 346 Division marched along the Beveland isthmus and reached an assembly area at Maria ter Heide about 3 miles north-east of Antwerp. Here they rested for four or five days, and reorganised the division with the help of the remnants of 331 and 344 Divisions. From these two shattered formations Diestel acquired three thousand soldiers, and 331 Artillery Regiment provided ten guns to make up what they had lost during the retreat. The division now had a strength of 8,000 men. Its faithful companion, 711 Division, was also resting and refitting at Maria ter Heide. On about 18 September both divisions were once again put into the line, this time under the command of LXVII Corps.

While these tired troops were resting, 719 Division, just down from Holland, with a mixture of battle groups and odd remnants, was holding a line north of Antwerp. Its task was to prevent the main road from the Beveland isthmus being cut, since it provided the only escape route for the divisions still trapped in north-western France and Belgium. This job it performed adequately, because British armour was not able to advance north from Antwerp at this time.

With the aid of the patched-up 346 and 711 Divisions, LXVII Corps took up the task of keeping the entrance to the Beveland isthmus open, so that 64 and 70 Divisions, the divisions left to defend the approaches to the Scheldt, could be properly supplied. The new line had 711 Division on the right flank, facing the West Scheldt from the main road into the Beveland isthmus to Lillo. 346 Division was on its left from Lillo to Merxem, and left again was 719 Division along the Albert Canal. This was the situation on 18 September.

348 Division (one brigade only) is shown as being part of LXXXIX Corps on 2 September. It is not listed by General Schwalbe, and it does not reappear on the northern bank of the Scheldt. We can assume that it was incorporated into another formation, and thus lost its identity.

712 Division was in LXXXIX Corps north of Lille on 2 September, and by 10 September it was part of the defensive force on the line north of Bruges. It was evacuated across the Scheldt, and was transferred to 1 Parachute Army. Under its divisional commander General Leutnant Friedrich-Wilhelm Neumann it fought against Operation Market Garden, and delayed British relief columns heading for Arnhem. It was in Army Group B until January 1945, when it had the misfortune to be transferred to Russia. It fought in the Battle of Berlin in April 1945, where it was destroyed.

Activation of 1 Parachute Army

On 1 July 1938 Major General Kurt Student was named commander of the first German airborne formation, 7 Flieger Division. The division comprised paratroop, glider and air-transport units, and came under the overall command of the Luftwaffe High Command – in German, Oberkommando der Luftwaffe (OKL). Student's paratroopers were largely responsible for the capture of Holland in 1940, when they parachuted onto the bridges of Rotterdam, Dordrecht and Moerdijk, and held them open for the ground invasion force. Out of a force of 4,000 men there were only 180 casualties.

The paratroopers' next action was a very different story, however. Student commanded XI Flieger Corps in the airborne invasion of Crete in 1941. The operation was in the end successful, but of the invasion force of 22,000 nearly one-third were casualties. These losses were so high that Hitler declared 'the day of parachute troops is over'. No major airborne operations were authorised after 1941, but the airborne forces remained in being. They became 1 Parachute Army, and by 1944 Student was in command. However, his forces were split up and fought in several theatres. The largest active formation was a Corps, but many parachute divisions were parts of infantry Corps.

Student as commander had under his direct authority only training units, convalescent depots and a rag-bag of other units. At 1500 hr on 4 September his responsibilities changed dramatically. He received a message from General Oberst Alfred Jodl, Hitler's operations chief, to activate his 1 Parachute Army, and bring it into action immediately along the line of the Albert Canal.

Student's troopers were spread out all over Germany, and apart from a few seasoned, fully equipped units, they were green recruits armed only with training weapons. His force of about 10,000 had almost no transportation, tanks or artillery. Student himself had no Chief of Staff.

Jodl stressed the maximum urgency of the situation, and ordered that Student rush his forces to Belgium and Holland with all possible speed. Weapons and equipment would be issued at the railheads of destination. Besides his paratroopers, two divisions had been earmarked for his

1 Parachute Army. They were the Limited Employment (LE) 719 Division, which was stationed along the Dutch coast; and 176 LE Division, composed mainly of semi-invalids and convalescents. He was also assigned sundry other troops scattered throughout Belgium and Holland, and twenty-five tanks.

All through the afternoon of 4 September, Student telephoned his far-flung subordinates with orders to muster and move out. He estimated it would take at least four days for his entire force to reach the front. But his toughest and best troops, rushed in special trains to Holland in a 'blitz move', would be in position on the Albert Canal in twenty-four hours.

Although Student's situation appeared black when he first looked at it, there were various factors to lighten it. He had von der Heydte's 6th Jaeger Regiment, a veteran formation which had been withdrawn from Normandy and refitted. There was a battalion of 2nd Jaeger Regiment, five new Parachute regiments, an anti-tank battalion and Parachute Army's service units. Behind that thin screen of veterans and recruits Student created a front, and to strengthen it he formed battle-groups (in German, Kampfgruppe, or KG) from non-Parachute splinter groups and military fragments which entered his area of command. By mid-September the worst of the crisis was past, and Student now commanded five divisions. These were strung out across Belgium roughly along the line of the Albert Canal, and linked up with the reconstituted 7th Army which was holding the Siegfried Line area. Student's battle line was made up of 719 Division on the right wing near Antwerp, KG Chill (about which more later), KG Walther (a paratroop group), Erdmann's Parachute Training Division, and 176 Division. Also under Student were 59 and 245 Divisions, and in a few days there would be a Panzer Brigade and II SS Panzer Corps, which was refitting near Arnhem.

One of the paratroopers was Adolf Strauch, who had been wounded in Russia and sent back to Germany. In August 1944 he volunteered to return to duty, although not fully recovered from his wounds. As a corporal he was ordered to take over a platoon of 8 Company, 2 Battalion, 2nd Jaeger Regiment. He was told that if his company commander was killed, he was to take over. On 5 September, 8 Company consisted of two heavy machine-gun platoons, one mortar platoon and some light machine-guns and Panzerschreck. The Panzerschreck was an infantry anti-tank weapon, firing a 3 kg grenade from a hollow tube.

On 7 September Strauch's unit reached Helchteren, 5 miles north of the Albert Canal, and was immediately in action against infantry and tanks of the Guards Armoured Division. They were in action again on the 8th, and on the 9th Strauch records:

The enemy repeated his attacks using flame-throwing tanks. We had only a few Panzerfaust and our Panzerschreck were out of action. By this time the company commander had been wounded, and I took over. We were attacked constantly, and were practically wiped out. We were ordered to withdraw, and by crawling through ditches a few of us managed to reach Battalion HQ.

There we learned that our company and one other had been destroyed, and I was told to collect little groups of men and regroup them.

Strauch, although only just promoted to sergeant, was put in command of 8 Company. He continued to fight in Holland, and his unit later took part in the Ardennes offensive. His account emphasises several things about the German Army. The NCOs were ready to take on officers' roles without hesitation, the paratroopers were determined fighters, soldiers regrouped automatically, and Student's scratch force became a hard nut to crack.

Kampfgruppe Chill
Student's orders to defend the line of the Albert Canal had been pre-empted by the determination of one man, General Leutnant Kurt Chill. He was in command of 85 Infantry Division, but that had been almost annihilated in the fighting in Normandy and after. He had been ordered to save whatever he could of his division, and move back to Germany. But he saw an opportunity to follow his own obstinate strong-willed nature and at the same time the spirit of Model's Order of the Day published on 3 September. That order read, in part:

To the soldiers of the Western Army
As your new Commander-in-Chief I direct this call to your honour as soldiers. We have lost a battle, but I tell you, we will win this war! I cannot say more now, although I know that there are many questions burning on the lips of the troops. Despite everything that has happened, do not allow your firm, confident faith in Germany's future to be shaken one whit.

I must however make known to you the gravity of this day and hour. This moment will and should separate the weaklings from the real men. Every single man carries now the same responsibility: when his commander falls out, he must take his place and carry on.

Take thought then that at this moment everything adds up to the necessity to gain the time the Führer needs to bring into operation new troops and new weapons. They will come.

Soldiers, we must gain this time for the Führer!

Chill decided to disobey his orders to return to Germany after he had concluded that the only way to avoid catastrophe was to set up a defensive line along the Albert Canal. He welded what remained of his 85 Division with the remnants of two others, and quickly sent these men to strategic points on the north bank of the canal. He then set up collection points at the northern exits of the bridges over the canal. In twenty-four hours he netted thousands of men from every branch of the Wehrmacht, including military government personnel and naval coastal units. This motley crew, armed at best with rifles, were on the canal when Student arrived.

Student was amazed and delighted at the way in which Chill had slowed down the German retreat, and had put the skeleton of a defensive line in place for 1 Parachute Army to build on. The line thickened up over the next few days, even under the Allied assaults recorded by Adolf Strauch. One of the units in that line, as we have seen, was Kampfgruppe Chill.

Chapter Ten

ALLIED OPERATIONS,
4–17 SEPTEMBER

Montgomery's orders of 3 September quoted in Chapter Eight nominate his instructions for 21 Army Group as:

1. British 2nd Army to secure area Brussels–Ghent–Antwerp.
2. 1st Canadian Army to advance to Bruges.
3. 21 Army Group to advance to and occupy the Ruhr, starting on 6 September.

There is no specific instruction to free the approaches to the port of Antwerp, which could have been done by the Canadian Army on the south bank of the Scheldt estuary and by the 2nd Army on the north. Had this order of 3 September required that such actions should be taken urgently and immediately to the exclusion of any other operations, they could have been done before the Germans had time to regroup and reorganise. While the reduction of the forts at the mouth of the estuary would still have been a major task, Antwerp docks could have been accessible from the North Sea in, say, six weeks rather than the twelve it actually took.

The force required to undertake the clearing of the banks in the early days of September would still have allowed the bulk of 21 Army Group to advance towards the Rhine. The clearing of the estuary and the advance to the Rhine could then have been done before the autumn weather began to slow down ground operations. Montgomery complained strenuously that there was no overall ground commander to make rapid decisions when there were fleeting opportunities to be grasped. *But he was the ground commander in the northern sector*, and *he* could have taken the decisions to clear the Scheldt immediately and then advance to the Rhine. Eisenhower would certainly have backed these decisions, and the quick freeing of Antwerp docks would have greatly increased the flow of supplies to all SHAEF forces.

What happened as a result of Montgomery's orders of 3 September now follows. Two items of particular importance to look at in the period

4–17 September are the attempt to establish a bridgehead over the Albert Canal in the northern Antwerp suburb of Merxem, and the movements of the Canadian Army along the Channel coast.

ANTWERP AND THE ALBERT CANAL

Antwerp was captured by 11 Armoured Division on 4 September. The war diaries and regimental histories give details of the contributions of the different units of the division to the capture. There are some inconsistencies between the accounts, but this is not surprising. There was the emotion of the capture, the extraordinary demonstrations of gratitude from the citizens, the continued exposure to hostile fire, and, because of the lack of maps, the uncertainty of a unit's location.

The Order of Battle of 11 Armoured Division as it was at the time of the capture of Antwerp is shown in Figure 6. (From here on, units are referred to by the abbreviations shown in this table.)

Extracts from the war diaries of some of the units, including the divisional War Diary, are given below. The entries cover the capture in

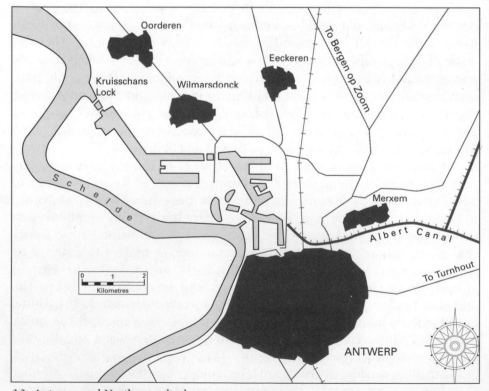

13. Antwerp and Northern suburbs.

Figure 6: Order of Battle, 11 Armoured Division, August–September 1944

Divisional Commander	Maj Gen Pip Roberts
Div Recce Regiment: 15th/19th Hussars	15/19 H
29 Armoured Brigade	
23rd Hussars	23 H
2nd Fife & Forfar Yeomanry	2 FF Yeo
3rd Royal Tank Regiment	3 RTR
8th Battalion, The Rifle Brigade	8 RB
159 Infantry Brigade	
4th Battalion King's Shropshire Light Infantry	4 KSLI
3rd Battalion The Monmouthshire Regiment	3 Mons
1st Battalion The Herefordshire Regiment	1 Herefords
Divisional Artillery	
13th Royal Horse Artillery	13 RHA
151st Field Regiment RA (Ayrshire Yeomanry)	151 Fd RA
75th Antitank Regiment RA	75 A/T RA

general, but focus on the attempts to establish a bridgehead over the Albert Canal to allow a rapid advance to the north.

The divisional War Diary for 5 September records the results of a night operation by 3 Mons to capture the main sluice gates of the docks. In this operation they were given substantial assistance by the Belgian White Brigade, both in military support and in guidance through the city, the docks and the suburbs.

11 Armoured Division War Diary
5 September: The night operation of 3 Mons was successfully carried out. The main sluice gates at Kruisschans Lock were discovered to be intact and with these in our hands occupation of the docks appeared to be complete. This morning a thorough reconnaissance was made of the whole area which revealed that the port was virtually undamaged. The clearing of the city itself was also continued until no enemy remained in it, but they were still active both west of the Scheldt and also north of the Albert Canal. All the bridges over the canal in the city and as far east as Herenthals were discovered to have been blown.

Numerous and persistent civilian reports told of large numbers of enemy still on our side of the canal, but when investigated these turned out to be grossly exaggerated. No indication had so far been given of the probable future course of our operations, and it seemed likely that we would either be ordered to rest and refit or to move east towards Germany.

However, at a Corps conference in the afternoon it was revealed that our objective lay to the north, and the division was ordered to establish a bridgehead over the Albert Canal as soon as possible, and then thrust north towards Hertogenbosch in Holland. We should thus be continuing to operate on the left of the Guards, who had now occupied Brussels and Louvain and were to cross the Meuse at Grave, the Waal at Nijmegen, and the Lower Rhine at Arnhem. Seizure of the bridges at these places was to be effected by the dropping of an airborne corps. [Note: This was Operation Comet, the predecessor to Market Garden.]

That this vast plan had not been long contemplated in its entirety is sufficiently demonstrated by the intention, abandoned only at the last minute, to use large numbers of the airborne forces on the Scheldt. Consequently it had been considered that the immediate task of the division was the securing of Antwerp docks and not of the Albert Canal bridges. Had any indication been given that a further advance north was envisaged, these could have been seized within a few hours of our entry into the city, when the enemy defences on the north bank were not coordinated. As it was, resistance in this area had appreciably stiffened, as 159 Infantry Brigade were soon to find out, because at daybreak on 6 September 4 KSLI were to assault over the canal.

6 *September:* At first light the attack went in. 4 KSLI established a small bridgehead against fierce opposition in the area of Merxem. At 1100 hr the enemy counterattacked with three infantry companies and five tanks, and isolated the KSLI in a factory. Enemy shelling continued on an increasing scale throughout the day, but at last light the factory position was still held.

Our troops had however run out of PIAT (Projectile Infantry anti-tank) ammunition, had had no food, and were running out of small arms ammunition. PIAT could be carried and used by one man, although that man had to be very strong to cock the weapon, and suicidal to use it. However, it was effective.] Owing to the shortage of PIAT ammunition, and the absence of any anti-tank guns, the enemy tanks had free play around the factory, and had thus been able to prevent supplies being brought across. 4 KSLI felt they should withdraw by night, but were ordered to hold on and try to get supplies across under cover of darkness.

Two companies of 3 Mons were sent to help from a flank, but they and two troops of tanks from 23 H were held up by a mined road-block. The intention was now for 11 Armoured Division to move north with 29 Armoured Brigade passing through the bridgehead and 159 Infantry Brigade clearing up Merxem before continuing in their wake. The Engineers were therefore ordered to construct one and if possible two bridges during the night.

At 1800 hr an enemy counterattack on the sluice gates was beaten off by 3 Mons, who were at that exact moment being relieved by a company of 2 Devons of 231 Brigade. This brigade was part of 50 Division, which had arrived during the day to take over Antwerp.

7 *September:* As it turned out 4 KSLI could not be reinforced during the night. 3 Mons could not get any further with their bridgehead owing to

strong machine-gun and infantry opposition, and 29 Armoured Brigade were unable to advance north through the dock area due to the going and enemy anti-tank guns. The Engineers were unable to construct a bridge either by night or day due to heavy shell fire. It was therefore decided that an advance north would be too expensive an operation to carry out, and 29 Armoured Brigade were withdrawn.

At 1530 hr, under cover of intense artillery fire 4 KSLI were brought back across the canal in assault boats, not a single casualty being incurred during this operation.

8 September: As the original plan of pushing north across the Albert Canal had now been abandoned, Division was ordered by XXX Corps to send 29 Armoured Brigade south to protect the Corps' right flank where enemy were infiltrating to the right rear of Guards Armoured Division. The rest of 11 Armoured Division was to follow shortly.

29 Armoured Brigade War Diary (WO 171/627)

On 4 September the Brigade arrived in Antwerp, and its regiments helped to capture the docks and round up the Germans in the city itself. On 5 September the tanks investigated and cleared areas outside the city to the south and south-east. None of the three units was ordered to push north. This changed on 6 September.

6 September: 1415 hr: one squadron 23 H put at thirty minutes notice to assist 159 Infantry Brigade to clear Merxem area. Orders were received late in the evening for the Brigade to pass over the canal at two bridges which had been constructed south of Merxem, and then break out of the 159 Infantry Brigade bridgehead.

7 September: Brigade moves two up through Antwerp to the line of the canal. Opposition from the northern bank of the canal proves too much, and armoured regiments find it impossible to get across.

1130 hr: As no bridge was available for us, and enemy holds line of railway north of the canal in strength, it was decided that a bridgehead will have to be made somewhere else. Units ordered to return to previous locations. One squadron of 23 H remains in dock area to cover 4 KSLI who are holding the bridgehead.

1840 hr: Warning order received to move at first light 8 September to Diest (30 miles south-east of Antwerp).

2115 hr: 23 H squadron withdrawn.

8 September: Orders confirmed. Move to begin 0900 hr. Route Malines–Louvain–Diest.

23rd Hussars War Diary and Regimental history

The War Diary of 23 H (WO 171/847) contains only the briefest entries for the days 5 to 8 September. They read:

5 September: At 1400 hr A Squadron sent to capture bridges and cross Albert Canal north of Antwerp; but any advance beyond railway impossible owing to heavy anti-tank and infantry opposition.

6 September: Other small enemy activity and infiltrations in the divisional area make it impossible for the Regiment as a whole to take advantage of the incredible generosity and enthusiasm of the people. One officer and four other ranks killed.

8 September: Move via Malines–Aerschot–Diest to protect Guards Armoured Division right flank and bridgehead over the Albert Canal.

The Regimental history, however, gives rather more detail after the 23rd Hussars' arrival in Antwerp late on 4 September:

When we arrived the enemy had let the main part of the town go with hardly a fight, vanishing in a panic. But he had as suddenly turned and dug in in the suburb of Merxem, north of the Albert Canal. Within a few weeks of his expulsion, he attacked the city with V-bombs. Only a few of us, therefore, were lucky enough to exploit the idolatry with which 11 Armoured Division was everywhere received.

All we had was one clear night. On 6 September, in the early afternoon, two troops of A Squadron went to support the infantry across the canal into Merxem. 4 KSLI had already established a bridgehead, and at first the leading troop under Lt Drake made good progress. But they very soon became badly involved with a thoroughly obstructive infantry position, supported by anti-tank guns. No progress could be made there.

Lt Unwin's troop was sent round another way but two of his tanks became bogged near the canal within view of the enemy. After a vain attempt to recover these – great help being given by 3 Mons – a most unpleasant night was spent there. On the following morning the remainder of this troop attempted to continue forward, but the leading tank was hit almost at once and the crew were killed in baling out.

As further progress was impossible, and as it had been decided to withdraw the KSLI bridgehead, A Squadron was recalled. At midday two troops and Squadron HQ from C Squadron were sent down to assist in KSLI's withdrawal over the canal. This was accomplished by a massed artillery and smoke barrage, thickened by fire from the tanks. No losses were sustained, and C Squadron rejoined the Regiment.

The following day the Regiment turned away to follow the general advance into Holland. The enemy, in fact, were not expelled from the Merxem position until the great Canadian offensive four weeks later.

4th Battalion King's Shropshire Light Infantry
The accounts in the war diaries and unit histories of 11 Armoured Division, 29 Armoured Brigade and 23rd Hussars all make it clear that

the main burden of establishing a bridgehead over the Albert Canal fell on 4 KSLI. The KSLI War Diary (WO 171/1326) contains only brief details of the bridgehead action, but the unit history is much more informative. Extracts taken from the history start on 5 September:

Until the morning of the 5th the Battalion was the only infantry unit in the city. Shortly after first light, however, 3 Mons and 1 Herefords arrived and were given the task of clearing the dock areas along the northern perimeter. As soon as that was done, we were to force a crossing of the Albert Canal and form a bridgehead on the far side.

C Company was despatched in an attempt to capture the bridge over the canal at Merxem, but came under very heavy fire from the northern bank. It was unfortunate that the Division had no maps that went as far as the Albert Canal. Most officers' knowledge of geography was so scanty that they did not even know where the canal was. The importance of the bridges over the canal was thus not realised.

As C Company advanced, covered by a troop of tanks, the bridge over the canal was blown. It was obvious that the far bank was strongly held and that any successful attempt to cross must be made under the cover of darkness.

There was little time for preparation, and only a few assault boats were available. As soon as darkness fell, D Company attempted to cross, but was pinned down by very heavy fire and could make no progress. A Company, however, found a crossing place, got across unobserved by the enemy, and began to fan out towards the west. B and C Companies both got across at the same place and moved north and east respectively. By first light a small bridgehead had been established. With the three Companies were Capt Hambley and Sgt Morris of the mortar platoon to control fire from two mortar sections set up near Sportspalatz south of the canal.

The situation facing the Battalion on the morning of the 6th was decidedly tricky, for the enemy was on the north in strength, with armour at call. As the three Companies moved off to enlarge the bridgehead, the leading platoon of A Company, advancing west along the canal bank, was attacked by five enemy tanks. They were engaged with PIATS and driven off. The whole of A Company, with a platoon of C Company under command, then continued the advance, but the enemy put in another attack, again supported by tanks, and hemmed the party in against the canal, cutting its line of retreat to the bridgehead. It had been impossible to get tanks across the canal, there were no antitank guns, and PIAT ammunition was running short.

In the meantime, B and C Companies, less the one platoon with A, had occupied two factories on the edge of the bridgehead. They were promptly engaged by enemy tanks, aided by snipers and machine-guns, which between them made one of the factories untenable and forced a withdrawal to the other.

Casualties were mounting rapidly, and although the three companies were promised tank support, the tanks never came. Some of the casualties were safely evacuated across the canal when a gallant barge skipper manoeuvred his craft so as to bridge the canal, but an enemy tank soon put a stop to that by firing the barge. It was impossible to move the casualties suffered by A Company, which remained cut off all day. They had taken refuge in another small factory, which was shelled by tanks at point-blank range. The whole street was in flames, but that night Maj Maddocks managed to lead two platoons across the road, which was swept by machine-gun fire, and join up with B and C Companies. The remaining platoon of A Company and one of C were never seen again.

The remainder of the night passed without incident. During the morning of the 7th the enemy attack was continued, but all his efforts to wipe out the three Companies were failures. It says much for the skill, endurance and courage of the Battalion that the enemy, although using tanks, two battalions of SS infantry, mortars, 88 mm and 155 mm field guns, failed to dislodge the three Companies.

Lt Col Reeves received a painful wound in the thigh during the shelling in the morning, and Maj Maddocks took over command of the party in the bridgehead. At 1300 hr orders came through for a withdrawal during the afternoon under a heavy artillery support programme. The Royal Engineers did a magnificent job of bringing the whole party back without a single casualty, and by 1545 hr all were once again on the south bank.

2nd Fife & Forfar Yeomanry War Diary (WO 171/853)

5 September: C Squadron remained on the canal north-east of Antwerp supporting 159 Infantry Brigade. The remainder of the Regiment moved into harbour south of the city, and during the next two days did much necessary maintenance on the tanks.

6 September: C Squadron rejoined the Regiment at 1200 hr.

7 September: The Brigade was ordered to move out to the north of Antwerp over the small bridgehead which had been established there, with 2 FF Yeo leading the right-hand axis of advance. However, the bridgehead had not been sufficiently cleared up, and after motoring into the middle of Antwerp the Regiment returned to its original harbour area less A Squadron who went off to watch the canal to the east of Antwerp.

8 September: At 0900 hr the Regiment led the Brigade to cross the Albert Canal by the bridgehead which the Guards had obtained at Beeringen, the route followed being Malines–Louvain–Diest.

3rd Royal Tank Regiment War Diary (WO 171/866)

4 September: 0630: Regiment moves continuing advance on Antwerp. Orders are to enter city with all speed and proceed straight to dock area with the object of preventing demolitions, 3 RTR on left axis. Routes are taken direct from Liaison Officer's maps.

1200: Reach Boom and make successful crossing of bridge against certain amount of opposition including mined crossing.

1600: Reach outskirts of Antwerp and within fifteen minutes have entered the city. Resistance from snipers and machine-gun fire increases as the centre of the city is reached.

1630: Bridge across canal reported mined and under heavy fire.

1645: Bridge successfully crossed by Lt Stubbs, who had already been first across at Boom.

1700: Orders received that only one Squadron plus a platoon of infantry should stay in Antwerp. By this time the whole of the Regiment was in the city with a troop down in the docks; order was therefore cancelled.

1800: Resistance in centre of city fairly consistent, but being dealt with.

5 September: 1100: Orders received from Brigade that 11 Armd Div is to clear Antwerp, 29 Armd Bde's role to liquidate enemy pockets. Probable stay two days. Units to concentrate on maintenance.

1200: Regiment moves to new harbour area outside city.

1800: Five 3-tonners to Antwerp for evening.

6 September: 1000: CO's conference. No news of further move received. Full maintenance to be carried out.

1400: 50 per cent of Regiment to Antwerp for afternoon. Raining heavily throughout afternoon and evening.

1900: Warning order; move tomorrow, not likely before 0800 hr.

7 September: 0715: Regiment moves into Antwerp. Head of column halted at bridge.

1100: Brigade ordered to return to original area pending change of plan due to Merxem being strongly held.

1900: Warning order from Brigade. Prepare to move first light tomorrow 8 Sept in SE direction.

8 September: 1030: Regiment starts on move to Diest.

1st Battalion The Herefordshire Regiment War Diary (WO 171/1307)

5 September: 0845: Battalion moved forward with two companies up to clear forts on south and east of city; forts used by Germans to store ammunition and flour. No opposition met, and by 1315 Battalion is established in area of Berchem, a southern suburb of the city.

2015: Information received that Germans have blown the bridges over the Albert Canal. KSLI are crossing canal to establish a bridgehead in Merxem tonight. Herefords will cross when ordered.

6 September: 0400: KSLI across canal. C Company Herefords move forward to occupy bridges south of canal.

1100: Information received that opposition is considered too strong. A brigade of 50 Division is moving in to relieve 159 Brigade. KSLI have been under fire all day.

7 September: 0800: Orders prepared for the relief of 4 KSLI by 1 Herefords supported by tanks passing through new bridgehead to be captured by 3 Mons. Mons bridgehead consisted of two platoons 150 yards in front of

defile caused by bridge over canal. This defile covered from both flanks and centre by machine-guns, mortars and antiaircraft guns.

1100: Order for Herefords attack cancelled, as bridgehead was not sufficiently large enough. Battalion returned to own location at Berchem.

2000: Battalion moved to new location south-west of city. 231 Brigade of 50 Division position in north of city.

8 September: Battalion now in semi-rest area at two hours' notice. Carrying on with maintenance, but prepared to provide mobile column of two companies with supporting weapons at half an hour's notice. Carrier platoon maintaining patrols every two hours to Hoboken.

1025: Carrier platoon located enemy position with light machine-guns and 20 mm cannon with self-propelled gun in area of factory west of River Scheldt. Enemy also firing on B Company.

9 September: 11 Armd Div to move over to the right flank of 2nd Army. Battalion under command 29 Armoured Brigade.

1015: Battalion commenced move.

COMMENTS ON THE WAR DIARIES AND UNIT HISTORIES

The entry in the War Diary of 11 Armoured Division for 5 September reading 'the bridge could have been seized within a few hours of our entry into the city' must surely have been written in hindsight. It has a tone of excuse which seems unlikely in an original entry. The Belgian White Brigade, whose contribution to the capture of Antwerp is described later in this chapter, pleaded with the British troops to help them seize bridges over the canal, but were told that 'they had no orders to mount an attack'.

When the assault over the canal was made by 4 KSLI thirty-six hours later, it seems to have been underprepared. A shortage of both PIAT and small-arms ammunition after less than twelve hours of action gives the impression of not taking the attack particularly seriously – which was certainly not the case for the troops themselves; KSLI suffered 150 casualties in the action, of which 31 were killed, and CO Ivor Reeves was badly wounded.

Throughout the 11 Armoured diary entries from 5 to 7 September, there is an impression of the advance north not being very important, and a willingness to give up if it seemed too difficult: 'tanks were unable to advance north due to the going and enemy anti-tank guns'; 'engineers unable to construct a bridge due to heavy shell-fire'. These were not situations that would have stopped them a few days earlier.

Intelligence about the German troops in front of them was what can only be described as optimistic. XXX Corps Commander, Gen Horrocks, said: 'The only troops to bar our passage northwards consisted of 719 Infantry Division, composed mainly of elderly gentlemen who had hitherto never heard a shot fired in anger, plus one battalion of Dutch SS and a few Luftwaffe detachments.' But as the KSLI history shows, they put up a stout defence.

The other curious thing about the Albert Canal battle in Antwerp is that there appeared to be plenty of Allied artillery available, which could presumably have been used to much better effect in supporting 4 KSLI and 23 H. In all the accounts there is a sense of a lack of interest in pushing north along the road to Woensdrecht and Bergen op Zoom. This lack of interest could only come from the senior formations, XXX Corps, British 2nd Army and 21 Army Group. The troops themselves, as the war diaries and histories attest, were still prepared to fight. They were undirected and unmotivated to push north.

THE BELGIAN RESISTANCE IN ANTWERP

Belgian Resistance forces were very helpful during the liberation of Antwerp. Had they been listened to with more understanding, the push to the north might have taken place while it could have been done easily.

The main advantages of resistance movements are local knowledge, patriotism and courage; the main disadvantages are security, communication and lack of weapons. In Belgium generally in 1944 there were four national movements, only one of which was in touch with the Belgian Government in exile in London. In Antwerp, however, a single loose framework had been set up to cover all resistance activities; it was called 'The underground Committee for resistance in Antwerp'. The president of this committee was Col Norbert Laude, and it assumed responsibility for civil resistance, aid to Jews, the Red Cross, and the coordination of armed-resistance groups.

Three other people were of particular importance to the Resistance in Antwerp. Lt Urbain Reniers of the Secret Army, codename Réaumur, was placed in charge of the armed groups, then numbering 3,500 men. M. Edouard Pilaet, codename François, was appointed Réaumur's assistant for militia and the partisans. M. Eugène Colson, codename Harry, had already established a resistance movement among those using and working the port; these included ship repairers, seamen stranded by the war, staff who operated the port, and the dock and river pilots. All these people were familiar with the operation of the docks, and were able to observe the preparations the Germans were making to demolish the dock installations.

Colson described what was done to prevent the demolitions:

One of my missions was to find out and report about the rumours and the idea that the Germans were intending to blow up, first of all the Scheldt

riverside quay, followed by the inside quays and structure of the port of
Antwerp. The Germans made holes in the riverside quays, and were
preparing concrete sleeves to fit inside the holes. Urbain Reniers gave orders
for the plant where these sleeves were being made to be blown up, and this
was duly done by the Secret Army.

My own group was sabotaging the finishing of the metal containers that
were to be filled with explosives and placed in the concrete sleeves. We also
knew that the explosives were stored on the lighter *Goro*. The metal
containers were never delivered, and we captured the *Goro* and held it until
Reniers was able to dispose of the explosives.

Although the Resistance was having some successes, it had one major
setback. On 25 August the Gestapo arrested Col Laude and several
committee members. Fortunately Reniers and Pilaet escaped, and were
able to set up a new committee to continue the work of resistance;
unfortunately the arrest of Laude severed communications with London,
and these were not re-established until the evening of 3 September.

By this time the BBC coded messages to the Resistance had told them to
distribute arms and take post, and finally to take action. Along the Scheldt
waterfront armed groups took post among the wharves ready to harass
German troops moving into the city from the west and to prevent
demolition of the pedestrian and vehicle tunnels. To their north along the
Albert Canal, others faced the Germans in Merxem. On the roads entering
the city from Brussels, groups stood ready to assist the Allied advance.
The first German prisoners were taken, and on the morning of
4 September Colson's group scored its first success, capturing the German
port commandant and his staff, and then proceeded to gain control of the
south-east corner of the dock area. Reports from Merxem told of the
Germans still firmly in control there.

On the day of liberation the Resistance was a great help to the units of
11 Armoured, as recorded in their war diaries and regimental histories.
That night they had secured a number of bridges in the dock area, and
the next morning Colson's men used the bridges to make an attempt on
Merxem from the west. However, they were unable to breach the German
positions facing them.

Another resistance group, the University platoon, tried to reach Merxem
from the south by crossing the Yserbrug over the Albert Canal. They were
assisted by 3 Mons, but found the bridge swept by accurate fire, and at
1330 hr the Germans blew it up. Then the only way to reach Merxem
was once again from the west.

It was clear now that to cross the Albert Canal would call for heavy
weapons and armour, but, to the dismay of Reniers and Colson, the
British had no orders to mount an attack, which the Belgians felt sure
would have opened the way to the Dutch border. Nor would they listen to

Pilaet's plea to secure a bridgehead a few miles east of Antwerp at Wijnegem, where his men had seized the bridge on the night of 4 September. Colson recorded: 'We were unable to act as we had planned towards Merxem through lack of firepower. We had twenty-one men inside the power station in Merxem. We had to leave them there because we were not given the support to get to them. All twenty-one were killed by the Germans; their names are engraved on a plaque on the wall at the place where they were shot.'

ANTWERP, 6–17 SEPTEMBER

From 4 to 6 September 11 Armoured Division was the only British formation in Antwerp. The Belgian Resistance provided very effective support, but it was not until 6 September that another British unit was engaged. This was 231 Infantry Brigade of 50 Division.

11 Armoured Division War Diary records that on 6 September: 'At 1800 hr an enemy attack on the sluice gates was beaten off by 3 Mons. They were at that exact moment being relieved by a company of 2 Devons of 231 Brigade (50 Div), which had arrived during the day to take over Antwerp.'

The entry in the 50 Division War Diary is not quite consistent with this, in that it records for 6 September at 2100 hr: 'Main HQ 30 Corps originated Most Immediate message to 50 Div which was received at 0705 hrs ordering 231 to under command 7 Armoured Division.' [Note: 7 Armoured Division is not a misprint; the role of 7 Armoured Division in Antwerp is not clearly documented, and must have been transitory.]

Whenever it was that 231 Brigade arrived in Antwerp, it was not long before it left. In *Normandy to the Baltic* Montgomery says: 'Orders were issued on 7 Sept for 50 Div to secure a bridgehead on the left of Guards Armoured, in some suitable area between Beeringen and Gheel. By nightfall on 8 Sept 50 Div had secured a small bridgehead over the canal south-west of Gheel; in this area also stiff resistance was encountered, and the enemy delivered a number of well-staged counterattacks.'

50 Division's War Diary entry for 2359 hr on 8 September states: '231 Brigade reverted to command of 50 Div.' In H.F. Joslyn's *Orders of Battle for the British Army* 231 Brigade is shown as being under command of 7 Armoured Division for the two days 7 and 8 September, after which it returned to 50 Division.

As the war diaries and unit histories show, 11 Armoured Division left Antwerp on 8/9 September and moved to the right of the Guards Armoured Division in the Beeringen bridgehead. They were then in position to provide right flank protection to XXX Corps in its projected advance to Arnhem. Who was to support the Belgians in Antwerp after

11 Armoured Division and 231 Brigade had departed? The answers are given in Gen Dempsey's diary and in the War Diary of 53 (Welch) Infantry Division.

Gen Dempsey (WO 285/9) records in his diary for 8 September: 'The leading brigade of 53 Div of XII Corps take over Antwerp this evening, thereby freeing the left of XXX Corps and enabling it to concentrate on its operations north-east of Diest.'

On 9 September his diary records:

1000: Saw C-in-C [Monty] at Tac HQ 21 Army Group with Commander Canadian Army and Commander First Army. We discussed future operations. Canadian Army will clear Havre, Boulogne, Calais and Dunkirk as soon as possible, and will clear the area north of Ghent as a second priority. They will take over the Ghent area from me at once.

   1300: Saw Commander XXX Corps at his HQ at Diest. His operations in the Albert Canal bridgehead [Beeringen] continue to be strongly opposed, and I told him to postpone the airborne landing until night 11/12 Sept at the earliest.

   1530: Saw Commander XII Corps at my HQ. The transfer of his Corps to the Antwerp area is proceeding satisfactorily, and he is planning an operation with 53 Div to strike north from Antwerp. He may be able to carry this out on 11 September.

His diary entry for 13 September reads:

Saw Commander VIII and Commander XII at my HQ and discussed the operations which their Corps will carry out [in Operation Market Garden]. VIII on the right will have 11 Armd Div and 3 Div. XII Corps on the left will have 7 Armd Div, 15 Div, and 53 Div.

   Canadian Army will relieve XII Corps in Antwerp as soon as possible. XII Corps will then be able to concentrate on their task.

The three infantry brigades of 53 Division were 71, 158 and 160. The divisional War Diary entries relevant to Antwerp begin on 7 September:

7 Sept:	0930:	158 Brigade Group started to move to Antwerp.
8 Sept:	0830:	158 Brigade (main force) started to move to Antwerp, accompanied by some div troops and 160 Bde Group.
9 Sept:	0615:	158 Bde report relief of 231 Bde.
	0800:	Further div troops incl 53 Recce start move to Antwerp.
	0900:	160 Bde report in position on Junction Canal.
10 Sept:	0300:	71 Bde report in position at Linthe, 10 km S of Antwerp.
	1425:	53 Recce in position at Vremde, 5 km SE of Antwerp.
	2315:	Op planned for area north of Antwerp is cancelled.

11 Sept: 1325:   53 Div to remain in present position for a few days.

              1700:   Belgian LO and Dutch LO join 53 Div HQ.

12 Sept: 0540:   160 Bde patrols cannot cross Albert Canal due to enemy activity on north bank.

13 Sept: Formations moved around, but no aggressive action during day.

14 Sept: 0315:   158 Bde ordered to move to Tongerloo, 30 km east of Antwerp.

              1417:   Ferry at Fort Lillo (10 km NW of Antwerp) being used by enemy. Each trip carries 20 men. Artillery tried to engage with one battery.

15 Sept: 0300:   Artillery reported enemy ferry active again tonight. Engaged with two batteries, but had to stop firing owing to ammunition restrictions.

              0400:   7 Armd Div responsible for defence of Albert Canal from Herenthals to Merxem.

              1755:   7 Armd Div confirmed that they will take over from 53 Div these tasks: 1. Security of Antwerp. 2. Watching line of Albert Canal from Gheel to Merxem. Relief of 53 Div to be complete by 1200 16 Sept.

16 Sept: 1000:   53 Div less 71 Bde move to Tongerloo to join 158 Bde.

17 Sept: 1640:   71 Bde relieved in Antwerp by 4 Can Inf Brigade, and move to join Div at Tongerloo.

The way the Belgian Resistance forces viewed the occupation/non-occupation of Antwerp by Allied troops in September is described by the Resistance leader Eugène Colson. He is talking initially about his team in the docks area, and then goes on to describe the military actions they undertook:

We were a bunch of specialists in the Port of Antwerp. Our knowledge of the terrain was such that foresaw the way the Germans would come to try to destroy the docks, and we were able to prevent them.

Our British friends left us on 8 Sept to go somewhere else, and we were alone for twelve very long days of twenty-four hours each until our Canadian friends came to occupy the ground and support us within the port area. We expected the Germans to harass us from the northern suburbs and villages of Merxem, Eekeren, Wilmarsdonk and Oorderen, and from across the Albert Canal towards the city. We prevented infiltrations from all of these places by constant patrolling.

I now [written in 1984] feel certain that the Resistance could have held the port area for only a short time without outside back-up. You must realise how grateful we are to our English friends, the 11th Armoured Division under General Roberts, and also my very dear Canadian friends, especially the Royal Hamilton Light Infantry, for the help and support they gave to safeguard our heritage.

We never pretended to be strategists, never. What we wanted to do was to give back to our community and our country that enormous heritage that the port of Antwerp represents, and to prevent its destruction by the Germans. What Generals Eisenhower and Montgomery wanted to do with it, I have no idea.

We lost a few men during the constant patrolling, skirmishing, and contact we had with the Germans to prevent them infiltrating our area. We had to do it without the weapons we had not yet received from the Allies by air, although we were given weapons by the Allies when they reached Antwerp, and we took plenty from the Germans.

COMMENTS ON ALLIED OPERATIONS IN ANTWERP, 6–17 SEPTEMBER

We saw previously that the higher command was apathetic about Antwerp and any moves north from the city. The troops themselves, especially 4 KSLI, were well and truly willing to have a go. But why no back-up? Why not commit either or both 50 and 53 Divisions with more conviction and more immediacy?

The answer given by Horrocks, as the senior commander who was in a position to do so, was that 'his eyes were fixed on the east and the borders of Germany'. While we may say that he was on the spot and should have realised the opportunity, we can also say that if Monty thought 'bouncing the Rhine' was the correct action, then nothing else was the correct action. There would be no point in putting forward any alternative view. And Monty would obviously have taken no notice of the Belgian Resistance, even if their ideas and requests had been conveyed to him.

The Belgian perception was that there were no Allied troops in Antwerp from 8 to 20 September. The war diaries suggest that there was always one infantry brigade in the city and dock areas, but it was concentrating on the protection of the docks, and was thus out of the view of the general population. The other two brigades of 53 Division were well outside the city, either to the east or the south.

Some of the War Diary entries show a lack of aggression and organisation: 'unable to cross the canal owing to enemy activity on the north bank'; 'artillery tried to engage ferries with one battery'; 'artillery had to stop firing owing to ammunition restrictions'. It all adds up to a lack of interest in Antwerp itself, or the idea of an advance north from the city. All eyes and almost all forces were concentrated on Arnhem. Arnhem took out Antwerp from 6 to 28 September, and the disaster at Arnhem was largely due to the Great Mistake at Antwerp on 4 September.

Chapter Eleven

RETRIBUTION: OPERATIONS, SEPTEMBER–NOVEMBER 1944

The failure to push north immediately after the capture of Antwerp on 4 September 1944 had a major impact on all subsequent operations in the northern sector of the Allied forces under SHAEF. The troops in the northern sector were 21 Army Group under FM (from 1 September 1944) Montgomery. The failure we have called the Great Mistake was compounded by other mistakes, especially in relation to the capture of the Channel ports.

The three operations that were principally affected by the Great Mistake were: Market Garden; the clearing of the south bank of the Scheldt estuary; and the clearing of the Beveland peninsula and Walcheren to free the north bank of the Scheldt estuary.

MARKET GARDEN: ARNHEM

The plan for the land element of Market Garden is described by Montgomery in *Normandy to the Baltic*.

The 2nd Army task involved establishing crossings over five major obstacles: the Neder Rijn at Arnhem, the Waal at Nijmegen, the Maas at Grave, and the two main transverse canals between the Escaut Canal bridgeheads and Grave, namely the Wilhelmina and the Zuid Willemsvaart. There were road and railway bridges at Nijmegen and Arnhem, and a road bridge at Grave, all of which were intact.

The essential feature of the plan was the laying of a carpet of airborne troops across these waterways on the general axis of the main road through Eindhoven to Uden, Grave, Nijmegen and Arnhem, culminating in a bridgehead force north of Arnhem. The airborne carpet and bridgehead force were to be provided by the Allied Airborne Corps, consisting of three airborne divisions and one airborne brigade. Along the corridor established by the airborne carpet, XXX Corps was to advance to the Arnhem bridgehead, whence it would develop operations to the north and east.

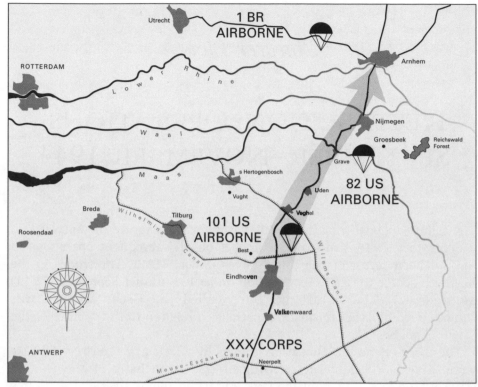

14. Market Garden plan.

As XXX Corps advanced north, VIII Corps was to relieve it of responsibility for the right flank of the corridor, and was to widen it to the east; on the left flank XII Corps was to perform the same function, this time widening the corridor to the west.

I Airborne Corps detailed 1 British Airborne Division, with Polish Airborne Brigade under command, to capture the Arnhem bridges. 82 US Airborne Division was to seize the bridges at Nijmegen and Grave, and 101 US Airborne was to capture the bridges and defiles on the XXX Corps axis between Grave and Eindhoven. The plan provided that 52 Division (Air Portable) was to be flown in north of Arnhem as soon as airstrips could be made available, in order to strengthen the bridgehead.

Allied resources in transport aircraft made it impossible to fly in the whole of the Airborne Corps in one lift, and in fact four days were needed to convey the Corps to the battle area, together with the provision of resupply by air.

Most of the accounts of Market Garden concentrate on the airborne operations in general, and on the efforts to reach 1 British Airborne Division in particular. These efforts were the task of the British 2nd Army, and they had to follow the axis Neerpelt–Eindhoven–Veghel–Grave–

Nijmegen. It was on this axis that they met 1 Parachute Army and survivors of the 15th Army. This account describes some of the results of allowing the 86,000 men of 15th Army to escape back into the mainland of southern Holland.

Market Garden order of battle
Airborne forces:
I Airborne Corps: 1 British, 82 US, and 101 US Airborne Divisions; Polish Para Brigade; 52 (Air Portable) Div
Ground forces:
Left flank: XII Corps: 7 Armd Div, 15 Div, 53 Div, 4 Armd Brigade
Centre: XXX Corps: Guards Armd Div, 43 Div, 50 Div, 8 Armd Brigade
Right flank: VIII Corps: 11 Armd Div, 3 Div

As a result of this concentration for the Arnhem thrust, there were only two British divisions available for other operations. These were 49 Div and 51 Div, both part of I British Corps, which in turn was part of the 1st Canadian Army.

51 Div had been grounded after the capture of Le Havre so that its transport could be used to help supply other formations. 49 Div had also taken part in the capture of Le Havre, and had also been grounded after the capture; but not for long. On 21 September the division moved to southern Holland, and commenced the task of clearing the country between the Arnhem corridor and the Maas.

This task was one of the responsibilities of the 1st Canadian Army, who were also required to free the Channel ports and the Scheldt estuary. As long as the Arnhem battle continued they could expect no help from the British 2nd Army, and their opposition had become stronger after the escape of various units of the 15th Army. 226 Div was in Dunkirk, 64 Div in Scheldt Fortress South, 70 Div in Scheldt Fortress North, and 346 and 711 Divs north of Antwerp. They all proved to be stubborn opponents. But they were not the only divisions from the 15th Army who were obstructive.

German troops opposing Market Garden
There were three other divisions from the 15th Army that got back across the Scheldt and escaped through the Woensdrecht isthmus, namely 59, 245 and 712. They were put under the command of 1 Parachute Army, who had been given the task of defending the line of canals from Antwerp to Maastricht. They had started this task by fiercely attacking any bridgeheads the Allies had established over the Albert or the Meuse–Escaut canals, such as those at Beeringen and Gheel. They continued these attacks, but at the start of Market Garden they had a higher priority in attacking the Arnhem corridor.

At the western flank of 1 Parachute Army's line was 719 Div, who were close to Antwerp. Progressing east, there was: Kampfgruppe Chill, largely composed of 85 Div under its Commander General Kurt Chill; Kampfgruppe Walther, mainly paratroopers; and Kampfgruppe Erdman, the Parachute Training Division. As back-up to this front line, Student had three of the divisions salvaged from the 15th Army, 59, 245 and 712. He also had II SS Panzer Corps refitting in the area of Arnhem; its two subunits were 9 SS Panzer (Hohenstaufen) Division, and 10 SS Panzer (Frundsberg) Division. They were more ready for action than Allied intelligence supposed.

THE ARNHEM CORRIDOR

Not much has been written about the battles to keep open the Neerpelt–Nijmegen corridor. On the first few days after Market Garden started on 17 September the corridor was very narrow, and was constantly attacked. Gradually it was widened by the efforts of VIII Corps on the right and XII Corps on the left, and by the contribution of 49 Division mentioned above. But it was a slow business.

Lt Gen Brian Horrocks commanded XXX Corps, and in his auto-biography *A Full Life* he has several comments to make on Market Garden. It was unfortunate, he says, that the landing at Arnhem was in full view of Field Marshal Model, commanding Army Group B. Model was able to institute immediate countermeasures, and he saw that the real threat lay in the rapid advance of the 2nd Army headed by XXX Corps. If he could delay this advance, then he could deal with the lightly armed troops of I Airborne Corps.

The second misfortune was that a copy of the Operation plans was taken from a shot-down glider, and within two hours it was on General Student's desk. Even though Student might have been short of troops, he now knew how to make the best use of them. These two pieces of bad luck were reinforced by Hitler's violent reaction to the landings, which he expressed by shouting 'Holland overshadows everything else'.

The weakness of the British 2nd Army's position during the whole operation was the long, slender and very exposed line of communication which ran south from Nijmegen to Neerpelt. Model instructed Student to do all he could to rupture this corridor, and Student was in a relatively strong position to carry this out. Attacks were made on the corridor continuously, and while it was kept open most of the time there were times when it was cut at one point or another. Horrocks records:

> The move of 43 Div, which I wanted to use for the final push to Arnhem, had been much delayed by congestion along our one and only road, caused to a large extent by the increasing enemy pressure which was coming in from the flanks. A heavy enemy attack on the bridge at Son had been beaten

back by the 101st, but on 20 September another German formation had penetrated into the village of St Oedenrode and halted all traffic on the lines of communication for some hours.

On 22 September Horrocks returned to his HQ after talking with the commanders of his leading troops. He was told by his Chief of Staff that contact was now established with 1 Airborne Division; they said they were short of ammunition, and if XXX Corps could not reach them within twenty-four hours they would probably be overrun. Horrocks continues:

While I was pondering over this unhappy situation, the same staff officer arrived thirty minutes later with the news that a German armoured formation had succeeded in cutting our road to the rear. So in addition to making no progress in front, we were now cut off as well. This was no fault of 101 Airborne, who had been fighting a series of difficult battles to keep our lines of communication open. But it was no easy matter to defend some 25 miles of road with a resolute enemy pressing in on both sides. In fact, many stretches of the road were constantly under shell fire, and at times the banks on either side became the actual front lines facing outwards. As might be expected, this slowed up the traffic moving along the road considerably.

It had been hoped that VIII and XII Corps on our left and right would have been able to have broadened these lines of communication, but they also were meeting stiff opposition and their progress had been slow. As it was vital to open communications with the rear, I was forced to turn 32 Guards Brigade back to start clearing the road from the north, while 101 Airborne and 50 Div advanced from the south. Though this operation eventually succeeded, for twenty-five fateful hours the road was closed to all traffic.

One of the formations on the left flank was 7 Armoured Division. The continued pressure on the corridor by the Germans is vividly portrayed by Rex Wingfield of 1st/6th Queens:

Next morning one regiment of tanks and an infantry battalion were left to hold our gains. The rest of us, mounted on Cromwells, turned back to clear the roads [the main supply route]. We soon found the targets of last night's firing – ten gutted Service Corps lorries, one blasted to fragments. That had been the ammunition truck.

Two hundred yards further down the road was a roadblock of logs. By it lay another burnt lorry and four blackened bodies. A chatter of tracer bounced and sang off the tank as a Spandau opened fire from the roadblock. Our tank's main gun fired, and cordite fumes blasted from the gun into our faces. One of our six-pounder shells hit right in the middle of the logs. The beams sailed upwards. A field-grey rag doll jerked high into the air. We burst through, firing Stens and heaving grenades into the back of the smoking roadblock.

The performance was repeated three times in 4 miles, and then we pulled into the relief column. Each morning we had to clear the roads in front and behind before we could move on.

1 Parachute Army effectively denied the capture of a bridgehead at Arnhem. Three of that Army's seven infantry divisions had come from the 15th Army. Resistance could have been much more easily brushed aside had those three divisions been absent.

CLEARING THE SCHELDT ESTUARY: SOUTH

This section records the general instructions given by 21 Army Group to the 1st Canadian Army, and then reviews the operations to capture the Channel ports and the south bank of the Scheldt estuary. The next section describes the operations north of Antwerp and the capture of Walcheren.

Montgomery issued various instructions between 26 August and 27 September, and the sections of those instructions relating to 'Intention' (of 21 Army Group as a whole), and the executive orders specific to the 1st Canadian Army, are reproduced below. During much of September, Montgomery's time was largely occupied with the planning and execution of Market Garden, as described in the previous section.

Perhaps because of his concentration on Arnhem, he gave much less attention to the Canadian Army on his left flank. One result of this lack of attention is an inconsistency in assigning priorities to the Canadians. And a result of the failure at Arnhem was to give them an additional task, that of protecting the 2nd Army's left flank.

Orders of particular relevance issued by 21 Army Group were:

M 520	26 August	WO 205/5G
M 523	3 September	WO 285/2
M 525	14 September	WO 205/5G
M 527	27 September	WO 205/5G

M 520: 26 August
Intention
To destroy all enemy forces in the Pas-de-Calais and Flanders, and to capture Antwerp.

1st Canadian Army
1. Having crossed the Seine the Army will operate northwards, will secure the port of Dieppe, and will proceed quickly with the destruction of all enemy forces in the coastal belt up to Bruges.

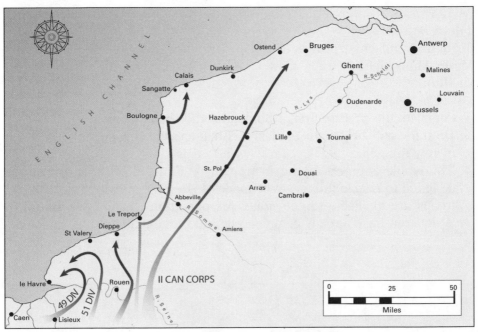

15. Orders for Canadian Army, 26 August and 3 September 1944.

2. One Corps will be turned westwards into the Havre peninsula to destroy the enemy forces in that area and to secure the port of Havre. No more forces will be employed in this task than are necessary to achieve the objective. The main business lies to the north, and in the Pas-de-Calais.

3. In order that Canadian Army can carry out its tasks to northward the more quickly, the Allied Airborne Army will cooperate with it in the Pas-de-Calais area. The airborne forces will be dropped well ahead of the advancing columns; under the conditions that will obtain they can well operate on their own for a week or ten days. [This airborne operation was cancelled.]

4. Generally, in its move northwards Canadian Army will operate with its main weight on its right flank, dealing with enemy resistance by outflanking movements and 'right hooks'.

M 523: 3 September
Intention
a. To advance eastwards and destroy all enemy forces encountered.
b. To occupy the Ruhr, and get astride the communications leading from it into Germany and to the sea ports.

Canadian Army
Canadian Army will clear the coastal belt, and will then remain in the general area Bruges–Calais until the maintenance situation allows of its employment further forward.

M 525: 14 September
Intention
To destroy all enemy west of the general line Zwolle–Deventer–Cleve–Venlo–Maastricht, with a view to advancing eastward and occupying the Ruhr.

Canadian Army

1. Complete the capture first of Boulogne, and then of Calais.
2. Dunkirk will be left to be dealt with later; for the present it will be merely masked.
3. The whole energies of the Army will be directed towards operations designed to enable full use to be made of the port of Antwerp. Airborne troops are available to cooperate. Air operations against the island of Walcheren have already commenced, and these include:

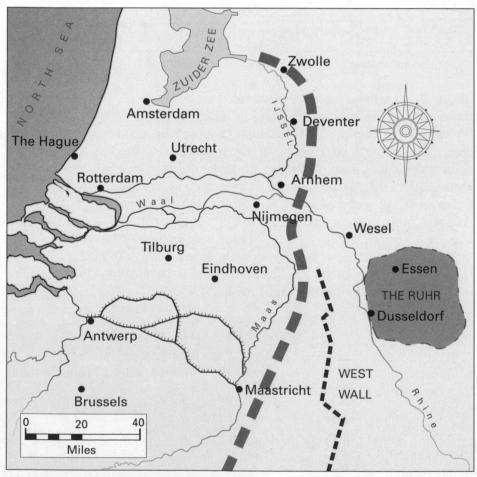

16. Montgomery's intention, 14 September 1944.

a. the isolation of the island by taking out road and rail bridges,
b. attacks on coast defence guns,
c. attacks on other artillery, including flak.

4. HQ I Corps and 49 Div will be brought up from the Havre area as early as possible to the Antwerp area. 51 Div will be grounded completely in the Havre peninsula, and its transport used to enable the above move to take place; the division will remain grounded as long as its transport is required by Canadian Army for maintenance or movement purposes.
5. Canadian Army will take over the Antwerp area from 2nd Army beginning on 17 September. The boundary between the two armies on completion of this relief will be decided by Canadian Army; 2nd Army to conform.

M 527: 27 September
Intention
a. To open up the port of Antwerp.
b. In conjunction with 1st US Army on the right, to destroy all enemy forces that are preventing us from capturing the Ruhr.
Canadian Army
1. The left wing of the Canadian Army will complete the operations that are now in progress to enable us to use the ports of Boulogne and Calais. Dunkirk will be masked, and will be dealt with later.
2. The Canadian Army will at once develop operations designed to enable us to have free use of the port of Antwerp. The early completion of these operations is vital.
3. The right wing of the Canadian Army will thrust strongly northwards on the general axis Tilburg–Hertogenbosch, and so free the 2nd Army from its present commitment of a long left flank facing west. This thrust should be on a comparatively narrow front, and it is important that it should reach Hertogenbosch as early as possible.

Comments on instructions M 520, M 523, M 525, and M 527
Reviewing the 'Intention' paragraph of these instructions, we can see that the emphasis changes as the campaign progresses. Between the dates of M 520 and M 523 the pace of 21 Army Group's advance accelerates massively, and new horizons open out. Between the dates of 523 and 525 the capture of Brussels and Antwerp is well and truly completed, and 1 Airborne Army has been assigned to 21 Army Group. Between 525 and 527 the Arnhem adventure was unsuccessfully undertaken.

M 520, paragraph of the orders for the Canadian Army, states that in turning west to capture Le Havre no more forces will be used than necessary. *The main business lies to the north.* It is reasonable to ask why all resources were not concentrated on the 'main business'. Could not everything else be left until the two major northward prizes, Antwerp and the overrunning of the V1 launching sites, had been won?

M 523 gives the first overt identification of the Ruhr as the objective, and Antwerp is not mentioned. M 525 is confusing and contradictory for the Canadian Army. They are required to take Boulogne and Calais *first*, but 'the whole energies of the Army will be devoted to the freeing of the port of Antwerp'. Which is more important? And Montgomery must have known that the whole of I Airborne Corps had been assigned to Market Garden, and there would be no airborne troops left for anything else.

In M 527, almost a fortnight later, Boulogne and Calais are still first priority. But at the same time the Canadians must *at once* develop operations to free the access to Antwerp. Also at the same time, more than half of the Canadian Army's strength is directed north to protect 2nd Army's left flank.

The formations on the right were 4 Canadian Armoured Division, Polish Armoured Division, and 49 Division. 51 Division had by this time been transferred to XII Corps. The task of freeing the north and south banks of the Scheldt estuary had therefore to be carried by one division only on the south, 3rd Canadian Infantry, and one division only on the north, 2nd Canadian Infantry. Antwerp was a long way behind in the priority stakes.

Capturing the Channel ports
The main purposes of this account of the Canadian Army's activities in September and October are to see what they were doing, how their resources were spread, and to what extent their activities achieved valuable results.

The Canadian Army crossed the Seine at three places, as shown in Map 1 in Chapter One. The two divisions in I Corps, 49 and 51, crossed at Vieux Port and Duclair respectively. II Canadian Corps crossed at Elbeuf, and immediately proceeded to Rouen.

The role of the various divisions in the capture of the Channel ports was as follows. 51 Division was sent to capture St Valery, where it had been forced to surrender in June 1940. As soon as it had taken St Valery, 51 Division turned west and joined 49 Division in the investment of Le Havre. The assault on the city started on 10 September, and the capture was complete on 12 September.

In this Operation (called 'Astonia') the two divisions were supported by 33 and 34 Armoured Brigades, and by large detachments of the specialised armour of 79 Armoured Division. The specialised armour included: Flails – tanks carrying devices to explode mines and thus clear paths through minefields; Crocodiles – Churchill tanks equipped with flame-throwers; AVREs, or Armoured Vehicles Royal Engineers – Churchill tanks with a variety of embellishments such as petards (super-heavy mortars), fascines for filling in anti-tank ditches, and bridge-layers of various types to provide rapid means of crossing canals, streams and other similar defiles.

The assault on Le Havre demanded a large percentage of the 79 Armoured Division equipment that was available in 21 Army Group's area, and until Le Havre was captured none of the specialised armour could be spared for the siege of any other Channel port.

After the capture, 49 and 51 Divisions were grounded outside the city. 49 Division stayed there until 21 September. It was then directed to the Antwerp–Turnhout Canal north-east of Antwerp to help relieve pressure on the Arnhem corridor. 51 Division stayed outside Le Havre until 7 October, when it was directed to help with the same task in the area of Eindhoven.

2 Canadian Division was directed on to Dieppe as soon as it had crossed the Seine. It was here in August 1942 that the division, supported by tanks and commandos, had carried out a divisional-strength raid. Of a total force of 6,000 there were 3,600 casualties, most of them Canadian. It was therefore completely understandable that they felt it was their right to recapture the port – although there was no absolute necessity for it to be done at once.

Dieppe was captured on 2 September, and on the next day there was a memorial service in the town, attended by Gen Harry Crerar, the Canadian Army Commander. The division stayed there to absorb 1,000 reinforcements, and it was not until 6 September that it moved out and travelled up the coast to capture Ostend on the 9th. It was then directed on to the capture of Dunkirk. Here the opposition was more determined, and it was decided that the division should leave Dunkirk, and move to Antwerp itself to relieve 53 Division. The move to Antwerp started on 16 September, and the division was established in Antwerp by the next day.

Third Canadian Division passed through Rouen on 30 August, capturing Le Treport on 1 September, and on 4 September the Divisional Recce Regiment reached the outskirts of Boulogne. Over the next two days they were joined by two of their infantry brigades, while the third infantry brigade was masking Calais.

Crerar and Guy Simonds, commanding II Canadian Corps, decided that Boulogne was to be captured by a deliberate, carefully planned attack to be called Operation Well-hit. Bomber Command and massive artillery support were needed, as well as the specialised armour of 79 Armoured Division; unfortunately, all of these elements were still committed to the battle at Le Havre. The problem with moving the specialised armour was described by Brig Churchill Mann, Chief of Staff to Crerar:

On completion of 'Astonia' time was at a premium in moving the special devices necessary for Well-hit. It was urgent that the limited transportation resources be utilised at maximum capacity to place the devices at the disposal of II Can Corps in sufficient time.

The problem was to provide in four days a lift of 119 equipments with 63 transporters, including eight supplied by 79 Armoured Div. This move entailed a distance of 200 miles.

The problem resolved itself into the need for all transporters doing one turn-around and covering 600 miles in four days. This could be accomplished only if the transporters drove continuously using relief drivers to enable drivers to get enough sleep.

The move of the specialised armour delayed the assault on Boulogne, and there were other delays due to the evacuation of the bulk of the population, 8,000 of whom were cared for by the Canadians.

The attack finally began on 17 September, when two brigades of 3 Canadian Division went in after a 3,000-ton bomber onslaught by the Royal Air Force. In support they had about 340 guns. The attack proceeded steadily, though it was held up by obstacles and by the heavy coastal batteries firing from Cap Gris Nez, 10 miles away. One by one the great concrete forts were reduced. The town itself, though not all the forts, was cleared by 20 September. Port operating parties who arrived on this day, having heard the wireless news of Boulogne's capture, were surprised to find that fighting was still in progress.

Six thousand prisoners, the number of the original estimate, had been taken, but there were still 4,000 more to be winkled out of various strong-points. The last of these to surrender, on 22 September, contained the Garrison commander.

The capture of Calais was also the mission of 3 Canadian Division, and had to wait until Boulogne had been dealt with. This assault included the capture of Cap Gris Nez and the cross-Channel battery at Sangatte, midway between Calais and Cap Gris Nez. In addition to the port's fixed defences, the Canadians found extensive flooding to the east, south and south-west. In consequence, they were forced to attack from the west of the town.

The operation was launched on 25 September with the support of a heavy air bombardment. It went well; on the following day the high ground south of Escalles, which dominated Sangatte and Calais, was occupied. Two days later, in spite of the minefields and inundations, Calais Citadel fell and the town itself was entered. After a truce to allow the evacuation of civilians, the attack was resumed on 30 September. The Cap Gris Nez position had been taken the previous day; Calais was entirely in Canadian hands by the morning of 1 October.

By this date all the Channel ports had been captured except Dunkirk, and it had been decided to contain but not capture that port; in fact it was still in German hands at the end of the war in Europe on 8 May 1945.

Clearing Scheldt south bank

The second task for the Canadian Army south of the Scheldt was to clear the southern bank of the estuary. We have seen that 3 Canadian Division was occupied for the whole of the month of September in taking Boulogne and Calais, and 2 Canadian Division was transferred out of the area on 16 September. 49 and 51 Divisions were either capturing Le Havre, grounded, or, in the case of 49 Division, transferred to the other side of Antwerp.

The only two divisions left to the Canadian Army were 4 Canadian Armoured Division and the Polish Armoured Division. They were following up the retreat of the German 15th Army to the Scheldt. Both armoured divisions crossed the Seine before the end of August, and by 4 September were on the Somme. The Germans were managing to withdraw in reasonable order, and from 6 September they started to evacuate troops over the Scheldt estuary. By 21 September all German formations except 64 Division had escaped and, as we have seen, they were directed to the defence of the Woensdrecht isthmus, the northern suburbs of Antwerp and the Albert Canal.

In this retreat they were pushed steadily, but not greatly harassed, by the armour of II Canadian Corps. After crossing the Somme, the Poles reached St Omer on 7 September, and on 12 September they relieved 7 Armoured Division in Ghent. They attacked north-east out of Ghent to clear the south bank of the Scheldt between Antwerp and Terneuzen. On 17 September they were repulsed at Hulst, but in a subsequent series of actions they took Hulst, Axel, and finally Terneuzen on 22 September.

On 24 September they were transferred to I Corps, which by then had been given the task of reducing the pressure on the left flank of the 2nd Army. This transfer took them to Turnhout, north-east of Antwerp, and completely removed them from further actions to clear the Scheldt south bank.

4 Canadian Armoured Division moved on from the Somme and by 8 September was on the Bruges–Ghent Canal at Moerbrugge, just south of Bruges. On the next day it captured Bruges and Zeebrugge, and then moved north-east to attempt to cross the Leopold Canal. It attacked with one of its infantry battalions, The Lincoln and Welland Regiment, but was repulsed with heavy loss.

After this repulse, Gen Simonds decided that 4 Division should confine its activities to maintaining contact and exerting pressure on the enemy, but 'without dissipating resources in driving out an enemy who might well be retreating'. The division was turned east to mop up the area from where it was to the Terneuzen Canal, and to keep a watch on the Leopold Canal until an assault could be mounted by an infantry division, a formation much more suited to such an operation.

There were two problems with this delay. First, the enemy, in the shape of General Eberding and 64 Division, was *not* retreating, but was making preparations for a determined stand; and second, the only available infantry division, the 3rd, would not be ready until after the capture of Calais. This was completed on 1 October, and 3 Division had moved up to the Leopold Canal by 4 October. As soon as 3 Division was relieved on the canal, 4 Armoured was transferred to help on the northern bank of the Scheldt.

The unfortunate 3 Division was left to clear opposition from the south bank. The forces against them were not much less in numbers, had a resolute commander, had an enormous advantage in the defensive terrain, and had had five weeks to prepare. They were also supported by the guns on the other side of the estuary.

The first assault across the Leopold Canal was made by two battalions of 7 Canadian Infantry Brigade just south of the village of Eede on 6 October. They met fanatical resistance. In spite of the efforts of a third battalion which crossed on the next day, it was four days before the bridgehead could be enlarged enough for the bridges to be built.

9 Canadian Infantry Brigade was loaded onto Buffaloes at Ghent, sailed 20 miles up the Ghent–Terneuzen Canal to its junction with the Scheldt, and on 9 October made a 5-mile trip up the heavily mined river to land just north of Biervliet. There was little opposition at first, but later they had to meet counterattacks and artillery fire from the batteries at Flushing and Breskens.

8 Brigade followed them, and against determined resistance and dreadful terrain gradually fought their way to link up the 7 Brigade bridgehead at Eede. The Germans were compressed back towards Breskens, and the town itself was taken on 22 October. The Germans continued to fight, and it was not until 3 November that the last enemy troops south of the Scheldt surrendered.

The conditions for fighting in this battle were most unpleasant, as recorded by Lt Col W.T. Barnard, the regimental historian of The Queen's Own Rifles of Canada, one of the battalions of 3 Canadian Division's 8 Infantry Brigade:

> The fighting in the Breskens Pocket was marked by the utter misery of the conditions and the great courage required to do the simplest things. Attacks had to go along dykes swept by enemy fire. To go through the polders meant wading, without possibility of concealment, in water that at times came up to the chest.
>
> Mortar fire, at which the Germans were masters, crashed into every rallying point. Spandaus sent their whining reverberations across the marshes. Our own artillery was deprived of much of its effectiveness because of the great difficulty in reaching an enemy dug in on the reverse slope of a dyke.
>
> Even that most potent weapon, the flame-throwing Wasp, was denied both cover and room to manoeuvre. The conditions for heavier supporting vehicles were so bad that at first little use could be made of them. It was particularly a rifleman's fight in that there were no great decisive battles, just a continuous struggle.

CLEARING THE SCHELDT ESTUARY: NORTH

Orders from 21 Army Group for these operations
We saw in the previous sections that the orders issued by Montgomery to
the 1st Canadian Army referred to Antwerp on the following dates:

M 525, 14 September: Whole energies of Canadian Army will be
directed towards opening the port of Antwerp (although the capture of
Boulogne and Calais had priority).

M 527, 27 September: This instruction was a restatement of M 525,
except that an additional major task, the protection of the left flank of the
2nd Army, diverted two-thirds of the Canadian Army's strength away
from the Antwerp operation.

Following on from M 527, Montgomery issued several orders to the
Canadian Army between 4 October and 2 November. Reproduced below
are the texts of those orders, including the intention, or, as it is
alternatively called, 'the general situation'.

M 529: 4 October
Intention
No general intention stated in these orders.

Canadian Army
1. Canadian Army is to destroy all enemy west of a line running north
and south through Tilburg.
2. As II Canadian Corps completes the operations designed to open up
Antwerp, so it will gradually be brought round to the Nijmegen bridgehead
area, and will take over that area. It will then operate northwards across
the Neder Rijn up to the Zuider Zee, and later westwards, clearing up all
country north of the Rhine and west towards the sea.
3. Once the Antwerp situation is cleared up, the further operations south
of the Rhine will be conducted by I Corps. II Canadian Corps will move up
to Nijmegen and will begin operations north of the Rhine.

7 October: A signal from Montgomery to Eisenhower explains the
difficulties of 21 Army Group:
1. I am not happy about the overall battle situation in the northern part of
   the Allied front. The enemy has reacted very violently to our threat to the
   Ruhr, and has concentrated strong forces against Second Army. I have
   three commitments which could become awkward and unbalance the
   whole business in the north:
a. The opening of Antwerp; we must get that place going, and I must have
   reserves of ammunition ready to throw in; I may need fresh divisions.
b. The bridgehead north of Nijmegen. This is daily threatened by the enemy
   and is none too strong; I must reinforce it by two divisions.

c. The enemy situation west of the Meuse; there is considerable enemy strength south of the line Maashees–Deurne. I must use VIII Corps to clean up this area and push the enemy back over the Meuse.

2. I could possibly carry Antwerp, plus 'b'; but I definitely cannot carry all three and also launch Second Army towards Krefeld.

3. If I carry on as we are now, and launch Second Army towards Krefeld on 10 October, that army will have two hostile flanks, as well as strong frontal opposition. A German threat north of Nijmegen, if successful, would unbalance me completely, and my thrust to Krefeld would cease.

   I would then find myself very stretched, and possibly unable to hold all my gains. I might then find that Canadian Army wanted more help to open Antwerp, and I would not be able to provide this help.

4. I have therefore decided to finish the operations to open Antwerp, push the enemy back over the Meuse, and postpone Second Army's move against Krefeld.

M 530: 9 October
General situation
[In this section Montgomery reiterates what was in his signal to Eisenhower on 7 October. He is more specific about Antwerp.] The use of Antwerp is vital to the Allies in order that we can develop our full potential. Therefore the operations to open the port must have priority as regards troops, ammunition, and so on.

Canadian Army
1. Will concentrate all available resources on the operations designed to give us free use of the port of Antwerp. The opening of this port will take priority over all other offensive operations.
2. Will ensure there is no interference by the enemy from the west with the Second Army main supply and communication route from Eindhoven to Nijmegen.
3. 52 (Lowland) Division begins to arrive through Ostend on 13 October, and is available for the Antwerp operations if so required by Canadian Army.

M 532: 16 October
General situation
1. The free use of the port of Antwerp is vital to the Allied cause, and we must be able to use the port soon. Operations designed to open the port will therefore be given complete priority over all other offensive operations in 21 Army Group without any qualification whatsoever.
2. The immediate task of opening up the approaches to the port of Antwerp is already being undertaken by Canadian Army, and good progress has been made. The whole of the available power of Second Army will now be brought to bear also.

Canadian Army
1. Will concentrate all available resources on the operations designed to give us free use of the port of Antwerp.
2. The right wing of the Army will be pulled over towards Antwerp, so that its operations can exert a more direct influence on the battle for possession of the area Bergen op Zoom–Roosendaal–Antwerp. Possession of this area is necessary in order to enable us to operate freely westwards along the Beveland Isthmus.

Comments on instructions M 529, M 530, and M 532
The task given in paragraph 1 of M 529 of 4 October was massive. 3 Canadian Division had only just completed the capture of the Channel ports, and 4 Canadian Armoured, Polish Armoured and 49 Division had been moved to the Turnhout area, where they found stubborn resistance on the line of the Antwerp–Turnhout Canal. The 1st Canadian Army did not have the resources to destroy the enemy nominated and free the Scheldt estuary at the same time.

In his letter to Eisenhower of 7 October, Montgomery is once again more interested in his push to Krefeld than in freeing Antwerp. In M 530 of 9 October Antwerp is given notional first priority, but at least half of the Canadian Army is required to protect the 2nd Army's supply route.

It is not until M 532 of 16 October that Antwerp is given unequivocal first priority. Paragraph 2 of M 532 is particularly revealing when it says: 'The right wing of the Army will be pulled over towards Antwerp, so that its operations can exert a more direct influence on the battle for the area Bergen op Zoom–Roosendaal–Antwerp.' The implication of this statement is quite clearly that the operations of 4 Canadian Armoured, Polish Armoured and 49 Division were only indirectly helping to liberate the Scheldt estuary, and had been mainly concerned with the protection of the 2nd Army, freeing that army for its push to the Ruhr.

Liberating the Scheldt was thus left to the 2 and 3 Canadian Divisions. They were on their own until 16 October. On the north bank 2 Canadian Division was opposed by the German 70 Division on the Beveland peninsula, and by 711, 346 and 719 Divisions north of Antwerp. There were also the artillery garrisons of the fortresses, sundry naval forces, and the flak units all over the area. These last could be used as antiaircraft, anti-tank or field artillery; they were particularly effective against tanks.

The Germans could also – and did – add mines and booby traps to the already appalling terrain of the polders, streams and marshes. And finally, all troops had to contend with the dreadful weather.

It is clear that either intelligence as to what the Canadian infantry might have to meet was faulty, or that the intelligence was misinterpreted or ignored. We will now see what this meant for 2 Canadian Division as they undertook operations to free the Scheldt north bank. As the operations unfolded, so it became clear that more troops were needed. Before the capture of Walcheren and the final freeing of the Scheldt north bank, these were provided in the shape of 52 (Lowland) Division, and for the assault on Walcheren 4 Special Service Brigade was added. This Brigade, whose name was converted at about this time to 4 Commando Brigade, consisted of: 4 Army Commando, supported by French troops; 41 Royal Marine Commando, 47 Royal Marine Commando and 48 Royal Marine Commando.

Stages of the battle for Scheldt north bank
There were four stages in the battle for the Scheldt north bank, with some overlap between stages 1 and 2:

1. Advance to Woensdrecht by 2 Canadian Division.
2. Clearing the area bounded by the Antwerp–Turnhout Canal, Bergen op Zoom, Roosendaal and Breda. This was to protect the back of 2 Canadian Division as it advanced along the Beveland peninsula.
3. Capture of South Beveland.
4. Capture of Walcheren.

Advance to Woensdrecht
11 Armoured Division left Antwerp on 8 September, and was weakly replaced by 53 Division, the last troops of which were withdrawn to take part in the Arnhem adventure on 17 September. Antwerp was a strange place in September. The civilian population was caught up in the euphoria of liberation and seemed almost oblivious to the presence of Germans in the northern suburbs of the city. Some civilians went about their affairs to the point of crossing back and forth over the Albert Canal from the German to the Allied sector. The Belgian Resistance, on the other hand, was active in attempting to extend the dock area perimeter.

The transfer of 2 Canadian Division from south of the estuary started on 16 September, and two battalions of 4 Brigade, the Essex Scottish and the Royal Hamilton Light Infantry (RHLI), took over the dock defences. On the night of the 20th the Essex were hit hard by a German attack, but after heavy fighting the enemy was beaten off.

The area around 4 Brigade positions had been flooded by the Germans until the Belgian White Brigade, supported by Canadian artillery, secured the sluice gates, allowing the tidal water to be drained. RHLI moved forward to the villages of Oorderen and Wilmarsdonck to protect this site on 22 September, and from then until 2 October no major initiative was taken by either side in this area. This lack of activity was much more beneficial to the Germans than to the Allies.

5 Brigade moved to the Antwerp area on 18 September, and took up positions at Wyneghcm, 3 miles east of Antwerp on the Albert Canal. Its

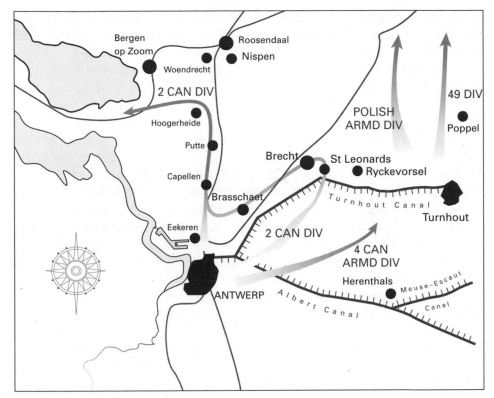

17. Advance to Woensdrecht – stage 1.

orders were to advance north with the resources available, but without incurring heavy losses. The Calgary Highlanders secured a bridgehead over the Albert Canal on 21 September, and the next day Le Régiment de Maisonneuve advanced from the bridgehead to the Antwerp–Turnhout Canal.

6 Brigade was now ordered to cross the Turnhout Canal at Lochtenberg. They achieved initial success on 24 September, but fierce German counterattacks caused heavy losses, and on 28 September the Canadians and supporting troops from the Belgian White Brigade were withdrawn back across the canal.

Further to the east, other attempts were made to cross the Turnhout Canal. I British Corps with 49 Division had moved up from Le Havre to the Albert Canal near Herenthals. They found the Germans in front of them were withdrawing, and followed them up to Turnhout. Between 24 and 29 September they established a firm bridgehead over the canal at Rijkesvorsel. 5 Canadian Infantry Brigade crossed just to the west of the bridgehead, and moved west through St Leonards, capturing Brecht on 1 October.

The 49 Division bridgehead was also used by the Polish Armoured Division. The Poles, with support from 49 Division, took Merxplas on

30 September, and for the next five days pressed forward against strong and growing opposition. They captured Baarle-Nassau on 4 October, and on the next day took Alphen, where they were temporarily halted.

To the right of the Poles' axis, 146 Brigade of 49 Division advanced to Poppel, which they took on 4 October. The Poles and 49 Division, the constituent formations of I Corps, then established a defensive line which ran through Brecht, Rijkvorsel, Merxplas, Baarle-Nassau, Alphen and Poppel. This line was part of the protection for the left flank of the 2nd Army, and would also serve as a jumping-off point for an attack to protect the right flank of the Canadians advancing to seal off the Woensdrecht isthmus.

The Canadian advance to do the sealing-off was in two prongs which aimed to join up. On 1 October it appeared that the Germans were preparing to withdraw from Merxem, the Antwerp suburb immediately north of the Albert Canal. The Belgian White Brigade were quick to start harassing the withdrawing enemy, and on 2 October they were joined by the Essex Scottish of 4 Canadian Brigade, who pushed forward to Fort de Merxem. On 4 October 4 Brigade reached Eeckeren.

6 Canadian Brigade advanced down the northern bank of the Turnhout Canal from their position at Brecht, and took Lochtenberg on 2 October. They took Camp de Brasschaet the next day, and on the 4th one of 6 Brigade's battalions, Les Fusiliers Mont Royal, took Capellen.

Here, 4 and 6 Brigades joined forces, captured Putte on 5 October, and on the 6th took Ossendrecht and Sandvliet. They now had to capture the three key villages blocking the entrance to the Beveland peninsula – Woensdrecht, Hoogerheide and Korteven. On the 7th the Calgary Highlanders got into Hoogerheide after a stiff fight, but the next day the Black Watch of Canada was forced back to its start line when it attempted to take Korteven.

Air reconnaissance reported a large German force with armour and guns in the woods south of Bergen op Zoom. Prisoners captured in the area were identified as being from Kampfgruppe Chill and from paratroop formations. That night and through the next day the Canadians in the Hoogerheide area had to beat off German attacks.

On 9 October a detachment from 4 Canadian Armoured Division came up to protect the long exposed flank of 2 Canadian Division. On 11 October the Canadian infantry reached the isthmus railway, all but cutting off the Germans in the Beveland peninsula. On 13 October the Black Watch of Canada got into Woensdrecht, but later was ordered to withdraw, having lost 145 officers and men, 56 of them killed. The Germans held on.

On 16 October the RHLI fought its way into Woensdrecht with intensive artillery support, and the next day the Essex Scottish beat off renewed enemy attacks, losing 121 in casualties, 21 of them killed. The enemy were not giving up, even though Rundstedt acknowledged that the land connection with Walcheren had been lost. For the moment, 2 Canadian Division was checked.

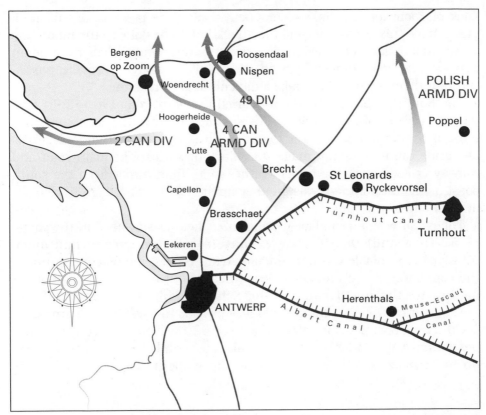

18. Advance to Woensdrecht – stage 2.

On 17 October 4 Canadian Armoured Division completed its concentration north-east of Antwerp and came under command of I Corps, and on the 20th attacked towards Esschen and Bergen op Zoom. In spite of determined resistance the former was taken on the 22nd, and the latter on the 27th. The other divisions of I Corps were pressing north and north-west to Roosendaal, Zundert and Breda, and the German formations around Bergen op Zoom began to retreat northwards. This reduced the resistance the Canadians were experiencing at Korteven, and on 24 October 2 Canadian Division was able to start its advance through the isthmus and along the Beveland peninsula.

South Beveland
Two flooded areas blocked the isthmus, and beyond them the South Beveland Ship Canal, a wide, deep canal, blocked the eastern tip of South Beveland. Early on 24 October the Royal Regiment of Canada, with massed artillery support, crossed the first floods. The next step was for the Essex Scottish, with the help of tanks from 4 Division, to rush the canal crossing.

Lack of room for the tanks to manoeuvre, and the presence of anti-tank guns, made this impossible, and the attack had to be done by the infantry.

Advancing across flooded polders over two days and nights, 4 Canadian Brigade reached Krabbendijke on 26 October, where 6 Brigade passed through them, prepared to make a difficult assault crossing.

The South Beveland Ship Canal varied in width from 190 to 290 feet. Its banks were raised well above the surrounding countryside, which like most of the central part of the island was below sea level. Drainage canals alongside the main canal made subsidiary obstacles. The main road and railway crossed by swing bridges rather more than a mile from the south coast of the island; there was another further north, and there were locks at each end of the canal.

The canal was a formidable obstacle, but help was at hand in the shape of 52 (Lowland) Division. As we have seen, Montgomery had made 52 Division available to the Canadian Army. Its first job on coming under the command of the Canadians was to carry out an amphibious landing further up the north bank of the Scheldt. This would draw off the Germans from the canal, and could well provide the element of surprise.

On 21 October 156 Infantry Brigade of 52 Division received a warning order that it would be required to make an assault landing. They moved up to Terneuzen, where they married up with the Buffaloes and other

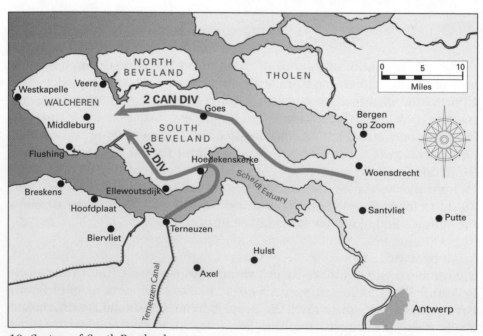

19. Capture of South Beveland.

amphibious craft that were to ferry them across the Scheldt and land them 12 miles west of the canal – that is, well behind the German positions on the ship canal.

At 0245 hr on 26 October the assault started, and by nightfall of that day 156 Brigade had established a bridgehead a mile deep and 3 miles wide. On the next day they captured the small port of Elleswoutsdijke, and on 28 October they made contact with patrols from the Royal Regiment of Canada, who had come from the crossing they had made over the ship canal.

To get across the canal, 6 Canadian Brigade had made a three-battalion assault. It took them two days to establish a bridgehead over the canal, but by then the engineers had finished a bridge on the line of the main road. On 29 October 4 Canadian Brigade advanced westward to meet 156 Brigade at 's-Gravenpolder. The Canadians and the Lowlanders then moved further west, until the only unfinished business in the clearing of the Scheldt was the island of Walcheren. This was the end of the battle for 4 Canadian Brigade.

The regimental historian of the Royal Regiment of Canada records:

> On 1 November a long line of weary, muddy infantrymen plodded slowly back down the road that would take them to a new area in Hofstade, a little village near Malines. The men were indescribably dirty. They were bearded, cold as it is only possible to be cold in Holland in November, and wet from having lived in water-filled holes in the ground for twenty-four hours a day. Their eyes were red-rimmed from lack of sleep, and they were exhausted from their swift advance on foot in terrible conditions. Yet all ranks realised with a certain grim satisfaction that a hard job had been well and truly done.

The difficulties and hardships of this battle were almost totally ignored by the Allied higher command. Montgomery could have recalled Gen Lancelot Kiggell's reactions in 1917. When he, a senior member of Haig's staff, finally viewed the battlefield of Passchendaele, he said to his guide, a front-line soldier: 'My God, did we really send men to fight in this?' To which the guide replied tonelessly: 'It's worse further up.'

Walcheren
The conditions on Walcheren were no better. This island contained the northern defence fortresses that *had* to be captured if supply ships were to be able to sail down the Scheldt estuary to the port of Antwerp.

Walcheren is approximately rectangular in shape, about 12 miles by 9 miles in size, and lies mostly below sea level. There is a rim of dunes up to 100 feet high connecting with an area above sea level in the eastern corner, where the causeway from South Beveland joins the island. On the dunes of the north-west and south-west coasts the Germans had mounted powerful batteries in concrete, covering respectively the sea approaches

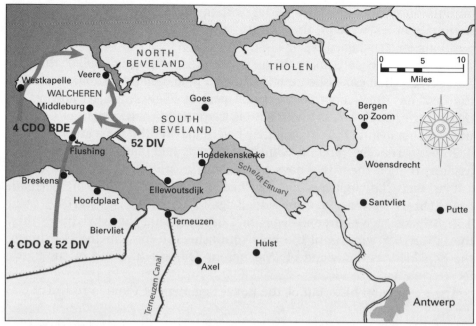

20. Capture of Walcheren.

and the mouth of the Scheldt. In addition, the coast was defended against infantry attack by barbed wire, mines and machine-guns, many of the latter in concrete emplacements.

The strength of the garrison was estimated at 7,000 men, and its reduction presented a very difficult problem. The nature of the terrain was unsuitable for an airborne landing; it was eventually decided to 'sink' Walcheren by breaching the dunes round its circumference. This would make many of the enemy artillery positions untenable, and restrict enemy movements. Also, if the breaches were large enough, assaulting forces could be launched into the island in amphibious craft and take the enemy in the rear.

Bomber Command carried out the dyke-breaching operations on 3 October at Westkapelle, on 7 October at Flushing, and on 11 October at Veere on the north-east coast of the island. In all, 9,000 tons of bombs were dropped on Walcheren, and by the end of the bombing the island looked like a saucer full of water. It ruined the rich polder land, but the stout-hearted Zeelanders averred that they would sooner have water than the Germans.

The plan was to make two assaults by sea, and another over the causeway from South Beveland to Walcheren. One seaborne force was to move from Breskens to secure Flushing, and the second was to embark at Ostend, assault the Westkapelle area, and then pass into the island through the breach in the dyke.

Operations began on 1 November. Early in the morning 4 Army Commando landed near Flushing and reached the waterfront without serious casualties. They were followed by troops of 52 Division, and the attack moved into the town. The Westkapelle force approached the coast supported by naval units and Continental-based air squadrons. On the east of the breach, 48 Royal Marine Commando quickly secured the major strong-points, and by evening had advanced 2 miles in the direction of Flushing. On the west of the breach, 41 Royal Marine Commando negotiated the gap in the dyke, dismounted, and captured Westkapelle. Later in the day they advanced towards Domburg.

The initial attack on the South Beveland–Walcheren causeway was made by 5 Canadian Infantry Brigade on 31 October. The causeway was 1,200 feet long and 40 feet wide, and afforded no cover whatsoever from the strong enemy positions at its western end. The first attacks were repulsed with very heavy loss. On 1 November the task was handed over to 52 Division, and 1st Battalion The Glasgow Highlanders of 157 Brigade was the unfortunate unit to whom it was allocated.

They also suffered, and the Divisional Commander, Gen Hakewill-Smith, decided to look for an alternative to a head-on assault. This he found in a ford across the Slooe Channel, 2 miles south of the causeway. It was a dangerous and unpleasant crossing, and the engineers worked heroically to clear mines and lay guiding tapes to show the safe path.

A bridgehead was established over the ford on the night of 3/4 November, and the troops then fanned out to join up with the western end of the causeway. The Germans now realised that they had lost control of the Scheldt, but there were still pockets of fanatical resistance that had to be mopped up. On 6 November the German Commander, General Wilhelm Daser, surrendered, and by 8 November all organised enemy resistance on Walcheren had ceased.

General Winter

One element of the retribution resulting from the delays caused by Montgomery's vacillation between Arnhem and Antwerp was the need to face deteriorating weather. The weather in north-west Europe in autumn and winter is characterised by cloud, fog and rain. These conditions start in mid- to late September, and are replaced by cold, frost and sometimes snow in early December. Obviously the weather is not consistent year to year, but the averages over a period of years are a guideline.

For campaigns in Europe the spring and summer favour the attacker and autumn and winter the defender. If the sky is mostly clear and the going generally firm, then attacking ground forces, especially tanks, can move forward rapidly and can be supported by their air forces. Thus the spring and summer months are the best times to attack, and the earlier the better.

In autumn and winter the going can become sticky, and present problems both for advances by the front-line troops and for resupply. The skies are often overcast, preventing close support of ground forces from the air, and making it difficult or impossible to drop airborne troops or supplies.

It is therefore highly desirable to use all speed possible in the spring and summer, and to leave any mopping-up operations for the time when it does not matter so much if movement is slow and deliberate. Operation Overlord could have been even more successful had the invasion been launched on 8 May 1944 instead of 6 June, thus giving the Allies an extra four weeks of summer weather.

However, the operations after 26 July, including the American break-out, the Falaise pocket, and the advance to the borders of Holland, all made good use of days of mainly fine weather. The delays after 4 September negated this advantage, and led to the forces under SHAEF becoming bogged down metaphorically and to some degree literally.

Montgomery complained about the weather on several occasions, almost as if it was deliberately interfering with his plans. We saw in Chapter Three that Monty and his opponent General Student both thought that bad weather was the most important factor causing the failure of the Arnhem adventure.

At the end of October the Scheldt estuary was about to be cleared, and the German forces south of the Maas pushed back over that river. One of the units helping to do the pushing back was 9th Royal Tank Regiment, one of the battalions of 34 Armoured Brigade. They arrived in south Holland in early October, and spoke about the weather they experienced (see *Tank Tracks* by Peter Beale).

'It was now October, and it was cold and often wet. Billets of any kind, and they were of many kinds, were certainly preferable to tank bivvies.'

War Diary, 20 October: 'No rain; dull; ground soft after heavy rain.'

Tank driver Cyril Rees: 'Ahead I could see the flat country receding into the gloom, with a few trees here and there and a hedge or two. It reminded me of the fens in so many ways.'

Of the advance to Roosendaal, tank commander Trevor Greenwood said: 'The surrounding country was very flat and quite open, but fairly well infested with ditches and drainage channels, as is most of this area; two or three vehicles had difficulty in the heavy ground and were ditched for a while.'

Bill Thompson was a tank wireless operator, and remarked on 29 October: 'We were fighting our way over bogs and dykes in pouring rain.'

Monty has this to say of the clearing of German troops from this area: 'The enemy's withdrawal from South-West Holland had been very greatly facilitated by the adverse flying weather. Under cover of mist and low clouds he had escaped the inevitably heavy punishment which in favourable conditions our Air Forces would have given him.'

The corollary of this observation is that bad weather is almost always an advantage to troops on the defensive. One of the Ultra intercepts quoted an OKW circular which referred to 'experiences gained during approach marches going into the battle area. Because of Allied air superiority precautionary measures had been ordered. Only energetic and circumspect leaders were capable of getting their columns forward. Bad weather was often not properly used for getting on with the march without incurring casualties.'

As winter closed in, so the overcast skies gave the Germans more and more protection from Allied air strikes, and as we saw in the Scheldt battles, so the increasing dampness made fighting much more unpleasant for everyone, but especially the attackers.

REVIEW OF RETRIBUTION

The failure to send troops north from Antwerp immediately after its capture on 4 September, or the Great Mistake as we have called it, had many consequences, all of them negative. Covered previously in this chapter, they can be summarised as:

1. The failure to reinforce 11 Armoured Division so that XXX Corps could send a force north from Antwerp to block the Woensdrecht isthmus allowed the escape of the German 15th Army. This was compounded by the insistence on capturing the Channel ports, including Le Havre. Had the Canadian Army with its full strength of II Canadian Corps and I British Corps been directed to ignore the Channel ports and push straight on for the Scheldt, most of 15th Army would have been eliminated before it had a chance to escape, and the Scheldt south bank would have been cleared of Germans in a few days. Those that were able to cross would have been stopped by a blocking force at Woensdrecht.
2. Even if the Canadians had not advanced rapidly to the Scheldt, the escaping German divisions would have been stopped at Woensdrecht. The divisions that did escape through the isthmus were 59, 245, 346, 711 and 712; they would not have been available to defend the northern suburbs of Antwerp and the Albert Canal, nor to harass the flanks of the Arnhem salient had the isthmus been blocked.
3. If the advance to Woensdrecht had been reinforced by either XII Corps or XXX Corps, then one or two divisions, supported by an armoured brigade, could have turned west along the Beveland peninsula. They could have moved on rapidly to the ship canal, established a bridgehead, and pressed on to the western shores of South Beveland. The capture of Walcheren would still have been a hard battle, but undoubtedly the number of casualties would have been much lower than they actually were.

The task of opening the Scheldt between 1 October and 8 November, six weeks of bloody, gut-grinding combat, cost the 1st Canadian Army 703 officers and 12,170 other ranks killed, wounded and missing, of whom almost exactly half were Canadians. The rest were Polish, American and British soldiers, and the gallant fighters of the Belgian and Dutch Resistance.

Added to those were earlier Canadian casualties on the Leopold Canal and south of it, casualties of 11 Armoured Division in the liberation of Antwerp, and those of other formations of XII and XXX Corps. There were also many casualties in the supporting Navy and Air Force units.

4. The delays in closing up to the south bank of the Scheldt and in sealing off the Woensdrecht isthmus allowed the Germans plenty of time to strengthen their defences. Not only did the five divisions listed above escape to the east, but 64 Division was able to make Fortress Scheldt South capable of holding out until early November, and 70 Division with its crew of invalids was able to do the same in Fortress Scheldt North.

5. The delay at the Scheldt meant that all subsequent operations had to take place in deteriorating weather. The tempo of advance slowed, and in many places came to a standstill. Had the Woensdrecht isthmus been blocked, and the Canadians closed up rapidly to the Scheldt, 21 Army Group could have reached the Rhine by the end of October.

They would still have had bitter fighting against 1 Parachute Army and Panzer units, but they could have prepared a jumping-off point for an advance into Germany. They could also have had the great benefit of the use of the port of Antwerp, which would have been available by mid-October rather than at the end of November.

Finally, it is just possible that the war in Europe could have been over by the end of 1944, with the Anglo-Americans in Berlin instead of the Russians.

Chapter Twelve

THE UNFORGIVING MINUTE

I may lose a battle, but I will never lose a minute.

Napoleon

No one realises the importance of the 'unforgiving minute' except me.

Patton

The best chance of a quick finish was probably lost when the 'gas' was turned off from Patton's tanks in the last week of August, when they were 100 miles nearer to the Rhine and its bridges than the British. Patton had a keener sense than anyone else on the Allied side of the key importance of persistent pace in pursuit. He was ready to exploit in any direction; indeed, on 23 August he had proposed that his Army should drive north instead of east. There was much point in his subsequent comment: 'One does not plan and then try to make circumstances fit those plans. One tries to make plans fit the circumstances. I think the difference between success and failure in high command depends upon its ability, or lack of it, to do just that.'

Liddell Hart

There are occasions in the course of a war or a battle when an opportunity presents itself for a brief moment of time. If not seized, the opportunity may disappear, never to return. As Patton implies, one of the qualities of an effective military commander is to appreciate that there is an opportunity, and then to seize and exploit it.

A word in the military vocabulary used to describe this is 'tempo'. The attacker has to maintain tempo for as long as it appears to be paying dividends, and the defender attempts to throttle the tempo of the attacker. The results of the throttling may be to discourage the attacker, and to give the defender a chance to strengthen his defences.

The operations of August to November 1944 in the northern sector of the Allied forces were characterised by three manifestations of tempo:

1. Positive forward tempo, where the tempo of the Allied advance was initiated and maintained, resulting in achievement of objectives more quickly than expected.

2. Self-inflicted reduction of tempo, where opportunities were either not recognised or not taken.
3. Defensive tempo: enemy reduction of tempo, where enemy action, often unexpected, forced a reduction in the speed of the Allied advance, and allowed reinforcements and other defensive measures to be put in place. There is a tempo in defensive measures, as well as in attack. The realisation that there is a gap in your defence, and the action to fill that gap, are the more effective the more quickly they are taken. This we have called 'defensive tempo'.

These three aspects of tempo have been demonstrated ever since wars have been fought. Each of the three will be discussed in turn. For each, some historical examples from a variety of campaigns are described, followed by examples from the northern sector battles from August to November 1944.

FORWARD TEMPO: CHARGE!

The exhilarating command 'Charge!' can result from calculated but instantaneous evaluation of a real opportunity, or from a mindless inability to think of anything else to say. The latter type of command is likely to cause a very courageous advance against impossible odds, as for example the charge of 9 Armoured Brigade in Operation Supercharge in the battle of El Alamein. It often happens in a unit's first battle, when the adrenalin is pumping hard, and the soldiers think they are invincible.

The examples discussed below are all situations where there was a calculated evaluation, a decision taken and acted on immediately.

At the battle of Salamanca on 17 June 1812 the British cavalry commander, Gen Le Marchant, breasted the skyline and saw below him two French divisions in square. He *at once* led his brigade in the charge to the destruction of the greater part of those two divisions. At the beginning of the same battle the British commander, Wellington, was observing the French column of divisions marching across his front along a low ridge about a mile away. Suddenly he noticed that the leading French division was racing away from those behind it. He at once saw an opportunity to fall on the French while they were stretched out and his own force was a compact mass directly under his own hand. He immediately gave orders for an attack, and the resulting British victory was described by the French General Foy as 'the catastrophe of the Spanish War'.

Similar opportunities arise in naval battles. Of the many occasions on which a naval commander has responded to such an opportunity, that of the United States Navy Admiral David Farragut is one of the most dramatic. It was during the action at Mobile Bay, Alabama on 5 August 1864. At the crisis of the action the Union monitor *Tecumseh* had just sunk, and the Union sloop *Brooklyn* had tried to pull out of the attack and was lying athwart the ship channel unwilling to proceed. Farragut, in charge of the Union forces, viewed the situation and immediately shouted 'I will take the lead!'

He was warned that there were torpedoes – the term then used for mines – but as his flagship *Hartford* and her consort *Metacomet* began to make headway he was heard to shout again, 'Damn the torpedoes! Full speed ahead!' Farragut's fleet entered Mobile Bay, forced the capitulation of the Confederate fleet there, and ended the usefulness of the bay to the Confederacy.

The career of Field Marshal Erwin Rommel demonstrates many instances of his ability to seize the moment. In his first action as a platoon commander in northern France on 8 August 1914, he and three of his men came round the corner of a hedge and saw twenty of the enemy standing about in the road. They attacked immediately, firing from the standing position, and the enemy broke.

In October 1917, moving continuously for fifty hours and seizing opportunity after opportunity, Rommel's company took Monte Matajur, the key to an enemy position in northern Italy. In the course of the action his company of 150 men captured 150 officers, 9,000 men and 81 guns. He repeated the same sort of performance between 10 May and 19 June 1940 as the Commander of 7 Panzer Division, leading one of the thrusts that destroyed the French Army and drove the British back across the Channel.

Moving back to the autumn of 1944, three examples of forward tempo in the Normandy break-out are shown, two from the British Army and one from the American.

British Army, Example 1: Normandy, 31 July 1944
Message from 1 Troop, C Squadron, 2nd Household Cavalry Regiment: 'At 1035 hrs the bridge at 637436 is clear of enemy and still intact.'

The bridge was over the River Souleuvre, and was 6 miles behind the German lines. The only Allied vehicles at the bridge were one armoured car and one scout car. 2 HCR was then the Reconnaissance Regiment of 11 Armoured Division, and 1 Troop had been patrolling ahead of the division. The two vehicles had crossed a road covered by an 88mm gun which was late in identifying them as enemy, and could not swing round quickly enough to knock them out. But it was now ready for anything else that crossed the road in either direction.

1 Troop Commander, Lt Dickie Powle, shouted to his corporal: 'We may as well keep going – we certainly don't want to go back past that lot.' The two cars went flat out down a track through the Forêt l'Evêque, a track which was the boundary between two German divisions. They found themselves – fortunately unrecognised – in a German column. The German vehicles eventually turned up a side-road, and Lt Powle and

Corporal Bland arrived at the bridge. They killed the guard on the bridge, concealed their vehicles in the nearby wood, and sent the message above.

The Divisional Commander saw at once a chance to seize the bridge in strength. The plan of attack was altered, and the advance of the 2nd Northants Yeomanry and 4th King's Shropshire Light Infantry was immediately switched to back up Powle and Bland at their lonely outpost. The original arrival at the bridge and the forceful follow-up were important factors in the successful execution of Operation Bluecoat.

British Army, Example 2: Normandy, 6 August 1944
Mt Pincon was a dominant feature of the Normandy landscape, and its capture would give the Allies command of the countryside for several miles into the German lines. But it was strongly held by the Germans, and its capture looked to be a bloody and expensive task.

However, in the evening of 6 August Gen Horrocks, commanding XXX Corps, saw his Chief of Staff, Brigadier Pete Pyman, running towards him – unusual for a Chief of Staff! 'We've got Mt Pincon, sir,' he called out as he ran. Gen Horrocks recounts how it happened.

> Captain Denny, who commanded the leading troops of 13/18 Hussars tanks working with 43 Division, discovered a narrow track winding up the hill, and reported by radio to his CO that the track was apparently undefended. He was immediately ordered to have a go. The track was so narrow that one tank toppled over into a disused gravel pit, but the others ground their way steadily up to the top. So, thanks to the initiative of one young officer the most important tactical feature in Normandy had been captured by six or seven tanks.

They were quickly reinforced by the 4th Wiltshire Regiment, who had been fighting almost continuously for forty-eight hours. Encouraged by their CO, who led the column himself, the battalion struggled to the top in single file.

The crewmen of the tanks were very pleased to see the infantry; because there was a thick mist swirling round them, they could hear Germans moving about, and they were beginning to feel exceptionally lonely. But Mt Pincon had been taken by seizing the opportunity when it was offered.

American Army:
The 3rd US Army under Gen George Patton showed many examples of great ability to maintain tempo. Russell Weigley says of Patton: 'He was one American General who believed that mobility must be exploited into the strategic manoeuvre of the indirect approach.' He implanted the belief in mobility in his subordinates, especially in the commanders of 4 and 6 Armoured Divisions, Gens Wood and Grow respectively. The account of

the battle to burst out of the Cotentin peninsula describes the actions of 4 Armoured Division.

During 29 July, 4 Armoured Division advanced with so much flair and speed as well as skill that by that evening the Corps Commander, Middleton, decided it was in a better position than the 6th to capture Avranches, the key road junction at the base of the Cotentin peninsula, and awarded it the prize.

Middleton, like Patton, could take personal satisfaction from the 4th's performance. Against the advice of tank experts, in early July Middleton had assigned it to a defensive role in his lines. The division had thereby received just enough seasoning to give it a battlefield sharpness uncommon to new divisions by the time it became a corps spearhead.

Brigadier Holmes Dager's Combat Command B (CCB) of the 4th discovered on 30 July that both bridges over the River See at Avranches were intact, and entered the undefended city early in the evening. Dager set guards round Avranches, and immediately sent a small force east along the north bank of the See to secure the bridge at Tirepied.

During the night and into the next day, CCB had to fight for Avranches after all, for a time giving up one of the See bridges. At first the enemy seemed to be mounting a serious counterattack, but he proved to be merely scrambling to get out of the Cotentin. So intent were the Germans on flight that on the afternoon of the same day, 31 July, Col Clarke's CCA of 4 Armoured Division sent a task force to race across the River Selune at Pontaubault, which dispersed a counterstroke and thus made sure that VIII US Corps could burst out of the Cotentin.

Forward tempo in the Antwerp battles

Night march to Amiens

Gen Brian Horrocks had commanded XXX Corps in North Africa. On one occasion he ordered his troops to make a night approach march. There was some opposition to the idea of a night march into hostile territory, but Horrocks reassured his subordinates by saying: 'It's moonlight tonight.' This became a code phrase to indicate that you were to treat night as if it was day, and accordingly move with all speed.

Gen Adair commanded the Guards Armoured Division in the crossing of the Seine and the advance to Brussels. He records:

On 29 August my Corps Commander, General Horrocks, summoned me to his HQ and said: 'I want you to get along as quickly as you can and seize crossings over the River Somme.' I replied: 'We're a hundred miles away. It'll take us a little time.' He said: 'Never mind. It's moonlight tonight. You've got to get up to the Somme and seize crossings over that as quickly as ever you can.' So we prepared and set off. It was pitch-dark and pouring with rain.

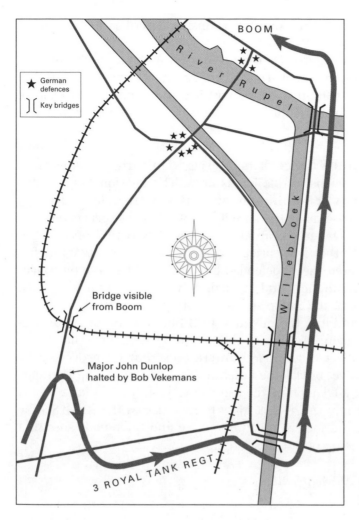

21. Rupel bridges at Boom.

Robert Vekemans and the bridges at Boom

Lt Robert Vekemans was a Belgian engineer officer and repatriated prisoner of war. He understood the importance of preventing the Germans from blowing up the road bridge over the River Rupel at Boom, just south of Antwerp, and also realised that the Germans would blow the bridge as soon as they saw Allied tanks approaching from the south. At a seminar held in 1984 on the liberation of Antwerp he described what happened:

> In the early morning of 4 September 1944 a sudden lull fell on the crossroads near the concentration camp at Fort Breendonk. The last German convoy had swiftly disappeared in the direction of Boom. Rapidly a tank troop arrived from the south. In the middle of the road, I tried to stop the first tank.

It moved past without the slightest sign of an answer, except turning its heavy gun turret. The second tank didn't stop either. The third one pointed to the fourth. From this fourth tank peered out a dusty black-bearded face in a black beret. The tank stopped, and the commander, pistol in hand, beckoned to me. After my short explanation he immediately stopped the leading tank.

A couple of hundred yards further, and it would have appeared on the overpass of the railway marshalling yard and have been seen by the German observer hiding in the roof of the bridge house. The alarm would have been given, and all the bridges blown up.

This tank commander [Maj John Dunlop, commanding C Squadron of 3 RTR], with prompt compliance as was his nature, pulled back his tanks at once, accepted my suggestion, and gave me a scout car. With his open-heartedness he convinced his colonel to venture the manoeuvre. Without his quick-wittedness, the entire action would have collapsed, as there was not a single minute to be lost.

INERTIA: SELF-INFLICTED DELAY

Napoleon at Waterloo
As Napoleon said, he might lose a battle, but would never lose a minute. Yet in the last stage of his last battle, he lost both.

In the Waterloo campaign Napoleon was opposed by the Prussians under Blücher and the British under Wellington. On 15 June 1815, after one of his swift and secret concentrations, Napoleon sprang like a tiger across the River Sambre. He drove in the outposts of Blücher's army at the point where its right touched the left of Wellington's force. Wellington was in the process of concentrating, but his forces were still scattered. When the first news of the crossing reached the Prussian and British commanders, they thought it was a feint. With the time they allowed Napoleon, he was able to drive a wedge between the two armies, and put himself in a position to attack each one separately with superior strength. Napoleon's campaign thus employed maximum tempo when it started.

On 18 June 1815 he was at La Belle Alliance facing Wellington's inferior force at Mont St Jean, close to the village of Waterloo. It was not until 1300 hr that Napoleon started his attack on the British lines, losing nearly half of that day's daylight. And it was not until 1800 hr that he began to assume tactical command himself. By then it was too late. The Prussians had arrived, and the combined allied strength overwhelmed him.

Balaclava: the charge of the Heavy Brigade, 25 October 1854
The British cavalry in the battle of Balaclava was commanded by Lord Lucan. Under him was the Light Brigade commanded by Lord Cardigan,

and the Heavy Brigade commanded by Gen James Scarlett. Scarlett had modesty and common sense, while Cardigan was a cavalry officer of whom the old saying about cavalry officers was certainly true: 'He was so stupid that his fellow officers noticed it.'

In the early part of the battle, before the legendary charge of the Light Brigade, the Heavy Brigade, some 500 men strong, faced an attack by 3,500 Russian horsemen. Instead of waiting to be attacked, the Heavy Brigade charged uphill and, fighting with courage and ferocity, routed the Russians.

As the Russians streamed back to where they had come from, Cardigan's Light Brigade was in a position to charge into the fleeing horsemen. Had Cardigan pursued, the cavalry action at Balaclava might have taken its place as a classic in military literature, and the host of the Russian horse might have suffered a discomfiture with few parallels in the history of war. As it was, Cardigan's total inability to see and seize the opportunity meant that the Russians escaped without further loss.

Normandy, 2 August 1944

11 Armoured Division captured the high ground around Le Beny Bocage and threw the Germans into a crisis when it penetrated the boundary separating Panzer Group West from the German 7th Army. An account of the operation makes it clear that Montgomery let a great opportunity elude him.

> The town of Vire, a key road junction in the rear of 7 German Army, was 7 miles further on, undefended and at the mercy of the British armour. Montgomery chose just that moment to change the Army boundary by placing Vire inside the American sector. The advance of 11 Armoured was directed south-east, with a warning not to trespass beyond the boundary 2 miles north of the town. Montgomery had allowed a great opportunity to pass him by.
>
> Had the British taken Vire on 2 August, 7 Army would have been forced to retreat. The next day troops of 1 US Army were to widen the Avranches gap at Brecy and push on south-east to enter Juvigny. They were 15 miles south of Vire. With the British in Vire and the Americans in Mortain the retreat of 7 Army would have been turned into a rout. The less mobile of the German troops would have been trapped. It was only Patton of the Allied generals who at this early stage saw the possibility of such a development. Seven more days were to elapse before the Allied command [Montgomery] was to see the great opportunity that was lost.

Rommel's rules of desert warfare

In a paper written by Rommel as an introduction to his account of the war in Africa, he gives his views on one of the reasons for 'inertia':

In my opinion the duties of a Commander-in-Chief are not confined to his staff work. He must also take an interest in the details of Command and frequently busy himself in the front line. One reason for so doing is that exact execution of the plans of the Commander-in-Chief and his staff is of the greatest importance.

It is a mistake to assume that every local commander will make as much of a situation as there is to be made out of it. Most of them soon succumb to a certain need for rest. Then it is simply reported that this or that can't be done for some reason or another – such reasons are always easy to think up. People of this kind must be made to feel the authority of the C-in-C, and be shaken out of their apathy by him. The C-in-C must be the driving motor of the battle. One must always have to reckon with his appearance in personal control.

Two of the generals who were particularly good at giving their troops the type of ginger that Rommel describes were Rommel himself and Patton. Their soldiers would often meet their commanders at the front line, and quite often beyond it. On several occasions soldiers would be gathering for an assault across an obstacle they thought to be held by the enemy, when their commander would appear on the enemy side and ask what they were waiting for.

Inertia in front-line units
This problem has been documented by Brigadier James Hargest of the New Zealand Army (PRO CAB106/1060). Hargest had a brilliant record with the NZ Army in the First World War, and in the Second World War he commanded the 5th New Zealand Infantry Brigade in Greece, Crete and Libya. He was appointed as an observer to British XXX Corps and served as such from 6 June to 10 July 1944 in Normandy. He was attached for much of that time to 50 (Northumbrian) Division, and was tragically killed on his farewell visit to that division. His observations are thus those of a person with immense ability and experience in 'sharp end' soldiering. Hargest comments on many aspects of the Normandy fighting, and selections from his report illustrate the attitudes and morale of infantry and tank soldiers.

The first extract relates to 50 Infantry Division:

The men are tired after 18 days of unrelieved strain (25 June). They are supposed to infiltrate the enemy's position – first by patrolling, then by moving on from one firm base to another. They achieve nothing – only sustain grave casualties. Their advances have no impetus. The moment the enemy Spandaus or mortars open up the troops go to earth and stay there, lose men and morale. It's all wrong. Had we young officers of spirit and training to push these patrols we might achieve something. The soldier from Britain will accept losses without losing morale providing he sees some results – but this niggling is hard on him.

Speaking with other officers I come to these conclusions. The morale of the infantry officer and soldier is not high. This applies to new troops as well as to veterans. Officers are not keen on patrol work as an example. Even senior officers grumble about being too long in the line and have the opinion that they are being 'used'. Last week I saw the 15th Scottish (Infantry Division) in action (26th June). They began their battle on Monday and by the next Saturday they were relieved – used up. The troops have not that spirit essential to victory. It appears to me that the Higher Command will do well to rely on air, artillery, and tanks. Our level of morale frightens me.

Any tank soldier who watched the infantry in action had the greatest sympathy for their wretchedly exposed task and the unflinching courage with which most of them carried it out. But Hargest was an infantry soldier, and he was observing what happened while it was happening. He also observed tank units in the early weeks of the Normandy invasion, and was not particularly impressed with them either: 'Our tanks are badly led and fought. Only our superior numbers and our magnificent artillery support keeps them in the field at all. They violate most of the elementary principles of war. They bunch up – they are the reverse of aggressive – they are not possessed of the will to attack the enemy. At the moment we suffer because of incompatibility and the lack of the will to fight in the Armoured Corps.'

He gives two examples of this lack:

On June 12 I came across a whole squadron of tanks in a field supported by SP guns. They told me there was a Tiger tank in Verrière about 1,000 yards to the left front, and in reply to my query why they did not attack they said it was very powerful. On June 17 a tank of the 8th Armoured Brigade sat passively at a British roadblock while several German scout cars and an SP gun moved down a straight road. The tank did not fire although the target was a perfect one. Neither did it call on the tanks in its troop nearby for support. The infantry Brigade Commander sent down a message asking that the gun and cars be taken on. The reply was 'If I do he will reply to my fire'. After a delay of 20 minutes and only after an infantry antitank gun had come into action beside it did the tank fire. Its third round got what looked like a direct hit on one vehicle – after a few shots it relapsed into silence and was only persuaded to fire again later.

Crerar and the Channel ports
In August 1944 Hubert Essame commanded an infantry brigade in 43 Division. He was thus in a particularly good position to observe, understand and analyse the actions of the Allied higher command. In his book *The Battle for Germany* he comments on the opportunities lost by the 1st Canadian Army and Gen Harry Crerar in late August and early September.

On 26 August Montgomery ordered the 2nd Army to force the Seine and drive ahead with all speed to Antwerp. At the same time the Canadian Army was to clear up the coastal belt as far north as Bruges. Dieppe, Le Havre and Boulogne were to be secured in the process. That the pursuit was on and that it called for an all-out effort by everyone to the limits of their endurance was made crystal clear by Montgomery.

And yet, when XXX Corps was on the point of entering Brussels on 2 September, it was difficult to detect in Gen Crerar's orders any feeling of urgency. The Polish Armoured Division, some 100 miles behind the spearheads of XXX Corps, was to cross the Somme and advance in the general direction of Ypres; 3 Canadian Division was to clear up the area around the mouth of the Somme; 4 Canadian Armoured Division was to halt and reorganise east of Abbeville; and 2 Canadian Division was to do likewise at Dieppe, which had fallen without a shot being fired. At a time when every minute counted, Crerar gave two of his divisions, one of them armoured, a period of repose. This did not impress Montgomery.

Crerar was the immediate cause of this inertia. His senior Canadian subordinate, Gen Guy Simonds commanding II Canadian Corps, was much more alert to the need to maintain tempo. He was convinced that had Crerar been content to mask the Germans in the Channel ports, II Canadian Corps could have raced the Germans to Breskens and cleared the south shore of the Scheldt. With Breskens in their hands they would have had a base for an assault on Walcheren, and would also have caught much of the German 15th Army in a pocket bounded by the Scheldt and the Channel coast.

There is no question that Crerar lacked the imagination and drive of Simonds. But there is also the Montgomery factor. Monty had a poor opinion of Crerar's ability, and was not slow to make his feelings known. Crerar would thus follow Monty's instructions slavishly, and hesitate to advance any ideas similar to those of Simonds – even if he had them. Crerar's inertia resulted in many thousands of Canadian casualties.

PARRY AND RIPOSTE: BLUNTING THE TEMPO

The tempo of the charge can be maintained only for so long. Sooner or later the advancing forces will have to pause to rearm, refuel and regroup. But the rapid advance, if continued hard enough, may result in such an objective being taken that the reorganising process can take place at leisure. When the Japanese captured Singapore, the tempo of that thrust had achieved all they could expect in that operation, and there was time enough to prepare for whatever was going to come next.

The capture of a Headquarters or a fortress, or the elimination of a significant portion of the enemy's forces, may mean that the 'charge' tempo can be temporarily wound back. It is while the charge tempo is in play that the 'parry' can be vital. The incidents that we are interested in are the short-term or tactical parries.

When the defender sees a weakness in the attacker's column he will try to cut the attacker's supply line, and thus delay or halt the advance. Another occasion for the parry is when the defender sees that a gap has been torn in his defences, and takes immediate steps to plug the gap.

While the defender parries and ripostes, the attacker, in order to maintain his tempo, must brush aside the riposte and thrust again. Whether the forward tempo is maintained or blunted depends on the perception, skill and determination of the opposing commanders. Examples of parrying are taken first from historical battles, and then from the battles of north-west Europe.

Wellington at Waterloo

One of the many crises during the battle of Waterloo, but perhaps the most important one, came just after 1800 hr. Wellington's centre had been underpinned all day by the farm buildings of La Haye Sainte and its garrison of King's German Legion under its British commander Maj George Baring. The garrison had tenaciously and courageously defied all attacks since the battle started. Now they were running short of ammunition, and after their last cartridges were spent they defended the farm with bayonets. Finally they were forced to give way, and the few survivors retreated to join the rest of the Allied army on the ridge to the north.

Attempts to save the farm were made, but a disastrous miscalculation ordered that the relieving force should attack in line, and they were terribly mauled by the French cavalry. The loss of La Haye Sainte and the destruction of the relieving force meant that a gap had been torn in the Allied line. This could have been turned into a chasm had the French seized the opportunity to do so. Even as it was, it was a situation of the greatest danger, and one where the need to parry immediately was vital.

Wellington was then with the Guards Division above Hougoumont on the Allied right flank. He was summoned urgently to the scene of the crisis, and as he galloped there he called up every remaining available unit. As all the Allied leaders in the centre had by now been killed or wounded, he temporarily took over command there himself. Leading five young Brunswicker battalions into the full storm of the French batteries, he rallied them when they broke under that hurricane of shot, and brought them steadily back into line.

The remnants of the Allied cavalry took post behind the Brunswickers and the other infantry to give them support and confidence. It was now a matter of holding the line. And hold it they did, until the Prussians arrived to ensure the complete defeat of the French and the flight of Napoleon. It was Wellington who executed the parry, doing it with total awareness of what had to be done, and doing it without wasting a moment.

Lanzerath, Ardennes, 16 December 1944
This action took place after the period of the Great Mistake, but it has two particularly interesting features: the parry was executed at the lowest level of a military formation; and it was instinctive.

Lt Lyle Bouck was in charge of seventeen men of an intelligence and reconnaissance platoon of 99 US Infantry Division. On the morning of 16 December he was in the US front line at Lanzerath, 15 miles north-east of Saint Vith, and came under heavy and unexpected artillery fire. He contacted his HQ, and was told that because his defensive position was a good one he should stay there and be on the alert for a German attack.

The attack duly came, and the position proved to be a good one. The Germans attacked three times during the day, and it was not until the fourth attack in the evening that Bouck's position was overrun. By parrying the thrust, Bouck's platoon had blocked one of the roads earmarked for the main effort of the German drive for some sixteen hours. They had put a serious crimp in the German offensive.

Belgium and Holland, September 1944
We have already seen several examples of the effects of parrying by the Germans as the Allies advanced into Belgium and Holland; three are repeated here.

Col Wysocki of the Polish Armoured Division noted that in their advance across Flanders: 'The Germans were not stupid. They were blowing bridges right before our very eyes, and slowed us up very effectively.'

Right at the beginning of Operation Market Garden, the landing of 1 British Airborne Division was in full view of Field Marshal Model, commanding German Army Group B. He was *at once* able to initiate countermeasures. He saw that the real threat lay in the rapid advance of XXX Corps; if he could delay this advance, then he could deal with the lightly armed airborne troops with ease. This he did very effectively with the formations of 1 Parachute Army, reinforced by the 15th Army divisions that had escaped back across the Scheldt.

General Leutnant Kurt Chill was one of the many German officers who gathered up stragglers and formed them into cohesive units, although he was probably the most effective. His action was immediate and instinctive, and in only two or three days he had put together a group that slowed the Allies from a gallop to almost a standstill. It was an impressive demonstration of blunting the tempo of an attacker.

Chapter Thirteen

THE REASONS WHY

A fundamental method for improving performance is to learn from our mistakes. However, it is much better to learn from other people's mistakes, and the purpose of this chapter is to examine the reasons for the Great Mistake – the failure to advance north from Antwerp on 4 September 1944 immediately after it had been captured. Having identified the reasons, we can then suggest ways for avoiding similar mistakes in the future.

In examining the events leading up to 4 September and what happened afterwards, we have seen that the Allies made several good decisions, particularly those relating to the successful battle of Normandy. At the same time there were three decisions that sent forces in the wrong direction:

1. The decision at Avranches, when three US divisions moved west to clear up the German forces in Brittany rather than east to the borders of Germany.
2. The decision that directed the 1st Canadian Army to capture the Channel ports, including turning west to Le Havre, rather than bypassing all the Channel ports and closing in on the Scheldt.
3. The decision not to advance north from Antwerp on 4 September, but to move east towards Germany.

The first decision, that at Avranches, affected the Great Mistake only indirectly. The three US divisions could have assisted in the assault on the borders of Germany by Patton's 3rd US Army. This would have made the defence of Germany's north-western borders even more difficult than it was, because the troops of the 15th Army and 1 Parachute Army would have to have been thinned out to the south to meet Patton's stronger thrust.

The second decision, determining the movements of the 1st Canadian Army immediately after it had crossed the Seine, was central to the Great Mistake. A rapid advance to the south bank of the Scheldt would have prevented the 15th Army from setting up the defences they did, and would have made it more difficult to evacuate troops over to Walcheren and South Beveland. Occupying the south bank would also have made it possible to harass, if not completely prevent, the mine-laying operations in the Scheldt waterway.

The third decision – the Great Mistake itself – not only allowed the escape of a large part of the 15th Army, but also condemned the Canadian Army to fight a long and bloody battle to clear the banks of the Scheldt estuary.

The purpose of this chapter is to identify the principal reasons for those decisions, especially that at Antwerp. Having identified the reasons, we can suggest what should be done to improve decisions in similar situations in the future.

T.E. Lawrence is reputed to have said that because mankind has been fighting battles for more than 3,000 years we should be able to do it right by now. But it is an unfortunate human trait that we find it very hard to learn from mistakes, particularly the mistakes of others. When Admiral de Robeck was in command of the naval assault on the Dardanelles in March 1915, he might have had more success had he remembered and adopted the 'damn the torpedoes' attitude of the US Admiral David Farragut at Mobile Bay in 1864.

Had Lord Cardigan studied any cavalry actions he would surely have seized the chance to complete the rout of the Russian cavalry after their repulse by the Heavy Brigade at Balaclava on 25 October 1854. But Cardigan was immediately afforded the admiration of the British public, which, in the well-chosen words of the *Encyclopaedia Britannica*, 'has habitually cherished valorous stupidity above economical skill in its military annals – and thus helped to ensure a recurrence of such follies.'

It would be a gross exaggeration to say that the decisions taken at Avranches, at the Seine, and at Antwerp were 'follies', as they all had reasonable justification. But what led to these less-than-optimal decisions? What information was lacking or misused, what factors were given inappropriate weight, what was the contribution of personal attitudes and relationships, and what was the effect of supply?

The reasons for the Great Mistake at Antwerp can be grouped under four headings:

1. Intelligence: what was the real situation, especially of the German forces; what was the situation as perceived by the Allied Intelligence services; how was the raw data analysed, and what use was made of it; what intelligence information was missing, or was in short supply?
2. Strategy: the overall mission of Operation Overlord, and the strategies proposed to achieve the mission; the balance between political and military objectives; the rigidity of the strategic plan, and the inability to modify the plan to take up unexpected opportunities; and the lack of contingent planning to exploit those opportunities.
3. Allied troops: the command structures of the Allied forces; differences in command culture between the Americans and the British; the effect

of supply; and the effect the relationships between the senior commanders had on the decisions that were made.
4. Execution of strategy, in particular the failure to maintain tempo at the vital moments, and to seize and exploit unplanned and fleeting opportunities.

INTELLIGENCE: SITUATIONS REAL AND PERCEIVED

German situation September 1944: the facts
We saw in Chapters Two, Five, Six and Seven the difference between the real situation and the perceived situation. Perceptions are what a commander has to use to make decisions, and perceptions by his subordinates will to some degree affect the execution of those decisions.

The real situation for the German Army at the beginning of September 1944 – as far as it can be judged from the German records – was bad, but with several opportunities for improvement. The German 7th Army and 5 Panzer Army had taken a terrible battering in Normandy, and were streaming back to the east in what appeared to be complete chaos. The chaos was real. Soldiers had to escape with what they could, and most heavy equipment had to be left behind. Commanders at all levels had lost touch with many of their troops, and the retreating armies were pounded by air attack, harassed by resistance forces, and pursued by Allied tanks and infantry.

In the northern sector of the front, however, the area of the Great Mistake, the German 15th Army was still in being, with six relatively untouched divisions, and the elements of several other divisions from the 7th Army and 5 Panzer Army. The overall command structure was still operating from OB West down to many divisional commanders, and Model was still able to make plans which could be at least partially executed.

Behind these troops in the front line there were also substantial resources in the Fatherland. Some of these would take time to come to the aid of the front-line troops, but others could be available in a matter of days. The longer-term actions included the combing-out of hospitals, cancellation of deferred service for some groups, reduction of age and fitness standards, and the release of men from some jobs by the substitution of women. [Note: It is significant that the Allied forces in the northern sector, those of Canada, Poland and Britain, were also suffering grave problems in finding replacements for their casualties.]

The German troops that could be brought up as reinforcements in only a few days – the first of which were on the north bank of the Albert Canal in two days, on 6 September – were those unexpectedly produced from Göring's Luftwaffe. Shortages of aircraft and fuel had left many aircrew with nothing to do, and while their infantry skills might be limited, they were tough, fit and dedicated.

Even better than the aircrew were the paratroops, also part of the Luftwaffe. They were widely spread through training, convalescence and reinforcement depots, but were under the single command of General Kurt Student's 1 Parachute Army, and many of them were seasoned fighters. The combined strength of the Parachute and Luftwaffe soldiers amounted to three immediately available divisions.

Two innate qualities of the German Army were the depth of its command structure and its resilience. The depth of its command structure was the product of the 'mission' system, whereby leaders from the most junior upwards were trained to take over the mission of their immediate superior should he become disabled. The training meant that not only could the junior carry out the more senior role, but also that he expected to do so; this in turn required that the junior should be constantly aware of his senior's mission.

The resilience of the Germans came partly from their experience of adverse situations over the two previous years, starting with their defeats at Alamein and Stalingrad, and partly from the comradeship of their primary group. In the German Army the primary group was generally company-sized, or 120 to 150 men. All members of that group saw it as their primary function to support each other, and the group was large enough to absorb a substantial number of reinforcements with ease.

The traditions of the German Army made it possible for determined officers such as General Leutnant Kurt Chill to rally and re-form soldiers retreating in disorder from Normandy. Chill's nucleus was the remnant of his own 85 Division, but on the banks of the Albert Canal he collected soldiers from all sorts of other formations, and in a matter of a day or two converted them into the fiercely battle-worthy Kampfgruppe Chill.

In less than a week after 4 September there was therefore a significant force to oppose 21 Army Group on the Albert Canal. There were seven divisions from the 15th Army, at least three from 1 Parachute Army, KG Chill, two divisions brought down from Holland, and any other ad hoc groupings similar to KG Chill. This is the equivalent of fourteen divisions. They were below strength, certainly, but so were some of the Allied divisions.

The Germans were short of equipment, their main disadvantage vis-à-vis the Allies. The only tanks they had in the northern sector were the battered remnants of 9 and 10 SS Panzer Divisions refitting in the area of Arnhem. But such tanks as they had, Mark IV H and J, Panther and Tiger, greatly outclassed the Allied tanks. The German factories were still producing 1,500 tanks every month, and so it would not be long before the Panzer divisions were rearmed.

There were many German 88s in their antiaircraft role in the Antwerp area. These could also be used immediately in a field role, and, more importantly, as a formidable weapon against Allied tanks. They also had two other simple but very effective weapons, the Panzerfaust and the multibarrelled mortar. The Panzerfaust was extremely lethal against tanks in close and easily defended country; and the 150 mm six-barrelled Nebelwerfer 41, known to Allied soldiers as the 'moaning minnie', was a devastating form of bombardment, and was easy to move and conceal.

In summary, the actual strength of the Germans in the northern sector by the second week of September consisted of fourteen divisions, each at something like 75 per cent of its establishment of combat soldiers. They had only about one hundred tanks, but they had reasonable anti-tank capability to take on the Allied armour. Measures had been taken to create new formations, and to rebuild those battered in Normandy and elsewhere; these were likely to be ready for the front line in a few weeks at most.

The Allied strength in the northern sector comprised nine infantry and five armoured divisions, and five armoured brigades. They also had available to them I Airborne Corps, consisting of three airborne divisions, a parachute brigade, and an air-portable division. The Allies were much stronger in tanks, and had overwhelming superiority in the air; they were about 50 per cent stronger than the Germans in ground combat troops.

But the Germans were not nearly as badly placed as the Allied intelligence reports suggested. They were defending country that was easy to defend, they were close to their manufacturing base of the Ruhr, and they were about to defend the borders of the Fatherland.

Topography

The country of Flanders, the Beveland peninsula and the area surrounding Antwerp was mainly featureless and flat, with innumerable waterways, which greatly reduced the mobility of tanks. In many areas, especially close to the banks of the Scheldt, the terrain generally was ideal for defence against infantry as well as tanks. The optimum plan for the Allies would have been to advance so quickly that the Germans would need the bridges intact for their own retreat, and the bridges could have been captured before they were blown.

The topography of Antwerp and its docks was a special problem. The layout of the docks was such that only experts could identify the crucial points that had to be taken and held, in particular the Kruisschans lock. The Albert Canal and all the bridges over it were of equal importance, and there were road and rail bridges whose capture would greatly ease the movements of the attacking Allies.

Allied Intelligence services had access to all the information on topography that they needed. It seems either that some of the information was not presented to the commanders, or that the commanders decided they could do without it.

Weather

The ideal time to fight a campaign in northern Europe, particularly the coastal areas of Belgium and Holland, is in the five months May to September inclusive. Outside those months the ground becomes less easy to traverse, and overcast skies restrict support of any kind from the air. The original date for the invasion was 8 May 1944, which would have allowed the full five months to develop Continental operations. The actual date was a month later, and initial progress in Normandy was slow. But the break-out and the rapid pursuit across France meant that the Allies had caught up with – and bettered – their operational schedule. It was important to maintain tempo during the period of reasonable weather.

The slowing of tempo at Antwerp suggests that the commanders were not aware of, or dismissed, the need to advance as quickly as possible during the few weeks that still remained before the weather began to turn. Ignoring information about the weather was one of the causes of the Great Mistake.

Resistance movements

Resistance movements in occupied countries have much knowledge that can be invaluable to liberating armies. The problem for those armies is to know what those movements are, what they can do, how to communicate with them securely, and how trustworthy they are – have they been compromised or infiltrated?

The Resistance in Belgium, and in Antwerp especially, was well-organised, had an enormous amount of local knowledge, and could produce fighting units of high quality and courage. They were prepared to act as guides, auxiliary combat troops and providers of information about the strength and nature of German forces in the area of Antwerp.

The Belgian government in exile in London had prepared a 'fantastic handbook about Belgium, complete with detailed maps and plans'. The intention was that this handbook should be available to all Allied formations that could benefit from it, obviously with reference to those at the spearhead of any advance. What had not been planned was the distribution of the handbook. When it could have been invaluable, all its copies were probably still in London.

Intelligence: Allied perceptions of the situation

The battle in Normandy had been a hard slog for the Allies. Many of those in the front-line units began to feel that a determined set-piece attack might gain a mile or two, and that the next attack could not be mounted for another four or five days at the least. Typical set-piece attacks in the 21 Army Group area from late June to mid-July were Epsom, Jupiter and Goodwood. At the rate the Allies were going, Berlin seemed a long way off.

There seemed to be no way in which the ferocious and tenacious German resistance could be broken. Goodwood, the southward attack by three armoured divisions east of Caen on 18 July, showed that even massive air bombardment was not enough to stop the Germans rallying soon after the bombing ceased. The three armoured divisions lost 400 tanks during the operation which advanced the front by 5 miles. The impression was that the Germans, if not invincible, were not going to be beaten until well into 1945, and then only with great difficulty.

When the 3rd US Army broke through at Avranches, pressure from the rear as well as the front forced the Germans to start withdrawing. The quicker advances all along the line were a great boost to Allied morale. There was still much hard fighting, for the Americans at Mortain and the Poles and the Canadians in closing the Falaise pocket. After the pocket was more or less closed, the tempo of the advance speeded up on the way to the Seine and, once across, became quite frenetic.

As we saw in Chapters Six and Seven, this change in the strength of the German opposition from rock-solid to an apparent disorganised rabble made the attitudes of Allied commanders and troops alike turn from muted pessimism to wild optimism. The atmosphere at all levels was euphoric. Here and there a few wiser heads, such as Winston Churchill, counselled that German resilience should never be underrated. But the views of the Allied commanders from Eisenhower down were that the Germans had been routed. All that was needed now was to push on smartly to Berlin, brushing aside any minor opposition.

The tone of the intelligence summaries in the early days of September is one of unconsidered and subjective exultation, almost as if the Intelligence staffs were writing what their commanders wanted to hear. There were very few objective assessments of the situation, although Colonel Oscar Koch of the 3rd US Army was notable for his cautious report – which was not what Patton wanted to hear.

To be fair to the Intelligence staffs, it was difficult to obtain the sort of information that has been presented in the first section of this chapter. Humint sources in Germany were largely inaccessible, and the reliability of those in Belgium and Holland, even if they could be accessed, was uncertain. The German units were all mixed up, and their overall Order of Battle was hard to discern.

On the other hand, it was known that nearly half of the 15th Army was still in play, and that there were units in Holland that could be reassigned to the Scheldt. It should have been known that 1 Parachute Army possessed considerable forces, and it could have been worked out that there were naval and Luftwaffe personnel with little or nothing to do who could be transferred to infantry units.

A major error in the intelligence summaries and commanders' beliefs was that they thought that the Germans had lost control of their forces, and that the troops themselves had lost the will and resilience to regroup and fight back. This is a very strange conclusion in the light of the German performance in adversity in Russia, North Africa, Italy and Normandy.

In making their decisions, the most senior commanders were aware from Ultra decrypts that Hitler realised the great importance of the port of Antwerp, and made the blocking of the Scheldt a first and immediate priority. Very little weight appears to have been given to this information.

In summary, incomplete and faulty intelligence was one of the major reasons for the Great Mistake. This was compounded by Allied commanders misinterpreting or ignoring the intelligence made available to them.

STRATEGY

In the Second World War strategy at the highest level had as its mission the destruction of the armed forces of Germany and Japan, and the removal of the governments that had led them into war. High-level strategy had to decide what resources should be deployed to the two parts of that mission, Germany and Japan, and the timing of operations.

The mission against Germany could be divided into a number of fronts: Russia, north-west Europe, Italy, the Balkans, the Baltic. In examining the Great Mistake, we are concerned with the north-west Europe front. The major operation here was Overlord, and we must review the mission of Overlord and the strategy developed to achieve that mission. One of the reasons for the Great Mistake was the failure to keep the Overlord mission firmly in mind, and adapt the strategy appropriately as circumstances changed.

In Chapter Eight we saw that the mission given to Eisenhower was: 'To enter the Continent of Europe, and in conjunction with other Allied nations undertake operations aimed at the heart of Germany and the destruction of her armed forces.'

While this appears a reasonable mission, there are at least two important questions that should be asked. Did the German troops have to be destroyed, or would it be equally satisfactory if they could either be persuaded to surrender, or left to wither on the vine? And could the 'operations aimed at the heart' be stated in more specific terms?

During the first two months of Overlord, SHAEF was concerned to obtain and expand a fairly limited foothold on French soil. The intention was to break out of that bridgehead, but the only two elements of the follow-up strategy that can be identified in the original planning are the clearing of Brittany and the freeing of its ports, and the advance to the Seine.

When 4 and 6 Armoured Divisions of the 3rd US Army reached Avranches on 1 August, a set of opportunities not envisaged by SHAEF planners suddenly opened up. They had assumed that the Germans would have fallen back to the Seine in a wheeling movement pivoting on Caen, and there would have been little chance to outflank their line. But that opportunity had arisen. Would Montgomery and his armies be able to seize it? The answer was no at the level of Montgomery and Bradley, and yes at the divisional commander level in the case of Gen John Wood of 4 US Armoured Division. At the higher level it was felt essential that the original Overlord plan should be maintained.

Strategy after crossing the Seine
When the Allies reached the Seine, rather sooner than expected, what did the Overlord plan say they should do? There was nothing so clear cut as advancing into Brittany and capturing the ports, and beyond the Seine were many more options. One of these was to capture the Channel ports, on the face of it a sensible thing to do. Another was to advance as rapidly as possible to the borders of Germany and then 'seize the Ruhr'. The Ruhr could have been seized from either the south or the north, or from both at the same time. And there were other options such as capturing and freeing Antwerp or Rotterdam, or advancing directly on Berlin.

The various options were not properly evaluated. Although movement at the end of August was very rapid and there was not much time for planning, without planning there was every chance that forces would go in unprofitable directions. In hindsight, it is easy to say that all of 21 Army Group should have ignored all the Channel ports, advanced through Antwerp and Brussels, cleared the banks of the Scheldt, and *then* have moved north to Nijmegen and Arnhem.

Such a strategy was in the mind of at least one senior Allied commander, the Canadian Gen Guy Simonds. All British commanders had been so conditioned to the infallibility of Montgomery that they were reluctant to put forward alternative plans. They knew that those plans would be rejected in favour of what Monty had decided.

One strategic objective that was frequently put forward at this time was the capture of the Ruhr, which was the centre of Germany's heavy industry, and its capture would have meant that the production of munitions of war would have been greatly reduced. But had thought been given to what the capture of the area entailed? It was heavily built up and industrialised, was some 40 miles from east to west and 25 from north to south, was intersected by canals and railways, and was strongly defended against attack from the air.

It was, in fact, a monstrously complicated target for military ground forces. It was much larger than Stalingrad, and had it been resolutely defended, as would certainly have been the case, it would have taken months to subdue and have caused huge Allied casualties.

The target of Berlin was equally illusory. Lines of communication would have become progressivcly more tenuous and, as we have seen, there were plenty of reserves in Germany that could have been mustered to pinch out the narrow corridor. A careful and objective evaluation should have made the first target the freeing of the port of Antwerp, followed by an advance in the direction of Arnhem. This would have been the optimum strategy to maintain the achievement of the Overlord mission.

Political and military objectives

In discussing the different strategies to be adopted after the break-out from Normandy, Montgomery often used to complain to Brooke that decisions were being taken on political rather than military grounds. But military commanders must always remember that wars are fought for objectives wider than purely military ones.

An objective of Overlord, although not explicitly stated, must have been to liberate the people whose countries had been overrun by the German Army, namely France, Belgium and Holland. It was important that those peoples, those nations, should feel that they were part of the liberation process.

The French, Belgian and Dutch servicemen and women who had been able to escape before they were overrun, or had been in one of their country's colonies such as French North Africa, were able to form units to fight with the Allies. The French formed the 1st French Army, which after fighting in North Africa landed as part of 6 US Army Group in the south of France on 15 August 1944. The Dutch had the Princess Irene Brigade, which was under the command of the British 2nd Army. The Belgians had a brigade under their Brigadier Piron, which at the beginning of September was under the command of Gen Horrocks' XXX Corps.

It was important for all these units, and for the soldiers, sailors and airmen from the three countries who were serving with the Allies all over the world, to feel that their efforts and sacrifices were appreciated. Failure to show appreciation could create political problems when the conflict was over.

Equally important were the political aims and needs of the USA and of Britain. By this time America was providing two-thirds of the combat forces, and American newspapers and politicians were demanding, quite fairly, that they should have an appropriate share of the command, the action and the recognition.

It would create all kinds of difficulties if Montgomery remained in command of significant American formations, or was given more than his fair share of supplies. Monty himself was adamant that only military factors should apply in the planning and conduct of operations. He appeared to ignore or not to understand how Eisenhower had to maintain political as well as military balance. In Monty's view, political considerations were irrelevant.

One result of Monty's attitude was that the possible contributions of the Belgian and Dutch Resistance were ignored. In relation to the Great Mistake, this had dire consequences in Antwerp. Had more understanding and sympathy been accorded to the knowledge and aspirations of the Antwerp resistance forces, then the British could have been guided and reinforced over the Albert Canal, and the benefits of blocking off the Woensdrecht isthmus would have been more apparent.

The actions of Maj John Dunlop at Boom show that being prepared to listen can pay enormous dividends. John Dunlop stopped to listen to the Belgian Robert Vekemans, and 3 RTR were able to cross the River Rupel before the Germans could blow all the bridges. Dunlop showed good sense and a willingness to believe that others could provide useful advice; it was a pity that others, particularly the senior commanders, did not display the same attitude.

ALLIED COMMAND WEAKNESSES

At the end of August and the beginning of September there were two major weaknesses which were having a bad effect on the conduct of operations. The first was the change in the command structure on 1 September, and the second was the relationship that had developed between Eisenhower and Montgomery. Both of these were causes of the Great Mistake, the second being the more important.

Command structure
The Overlord plan assigned overall control of the ground forces of the Allied Expeditionary Force to Montgomery for the battle of Normandy. It was felt that the area in which the battle was to take place was of such a size that there could be only one ground force commander. It turned out that this was a sensible decision, and Montgomery executed his task competently.

When the area of battle had expanded to allow the employment of three Army Groups, the planners had nominated that the Supreme Commander, Eisenhower, should take over direct command of those three Army Groups, 21 under Montgomery, 12 under Bradley and 6 under Devers. He would have support from sea and air, would assign missions to the three groups, and would apportion supply according to the needs of each.

The change in ground force commander took place on 1 September. On the same day, Eisenhower moved his Forward HQ from Tournières in Normandy to Jullouville, on the Atlantic coast of Normandy. This move was to the west, while most Allied forces were moving east towards Germany. As well as being further away from the main battle, the communications systems at Jullouville functioned very poorly for the first weeks of their installation.

Commanders at every level must be in close enough contact with what is happening ahead, so that reverses can be addressed quickly and unexpected opportunities exploited immediately. A commander, however, cannot be at every point of the front for which he is responsible.

A company or squadron commander can perhaps see the action across his complete front, but going up the scale of command this overall view of the battlefield becomes more and more difficult to grasp. Some senior commanders, such as Rommel with 7 Panzer Division and Patton with the 3rd US Army, seemed to know by instinct where their presence would do the most good. But even they needed systems that would keep them in touch with the whole area for which they were responsible.

The senior commander, then, needed a communication system that provided timely and accurate information. There were at least two systems available to Eisenhower and Montgomery, to which Montgomery added a third. The first was the normal hierarchical channel, transmitting situation reports (sitreps) up the chain of command. Because of the need to collate information from all subunits at each level, this was often a slow process. The second system was the high-grade sigint system of Ultra, which provided commanders at the highest level with up-to-date information on the enemy's intentions and dispositions.

However, a danger had developed with the use of Ultra. Its beneficiaries had begun to believe that it was omniscient, and reported the *complete* German situation. This could lull senior Allied commanders into a false sense of security, and tended to make them rely less on traditional intelligence systems.

The third system, used very effectively by Montgomery, was that of skilled liaison officers keeping in direct touch with selected units in the front line. Their daily reports provided a real feeling for what was happening, and what were the current threats and opportunities.

Montgomery complained many times that a Ground Force Commander was essential, so that those threats and opportunities could be dealt with or seized without delay. As has been suggested, it was much more important for a commander to be in touch with the whole of his front rather than be there at one particular spot. Having made a decision to defend or exploit, he could then visit the spot if he wanted to boost morale. The decision-making depended on information, not location.

When the command structure changed on 1 September, Montgomery was still in charge of the northern sector of the Allied armies. He was there, and he could make decisions to meet the changing circumstances. After the capture of Antwerp he could have ordered the exploitation north, the crossing of the Albert Canal and the advance to Woensdrecht. Only he can be blamed for the failure to act, and he had complete authority to do so.

The change in command structure on 1 September, and the remote location of Eisenhower, were irrelevant to the Great Mistake. It was Montgomery who failed to grasp the opportunity.

Personal relationships: the Monty factor

The nature of the relationship between Eisenhower and Montgomery was one of the main reasons for the Great Mistake. In Chapter Four we discussed their different backgrounds and temperaments. Their opinions of each other were such as to make team-work difficult. Eisenhower was aware that both Brooke and Monty thought that his strategic grasp and military capability were inadequate for either Supreme Commander or Ground Force Commander. Even though Eisenhower was a very confident person, he could have felt somewhat overawed by the historical weight of Britain's strategic experience and by Montgomery's reputation as a successful field commander. Additionally, Monty was the representative of the USA's major ally after Russia.

Viewing these two points objectively, we have to question Britain's strategic record and Monty's ability as a commander. In the Boer War and the First World War Britain's strategy was abysmal until the final stages, and there was no opportunity to improve between 1919 and 1939. The first three years of the Second World War demonstrated strategies always ending in defeat, with the two exceptions of O'Connor in North Africa and Cunningham in East Africa, both of which victories were against the Italians. This record gives little confidence in Britain's strategic competence, vaunted so patronisingly by Brooke and Montgomery.

Monty was a careful, painstaking commander who could train and motivate his troops, and lead them effectively in battle. He was good at the set-piece attack and the controlled defence, but he lacked the ability to seize the moment and run with it. The three examples discussed earlier – Avranches, the Seine and Antwerp – show a commitment to previously made plans, rather than adapting the plans to the circumstances that had arisen.

Eisenhower's opinion of Montgomery was one of respect, irritation and exasperation. He recognised Monty's ability and record as a commander, and was quite happy for him to command the land battle in Normandy. But he was unable to get close to Monty in the same way as he was close to Bradley. With Bradley he could discuss matters, whereas Monty's method of discussion was to lecture. Monty's subordinates had to subject themselves to the lecturing; but it was profoundly irritating to a superior to be constantly lectured by a subordinate.

Inevitably, matters came to a head. Since late August 1944, Monty had been bombarding Eisenhower with requests, some of which were almost orders, relating to two matters: broad versus narrow front, and single Ground Force Commander. Monty would not agree to any opinion other than his own. This was totally hypocritical, in that he refused to tolerate the attitude in his subordinates that he was continually taking to his superior.

During the battle of the Ardennes the differences between the two became so acute that Eisenhower drafted a cable to the Joint Chiefs of

Staff saying that 'the rift between Montgomery's thinking and mine has become so deep that one of us will have to be relieved from duty'. Had the cable been sent, Monty would have been dismissed at once.

He was rescued by his Chief of Staff, Freddie de Guingand, who flew to SHAEF in a snowstorm as soon as he had become aware that something was amiss. He persuaded Eisenhower not to send the cable, and Monty retained his position. But Monty never showed any gratitude to de Guingand, denying him attendance at the surrender ceremony, and doing nothing to help progress his postwar military career.

The period from late August to mid-October was one in which the constant arguments between Eisenhower and Monty distracted their attention from the battles they and their subordinates were fighting. In respect of Antwerp, Monty was so obsessed with strategy and command questions that he took his eye off the immediate possibilities of the main game, and on 4 September allowed everyone to relax.

His failure to insist on the maintenance of the tempo that had been reached was the major cause of the Great Mistake. It was unfortunate that his failure of 4 September was the prelude to the disaster at Arnhem and the destruction of 1 British Airborne Division.

SUMMARY

The principal reasons for the Great Mistake were:

1. Intelligence
The ability of the Germans to resist the Allies in September 1944 was greatly underestimated. The actual strength of the 15th Army and the potential reserves in Germany, especially from the Luftwaffe, were discounted to almost nothing. The resilience of the German command structure and of the German soldier were forgotten. Many of the intelligence sections lost their objectivity and gave their commanders a very misleading picture of the real situation. Those that were more objective were ignored by their commanders.

There was no doubt that Ultra provided senior commanders with extremely useful information. However, there was a tendency to think that the utterances of Ultra were not only accurate but also complete, and that there was no need to cross-check the high-grade sigint against information from less sophisticated sources.

In addition to misinformation about German troops, not enough attention was paid to the topography that would be encountered in the low-lying ground around Antwerp, and the need to overrun that ground before the autumn weather set in. And the potential help from the resistance movements was not considered.

2. Strategy

Overlord strategy as originally planned was vague about what should happen after the break-out from the Normandy bridgehead. As far as it went, the Overlord strategy was rigidly followed to include the overrunning of Brittany and the capture of the Channel ports. In the event, both of these were of little value compared with the time they wasted.

The main strategic failure was not to seize the opportunity to go straight for Antwerp and its approaches from the North Sea. Besides providing a major port facility, this would have neutralised the German 15th Army.

3. Relationships

The command cultures of the American and the British Armies were not identical, and little discussion was held on developing a common command culture, at least for Operation Overlord. Eisenhower did his best to coordinate conflicting views, but he was greatly hindered by the contemptuous attitude of Brooke and Montgomery.

Montgomery gave little support to Eisenhower. For much of the two months mid-August to mid-October he was criticising, with lofty condescension, the plans that Eisenhower made and the execution of those plans. These constant arguments diverted both commanders away from the business of running the war. The solution was in Montgomery's power, but he did not care to exercise it. The principal blame for the Great Mistake can be assigned to Montgomery.

Chapter Fourteen

ENVOI:
TEACHING GRANDMOTHER

The principle of corrective action is that if a mistake has been detected and identified, action should be taken to ensure that it does not happen again. The lesson that has been learnt should be taught to those who may have to face the same situation in the future, so that they are less likely to make the same mistake.

One of the regrettable things about people is that each generation seems to have to make the same mistakes as previous generations. We have to wait until we have made a mistake ourselves to learn from it, rather than reaping the benefit of past experience. One of the reasons why the learning process is so inefficient is that many mistakes are covered up or not acknowledged. Montgomery, for example, maintained that everything always went according to plan. He therefore never made a mistake, and had nothing to learn.

The three major areas where lessons could have been learnt from the events of the Great Mistake were: intelligence; strategy; and command structure and execution.

1. INTELLIGENCE

The two principal components of military intelligence are sigint (signal intelligence) and humint (human intelligence). The Allied systems for obtaining intelligence from signals were very good at all levels. They were particularly strong at the highest level, where Ultra was able to tap into messages transmitted by Hitler and the German High Command. This knowledge was so powerful that it may have caused Allied senior commanders to rely on it to the exclusion of other sources. If the OKW was using other methods of communication, for example land lines, then there might be no fall-back system to replace Ultra. This was made very clear when the Germans launched the Ardennes offensive on 16 December 1944, taking the Allies completely by surprise.

Humint, or the collection of intelligence by people on the ground, is generally much more difficult and dangerous. There is the difficulty of being on the ground in the places where information can be gathered, and the danger of betrayal or capture. There is the equally difficult and dangerous task of transmitting the information to those who can make effective use of it.

But humint is so valuable that it must form a major part, if not *the* major part, of any system of military intelligence. Its first value is intrinsic, in the information that has been gathered itself. Its second value is to provide confirmation and validation of sigint – for example, are signals purporting to come from II Panzer Corps real, or do they relate to formations of dummy tanks?

In his *History of British Intelligence in WWII*, F.H. Hinsley comments on the Intelligence obtained from various sources before the Germans launched the Ardennes offensive:

> Before reviewing the intelligence obtained from the most productive source – high-grade military sigint – we may note what little information was obtained from the others. The Special Intelligence Service and Special Operations Executive supplied no reports of German preparations or intentions. Nor did the US Office of Strategic Services, and it is recorded that in its efforts to penetrate Germany it did not succeed in placing any agents in the Eifel area before the German attack. The Dutch Resistance gave some information about the transfer of HQ 15 Army, and about movements of the Parachute divisions.

In December 1944, then, sigint provided little information, and this was ignored; and humint provided effectively none. The lesson to be learnt from the Great Mistake in respect of Intelligence is that there must always be a strong humint system to provide primary Intelligence and to confirm information from sigint systems. It is not easy to set up an adequate humint system, as Hinsley implies in respect of the Ardennes operation. In countries where there is totalitarian control, such as Hitler's Germany, gathering information demands nerve and skill, and transmission is fraught with danger.

Gathering information is to some extent done automatically by the inhabitants of the area where there are operations or installations of military interest. In the autumn of 1944, the Germans in Germany would have been able to see the movements of troops, the sites of antiaircraft guns and many other items concerning the German Army. But it would have been most unlikely that they would have wanted the Allies to share their knowledge.

As for the French, however, and the Belgians and the Dutch, many of them were keen to observe and report items of military importance. In these three countries, and many others that had been overrun and occupied by Germany, there were resistance fighters who both actively sought useful information, and looked for ways to transmit to those for whom it would be valuable.

The analysis of the Great Mistake shows that the potential of all resistance movements, and especially the Belgian Resistance in Antwerp, was grossly underused or ignored. The very understandable problem for the Allies was to know who the resistance fighters were, to what extent they could be trusted, and how secure communication could be established.

When a country is ruled by an oppressive government, be that of the country itself or from a foreign country, there will generally be a group of people who want to overthrow or evict that government, and who will be prepared to work for a 'liberator'. The liberating power must know who those people are, what their quality and strength is, and how they can be contacted. The only reliable way of doing this is to have agents in the country. Once again, it is a task for humint.

The major lesson to be learnt in respect of Intelligence is therefore: that governments – and we are talking here of the governments of the USA and the UK – invest substantially in agents on the ground in all countries that could potentially become hostile in the future; and that information is verified and then objectively presented to the commanders who need to use it.

2. STRATEGY

Every organisation has to formulate, implicitly or explicitly, the objectives it is aiming to achieve. This requirement applies just as much to nations. Without clear objectives it is difficult to make realistic plans or to allocate material and human resources. In time of peace, national objectives are harder to state than they are in wartime. For example, where was England headed between 1919 and 1939? Was it important to maintain the Empire, and why? What were the benefits of having half the map of the world coloured in red?

Uncertainty as to how to answer these questions made for vacillation, shifting relationships with other countries, disarmament and then frantic rearmament. Strategy was much easier to state when Britain was at war. The objective was, in the thundering resonance of Churchill's speeches, 'Victory!' As an emotional rallying cry, nothing could have been better to give heart to a nation made despondent by the overrunning of France in June 1940. But what was victory? And how could it be achieved?

Victory could comprise one or more of the following: the liberation of all areas overrun by Germany since 1936 (would that include Sudetenland, Austria, the Rhineland?); the defeat of the German armed forces, either by death, capture or capitulation; the destruction of installations of military significance; the elimination of the sources of the sinews of war; the removal of Hitler and the Fascist system of government; or the destruction of the cities of Germany.

An extreme statement of what the consequences of victory for the Allies and defeat for Germany should be was proposed by Henry Morgenthau, President Roosevelt's Secretary of the Treasury. The statement was endorsed by Roosevelt and Churchill on 15 September 1944.

The essence of the plan was that Germany should be dismembered and converted into a country primarily agricultural and pastoral in its character. In execution of this policy, Morgenthau proposed that the Ruhr should not only be stripped of all existing industries, but so weakened and controlled that it could not in the foreseeable future become an industrial area. All industrial plant and equipment not destroyed by military action should either be completely dismantled or removed from the area, or completely destroyed.

Fortunately, this draconian plan was never put into effect, because it would have completely destabilised Europe and made the westward advance of Russia even more likely. Even as it was, it was a most generous gift to Goebbels, who was able to tell the German people that they could expect no more mercy from the Western Allies than they could from the Russians.

In 1944, the major components of the strategy to defeat Germany were: the bombing of Germany; the Italian campaign; support of resistance movements; and Operation Overlord, the landing in France. In analysing the Great Mistake we are concerned only with Overlord, and we have seen that the objectives of Overlord as given to Eisenhower were: 'To enter the Continent of Europe, and undertake operations aimed at the heart of Germany and the destruction of her armed forces.'

This is stated very broadly, and thus gives Eisenhower plenty of flexibility. Its generality, however, makes it difficult to assess whether a particular action is going to make a contribution. The capture of the Brittany ports, for example, did nothing in the heart of Germany, and while it eliminated the German garrisons it did so at considerable cost in men and time.

At the next level below in the hierarchy of military objectives there was some vagueness as to what was the appropriate strategy to follow, especially after the clearly defined objective of a secure lodgement had been executed. Were the Channel ports important compared with Antwerp or Rotterdam, were the Ruhr or Berlin realistic objectives, and should the advance be on a narrow or a broad front?

The lesson to be learnt from looking at strategies employed in north-west Europe, and particularly as they affected the Great Mistake, is that the overall objective must be clearly defined. It must be broad enough to allow flexibility as circumstances change, but be precise enough that the contributions of various alternative operations can be quantitatively evaluated against it. For example, at Antwerp on 4 September 1944 Montgomery had several alternatives. One of these was to thrust to Arnhem, and another to free access to the port of Antwerp.

Taking into account all the information that could have been available to him, the choice must have been that the rapid freeing of Antwerp would have made the greater contribution to enabling an Allied advance into the heart of Germany.

In any military operation, therefore, there needs to be a clear statement of objectives, and an unbiased and thorough system for evaluating which plans best help the achievement of those objectives. Quite obviously such systems exist, but they need to be carefully examined to see how they can be improved so that 'great mistakes' occur less frequently.

3. ALLIED COMMAND WEAKNESSES

The command of an army composed of formations from different nations demands a level of tolerance and understanding rarely possessed by senior military commanders. The Allies were extremely fortunate to have Eisenhower as the Supreme Commander in Europe. His confidence in himself made him able to withstand the disagreements between his subordinate commanders, and the denigration of his own performance, particularly by Brooke and Montgomery.

A major cause of the Great Mistake was the abrasive relationship between Eisenhower and Montgomery, which at times, and especially at the beginning of September 1944, distracted the attention of both men from the main game. Montgomery contributed almost all the abrasion to this relationship. While he was a very competent commander, and a brilliant trainer and motivator, he had difficulty in establishing good relations with his equals and his superiors. Norman Dixon, in *The Psychology of Military Incompetence*, comments on letters written by Monty to his brother Brian:

> At a superficial level the letters are certainly those of the braggart schoolboy brimming with self-confidence, but at a deeper level of analysis and in the context of his other characteristics these really rather pathetic and naïve pieces of conceit betray an underlying need to prove himself to others and thereby to himself. People who are really self-confident do not need to boast to their younger brothers, particularly when they are intelligent enough to realise that boasting detracts from, rather than enhances, their image in the public mind.

The innate but carefully concealed lack of self-confidence resulted in his working against rather than with Eisenhower. Had Monty been able and willing to take the time to talk regularly with Eisenhower, and talked as an adviser rather than a lecturer, their relationship might have been brilliant. Unfortunately for the soldiers killed in the Scheldt operations, this never happened.

The job of the commander of thousands of men in time of war is one which demands special qualities, and we can all be thankful that Monty had many of these. Further, we cannot expect to change people's personalities. But there is a lesson here that a senior commander can often be more lastingly successful if he can be tolerant of others he has to work with, and can use their strong points for support rather than their weak ones for criticism. There is much to learn for future generations of military leaders from the positives and negatives of the relationship between Eisenhower and Montgomery.

The second lesson to be learnt from the performance of the Allied High Command is the importance of clear and prompt communication between all levels of command. At the critical time of the first week of September 1944, the performance of Eisenhower's communication system at Jullouville was extremely erratic. Communication systems have obviously improved enormously since then, but there have been many times over the last sixty years when operations have been jeopardised because of system breakdowns. The corrective action that should be taken is to thoroughly, rigorously, and if necessary destructively test communication systems before they are put into field service.

The third lesson is the importance of tempo. Forward tempo, as discussed in Chapter Twelve, requires a commander to identify an opportunity, and to seize and realise it with all possible speed. Among the Allied commanders in north-west Europe who had this ability were Patton, Guy Simonds, John Wood, and Joe Collins ('Lightning Joe'). Among those who lacked the ability were Harry Crerar and Montgomery.

Some people are born with the ability. The question is, can it be implanted in others by training? It is such an important quality that the third lesson to be learnt from the Great Mistake is to develop the ability to seize the moment by all possible methods of training.

Appendix One

GERMAN FORMATIONS IN THE GREAT MISTAKE

The infantry divisions shown on Map 14 and in General Leutnant Schwalbe's list of successfully evacuated formations fall into four categories. The differences between the categories can include such factors as: intended use, establishment (number of troops in division), age, origin, scale of armament and mobility. The descriptions given are those that applied in June 1944. The term 'regiment' is equivalent to the British 'brigade', a formation containing three, or sometimes two, battalion-sized subunits.

At the beginning of the war in 1939 the German infantry division was what was called the 'old type'. It had three regiments of three battalions each, a regiment of artillery, and other supporting fire in the form of anti-tank guns and mortars. Going by their numbers, 59, 64 and 70 fell into this category. Their strength at the end of August 1944 was undoubtedly a great deal less.

245 Division was an LE (Lower Establishment) division, although it still consisted of three regiments of three battalions each. It was formed in the summer of 1943 as a *bodenstandig*, or static, division, intended mainly for a defensive role. It could provide the equivalent of a regimental group for mobile counterattack. Some of its troops were recruited from areas of east Europe and Russia that had been overrun by the Germans. These foreign troops were collectively called the 'Ostlegion'.

345, 346 and 348 Divisions were also Lower Establishment, but consisted of only two regiments of infantry plus a regiment of artillery. They were formed in late 1942, and were sent from Germany to occupy coastal areas in the West. They contained a number of personnel from older age groups, as well as Ostlegion soldiers.

711, 712 and 719 Divisions were three of the fifteen divisions of the 'Fifteenth Wave', all of which were formed in the spring of 1941. They were also LE divisions of two infantry regiments and one artillery regiment, and possessed limited mobility.

GERMAN FORMATIONS AND COMMANDERS

This list shows the German formations relevant to the Great Mistake, showing their commanders at the beginning of September 1944.

Abbreviations: AK: Armee Korps; Res K: Reserve Korps; KG: Kampfgruppe; VG: Volksgrenadier; GAF: German Air Force.

Formation	Commander
15th Army	Gen Oberst Hans von Salmuth
–	Gen Gustav von Zangen (from 27 Aug 1944)
67 Res K	Gen Otto Sponheimer
86 AK	Gen Bruno Bieler
88 AK: formed in Holland, 1942	Gen Hans Reinhard
89 AK: formed as 'Scheldt' Korps, January 1943	Gen Alfred Hubicki
59 Inf Div	Gen Lt Walter Poppe
64 Inf Div: Scheldt Fortress South (Breskens)	Gen Lt Kurt Eberding
70 Inf Div: Scheldt Fortress North (Walcheren)	Gen Lt Wilhelm Daser
85 Inf Div: KG Chill	Gen Lt Kurt Chill
176 Inf Div	Gen Lt Berthold Stumm
226 VG Div: retreated to Dunkirk and stayed there	–
245 Inf Div	Gen Lt Erwin Sander
331 Inf Div	Gen Maj Karl Rheim
344 Inf Div	Gen Maj Eugen-Felix Schwalbe
345 Inf Div	–
346 Inf Div	Gen Lt Erich Diestel
347 Inf Div	Gen Lt Wolf Treierenberg
348 Inf Div	Gen Lt Paul Seyffardt
711 Inf Div	Gen Lt Josef Reichert
712 Inf Div	Gen Lt Friedrich-Wilhelm Neumann
719 Inf Div	Gen Lt Karl Sievers
17 GAF Div	–

Appendix Two

ALLIED ORDERS OF BATTLE

The Orders of Battle in this appendix show the structures of some of the formations that took part in the operations before and resulting from the Great Mistake. The general date of their currency is the beginning of September 1944.

21 ARMY GROUP

21 Army Group: Gen Bernard Montgomery
British 2nd Army: Gen Miles Dempsey
  VIII Corps: Lt Gen Richard O'Connor
  (VIII Corps did not take part in this operation)
  XII Corps: Lt Gen Neil Ritchie
    7 Armoured Division
    15 Infantry Division
    53 Infantry Division
    4 Armoured Brigade
  XXX Corps: Lt Gen Brian Horrocks
    Guards Armoured Division
    11 Armoured Division
    43 Infantry Division
    50 Infantry Division
    8 Armoured Brigade
1st Canadian Army: Gen Harry Crerar
  II Canadian Corps: Lt Gen Guy Simonds
    4 Canadian Armoured Division
    Polish Armoured Division
    2 Canadian Infantry Division
    3 Canadian Infantry Division
    2 Canadian Armoured Brigade
  I British Corps: Lt Gen John Crocker
    49 Infantry Division
    51 (Highland) Infantry Division
    33 Armoured Brigade
    34 Armoured Brigade

2 CANADIAN INFANTRY DIVISION (2 CAN)

Toronto Scottish Regiment (Machine-gun Battalion)   TSR
8th Reconnaissance Regiment   8 CAN RECCE

   4 Canadian Infantry Brigade
      Royal Regiment of Canada   RRC
      Royal Hamilton Light Infantry (Wentworth Regiment)   RHLI
      The Essex Scottish Regiment   ESR

   5 Canadian Infantry Brigade
      Black Watch (Royal Highland Regiment of Canada)   RHR of C
      Calgary Highlanders   CH
      Le Régiment de Maisonneuve   RDM

   6 Canadian Infantry Brigade
      Les Fusiliers Mont-Royal   FMR
      Queen's Own Cameron Highlanders of Canada   QOCH of C
      South Saskatchewan Regiment   SSR

3 CANADIAN INFANTRY DIVISION (3 CAN)

The Cameron Highlanders of Ottawa (Machine-gun Battalion)   QHD
7 Reconnaissance Regiment   7 CAN RECCE
(17th Duke of York's Royal Canadian Hussars)

   7 Canadian Infantry Brigade
      Regina Rifle Regiment   RRR
      Royal Winnipeg Rifles   RWR
      1st Battalion The Canadian Scottish Regiment   1 CSR

   8 Canadian Infantry Brigade
      Queens Own Rifles of Canada   QOR CAN
      Le Regiment de la Chaudiere   LRC
      North Shore Regiment   NSR

   9 Canadian Infantry Brigade
      Highland Light Infantry of Canada   HLI CAN
      Stormont, Dundas, and Glengarry Highlanders   SD & GH
      North Nova Scotia Highlanders   NNSH

4 CANADIAN ARMOURED DIVISION (4 CAN ARMD)

29th Reconnaissance Regiment (The South Alberta Regiment)

4 Canadian Armoured Brigade
   21st Armoured Regiment (The Governor General's Foot Guards)
   22nd Armoured Regiment (The Canadian Grenadier Guards)
   28th Armoured Regiment (The British Columbia Regiment)

10 Canadian Infantry Brigade
   The Algonquin Regiment
   The Lincoln and Welland Regiment
   The Argyll and Sutherland Highlanders of Canada

Sources

The two major sources of information for *The Great Mistake* were the National Archives at Kew and published works relating to the topic. The list of books that were consulted is included in the Bibliography.

NATIONAL ARCHIVES

All categories of record held at Kew were scanned for possible relevance. Those categories containing documents that appeared to be useful are shown below, and a detailed list of documents follows.

CAB	Records of the Cabinet Office
DEFE	Records of the Department of Defence
EN	Records of the Imperial War Museum
FO	Records of the Foreign Office
GFM	Copies of captured German records
HS	Records of Special Operations Executive
PREM	Records of the Prime Minister's Office
WO	Records of the War Office

CAB: Records of the Cabinet Office

CAB 44: Committee of Imperial Defence Historical Branch & Cabinet Office
44/56: Orders of Battle down to Divisions
44/57 and 44/58: Orders of Battle; Brigades
44/252–3: Advance from the Seine to the Siegfried Line

CAB 88: Combined Chiefs of Staff Committees: minutes and memoranda
88/59: Combined Intelligence Committee (CIC): memos 14 December 1943 to 6 July 1945
88/60: CIC memos 22 April 1944 to 16 October 1945

CAB 101: War Cabinet & Cabinet Office Historical Section
War Histories, WWII, Military
101/315: Air Operations, 1–16 September 1944
101/316: The Lower Rhine, 17–30 September 1944
101/317: The advance up the Channel coast, 17–30 September 1944
101/318: Operations in support of 2nd Army, 1 October–8 November 1944
101/319: The opening of the Scheldt Estuary 1 October–8 November 1944

CAB 106: Records of the Historical Section
106/960: Operation Sabot: the advance of XXX Corps to Antwerp and Brussels
106/962: Operation Market Garden
106/970: Report on clearing the Scheldt estuary, October–November 1944
106/1041: Directives for operations July–December 1944 by Gen M.C. Dempsey
106/1057: Account of A/A defences in Brussels and Antwerp, 4 September 1944–23 January 1945
106/1061: Notes of conversations, Gen Miles Dempsey
106/1067: Telegrams HQ 21AG and War Office, June–September1944
106/1091: Extracts from Gen Eisenhower's personal papers, including telegrams to and from Montgomery
106/1106: The broad front versus the narrow front controversy

DEFE: Records of the Department of Defence

DEFE 3: Intelligence from radio intercepts
3/112–128 and 3/220–239: Intelligence from intercepts, 2 August to 18 October 1944

WO: Records of the War Office

WO 171: War Diaries
The diaries for Army and Corps cover several aspects of their activities, e.g. operations, admin, signals, ordnance, etc. The diaries listed are those concerned with operations.

171/132: 21 Army Group G (Int) July to August 1944
171/133: 21 Army Group G (Int) September to October 1944

171/200–205: 2 Army G (Ops) August 1944
171/206–209: 2 Army G (Ops) September1944
171/310: XII Corps G.S. January–September 1944
171/339, 340: XXX Corps G and G. Apps August 1944
171/341: XXX Corps G September 1944
171/456: 11 Armoured Division G January–December 1944

171/514: 50 Inf Div G August–September 1944
171/554: 53 Inf Div G September–October 1944
171/860: 11 Armd Div Recce Regt (2 Northants Yeo)

171/627: 29 Armoured Brigade
171/866: 3 RTR
171/853: 2 Fife & Forfar Yeo
171/847: 23 Hussars
171/1359: 8 Rifle Brigade (battalion-sized unit)
171/691: 159 Infantry Brigade
171/1349: 3 Monmouthshire Regt
171/1326: 4 King's Shropshire Light Infantry
171/1307: 1 Hereford Regt

WO 205: 21 Army Group Papers
205/5D: C-in-C demi-official correspondence
205/5G: C-in-C directives to Army commanders

WO 285: Gen M.C. Dempsey papers
285/3: 2 Army intelligence summaries May to September 1944
285/4: 2 Army intelligence summaries September to December 1944
285/9: Personal war diary June to September 1944
285/10: Personal war diary September to December 1944
OCMH, DA: Office of the Chief of Military History, Department of the Army, Washington, DC.

Bibliography

(Unless otherwise stated, all books published in London)

Alexander, Field Marshal Earl (1962) *Memoirs*. Cassell.

Ambrose, Stephen (1984) *Pegasus Bridge*. Allen & Unwin.

Ambrose, Stephen (1971) *The Supreme Commander: The War Years of Gen Eisenhower*, Doubleday, Garden City.

Barclay, Brigadier C.N. (1952) *Royal Northumberland Fusiliers 1939–1945*. William Clowes.

—— (1956) *History of the 53rd (Welsh) Division in World War II*.

Barnard, Lt Col W.T. (1960) *The Queen's Own Rifles of Canada 1860–1960*. Ontario Publishing Co., Ontario.

Barnett, Corelli (1962) *The Desert Generals*. Pan Books.

Beale, Peter (1995) *Tank Tracks: 9th Battalion Royal Regiment at War, 1940–1945*, Sutton, Stroud.

Bell, Noel (1947) *G Coy, 8th Battalion The Rifle Brigade, 1944–45*. Gale & Polden, Aldershot.

—— (1947) *From the Beaches to the Baltic*. Gale & Polden, Aldershot.

Bennett, Ralph (1979) *Ultra in the West*. Hutchinson.

Bevan, D.G. (1946) *1st and 2nd Northants Yeomanry 1939–1946*. J.H. Meyer, Brunswick.

Blumenson, Martin (1961) *The US Army in WW2: The European Theatre Operations: Breakout and Pursuit*. OCMH, DA.

Blumentritt, G. (1975) *Von Rundstedt: The Soldier and the Man*. Natraj, Dehra Dun.

Boscawen, Robert (2001) *Armoured Guardsmen*. Leo Cooper.

Bradley, Omar N. (1951) *A Soldier's Story*. Eyre & Spottiswoode.

Brett-Smith, Richard (1976) *Hitler's Generals*. Osprey.

Brower, Charles F. (ed.) (1998) *World War II in Europe: The Final Year*. St Martins Press, New York.

Brownlie, W.S. (1964) *The Proud Trooper*. Collins

Bryant, Arthur (1959) *Triumph in the West*. Collins.

Butcher, Harry C. (1946) *Three Years with Eisenhower*. Heinemann.

Calvacoressi, P. (1980) *Top Secret Ultra*. Pantheon.

—— (1989) *Total War* (2nd edn). Penguin.

Chalmers, W.S. (1959) *Full Cycle: The Biography of Admiral Sir Bertram Ramsay*. Hodder & Stoughton.

Chandler, A.D. (ed.) (1970) *The Papers of Eisenhower*. John Hopkins Press, Baltimore.

Churchill, Winston (1954) *The Second World War 1939–1945, Vol. VI: Triumph and Tragedy*. Cassell.

Clarke, Dudley (1952) *The 11th at War*. Michael Joseph.

Close, Bill (1998) *View from the Turret: History of 3 RTR in WWII*. Dell & Bredon.

Copp, Terry (1984) *Maple Leaf Route: Antwerp*. Maple Leaf Route, Alma, Ontario.

—— (1985) *Maple Leaf Route: Scheldt*. Maple Leaf Route, Alma, Ontario.

Cunningham, Admiral Lord (1951) *A Sailor's Odyssey*. Hutchinson.

Darby, Hugh and Cunliffe, Marcus (1949) *A Short History of 21 Army Group*. Gale & Polden, Aldershot.

De Guingand, Francis (1947) *Operation Victory*. Hodder & Stoughton.

Delaforce, Patrick (1994) *The Fighting Wessex Wyverns*. Sutton, Stroud.

—— (2001) *The Black Bull*. Chancellor Press.

—— (1995) *The Polar Bears*. Sutton, Stroud.

Dempsey, Gen Sir Miles. *Intelligence Summaries*. Held in Liddell Hart Archives, King's College, London.

D'Este, Carlo (1983) *Decision in Normandy*. Collins.

Dixon, Norman (1994) *On the Psychology of Military Incompetence*. Pimlico.

Ehrman, J. (1956) *History of the Second World War*. UK Military Series: Grand Strategy, Vol. V. HMSO.

Eisenhower, D.D. (1948) *Crusade in Europe*. Heinemann.

—— (1946) *Report on the Operations in Europe*. HMSO.

Eisenhower, David (1987) *Eisenhower at War 1943–45*. Vintage, New York.

Ellis, L.F. (1946) *Welsh Guards at War*. Gale & Polden, Aldershot.

—— (1968) *Victory in the West* (2 vols). HMSO.

Essame, Gen H. (1969) *The Battle for Germany*. Batsford.

Evans, Roger (1951) *The Story of The 5th Dragoon Guards*. Gale & Polden, Aldershot.

Ferral, R.H. (1981) *The Eisenhower Diaries*. New York.

Fitzgerald, D.J.L. (1949) *History of the Irish Guards in WWII*. Gale & Polden, Aldershot.

Fuller, J.F.C. (1954) *The Second World War 1939–45*. Eyre & Spottiswoode.

—— (1961) *The Conduct of War, 1789–1961*. Eyre Methuen.

Gilbert, Martin (1989) *Second World War*. Weidenfeld & Nicolson.

Gill, R. and Groves, J. (1945) *Club Route in Europe*. Privately published.

Goodspeed, Maj D.J. (1962) *Battle Royal: A History of the Royal Regiment of Canada 1862–1962*. Royal Regiment of Canada Association, Ottawa.

Goolrick, William and Tanner, Ogden (1979) *The Battle of the Bulge*. Time-Life Books, Virginia.

Graham, Andrew (1964) *The Sharpshooters at War*. Sharpshooters Association.

Graham, Dominic (1993) *Price of Command: A Biography of General Guy Simonds.* Stoddart Publishing, Toronto.

Greenfield, K.R. (1960) *Command Decisions.* Washington.

Hamilton, Nigel (1987) *Monty: Master of the Battlefield.* Sceptre.

—— (1986) *Monty: The Field Marshal 1944–76.* Hamish Hamilton.

Hastings, R.W.H.S. (1950) *The Rifle Brigade in WWII.* Gale & Polden, Aldershot.

Heichler, Lucian (No date) *German Defence of the Gateway to Antwerp.* OCMH MS R-22

Hesketh, Roger (1999) *Fortitude: The D-Day Deception Campaign.* St Ermin's Press.

Hibbert, Christopher (1962) *Arnhem.* Batsford.

Higham, Robin (1972) *A Guide to the Sources of British Military History.* Routledge & Kegan Paul.

Hinsley, F.H. (1979) *British Intelligence in WW2: Its Influence on Strategy and Operations*: Vol. III, Part 2. HMSO.

Hogg, I.V. (1994) *German Order of Battle, 1944.* Greenhill Books.

Horne, Alistair (1994) *Monty: The Lonely Leader 1944–45.* Macmillan.

Horrocks, Brian (1960) *A Full Life,* Collins.

How, J.J. (1954) *3rd Battalion the Monmouthshire Regiment.* Griffin Press, Pontypool.

Ingersoll, Ralph (1946) *Top Secret.* Partridge.

Irving, David (1977) *Hitler's War.*

—— (1981) *The War between the Generals.* Allen Lane.

Jacobsen, H.A. and Rohwer, J. (1965) *Decisive Battles of WWII.*

Johnson, Curt and McLaughlin, Mark (1981) *Civil War Battles.* Fairfax Press, NY.

Joslen, H.F. (1960) *Orders of Battle 1939–45.* HMSO.

Keegan, John (1974) *Rundstedt.* Ballantine Books, New York.

—— (1997) *The Second World War.* Pimlico.

Kemp, P.K. (1955) *King's Shropshire Light Infantry: The History of the 4th Battalion, 1745–1945.* Wilding & Son, Shrewsbury.

Kennedy, Maj Gen Sir John (1957) *The Business of War.* Hutchinson.

Kirby, Norman (1989) *1100 Miles with Monty.* Sutton, Stroud.

Lamb, Richard (1983) *Montgomery in Europe, 1943–45.*

—— (1991) *Churchill as War Leader.* Bloomsbury.

Lauwers, B. (1989) *The British Advance from Normandy to Antwerp.* (No publisher) Belgium.

Lawrence, Vic and Hill, Peter (1994) *Two Hundred Years of Peace and War: A History of the Northamptonshire Yeomanry.* Orman Publishing.

Lewin, Ronald (1971) *Montgomery as a Military Commander.* Batsford.

—— (1978) *Ultra Goes to War.* Hutchinson.

Liddell Hart, Basil (1973) *The Other Side of the Hill.* Cassell.

Lucas, James (1988) *Storming Eagles.* Arms & Armour Press.

Lyon, Margot (1971) *Belgium.* Walker & Co.

McDonald, Charles B. (1963) *US Army in WWII: The Siegfried Line Campaign.* OCMH, DA.

McKee, Alexander (1971) *The Race for the Rhine Bridges*. Souvenir Press.

Macksey, Kenneth (1987) *Military Errors of WW2*. Arms & Armour Press, Poole.

MacMahon, J.S. (1985) *Professional Soldier: A Memoir of Gen Guy Simonds*. Winnipeg.

Madej, W. Victor (ed) (1984) *German Army Order of Battle 1939–1945*. Game Book Marketing.

Mitcham, Samuel W. (1985) *Hitler's Legions: The German Army Order of Battle, World War II*. Stein & Day, New York.

Montgomery, Viscount (1948) *Normandy to the Baltic*. Houghton Mifflin, Boston.

—— (1958) *Memoirs*. Collins.

Moore, William (1991) *Panzer Bait: With 3 RTR 1939–1945*. Leo Cooper.

Moorehead, Alan (1946) *Montgomery*. Hamish Hamilton.

Moulton, J.L. (1978) *Battle for Antwerp*. Ian Allan.

Murray, G.E. Patrick (1996) *Eisenhower versus Montgomery: The Continuing Debate*. Praeger, Westport, Connecticut.

Nafziger, George F. (2000) *German Order of Battle: Infantry in World War II*. Greenhill Books.

Nicolson, Nigel and Forbes, Patrick (1949) *The Grenadier Guards in the War of 1939–1945. Vol. 1: The Campaigns in NW Europe*. Gale & Polden, Aldershot.

North, John (1953) *North-West Europe 1944–5: The Achievement of 21 Army Group*. HMSO.

Orde, Roden (1953) *The Household Cavalry at War: 2 HCR*. Gale & Polden, Aldershot.

Pillinger, Capt H.R. (1944) *11th Armoured Division Signals*. Personal diary held by Imperial War Museum.

Pogue, Forrest C. (1954) *The US Army in WW2: The European Theatre Operations: The Supreme Command*. OCMH, DA.

Ramsay, Admiral Sir Bertram (1994) *Diary: The Year of D-Day* (edited by Robert Love and John Major). University of Hull Press.

Randel, P.B. (1945) *A Short History of XXX Corps in the European Campaign*. Privately published in a limited edition.

Roberts, G.P.B. (1987) *From the Desert to the Baltic*. Kimber.

Rosse, The Earl of and Hill, E.R. (1956) *The Story of the Guards Armoured Division*. Geoffrey Bles.

Ruppenthal, Roland G. (Vol. 1 1953, Vol. 2 1959) *The US Army in WWII: The European Theatre: The Logistical Support of the Armies*. OCMH, DA.

Ryan, Cornelius (1974) *A Bridge Too Far*. Simon & Schuster, New York.

Schramm, Percy E. (1979) 'OKW War Diary'. In Vol. 10 of Detwiler, Donald S. (ed.) *World War II German Military Studies*. Garland, New York.

Sellar, R.J.B. (1960) *Fife and Forfar Yeomanry 1919–1956*. William Blackwood.

Shulman, Milton (1947) *The German Defeat in the West*. Secker & Warburg.

Stacey, C.P. (1960) *The Victory Campaign: The Operations in NW Europe 1944–45*. Queen's Printer, Ottawa.

Tedder, Marshal of the RAF (1966) *With Prejudice*. Cassell.

Thompson, R.W. (1957) *The Eighty-Five Days*. Hutchinson.

Thornburn, Maj 'Ned' (1987) *First into Antwerp: The Part Played by 4 KSLI in the Liberation of the City in September 1944*. 4 KSLI Museum Trust, Shrewsbury.

Trevor-Roper, H.R. (1964) *Hitler's War Directives 1939–1945*. Sidgwick & Jackson.

23rd Hussars (Members of the Regiment) (1946) *The story of the 23rd Hussars*. Privately published.

Urquhart, Sir Brian (1987) *A Life in Peace and War*. HarperCollins.

Verney, Maj Gen G.L. (1954) *The Desert Rats*. Hutchinson.

Verney, Peter (1970) *'The Micks': The Story of the Irish Guards*. Peter Davies.

'Views and Surveys' No. 195 (1985) *Belgium, September 1944*. Ministry of Foreign Affairs, External Trade and Cooperation in Development, Brussels.

Weigley, Russell (1990) *Eisenhower's Lieutenants*. Indiana University Press, Bloomington, Indiana.

Westphal, Gen Siegfried (1951) *The German Army in the West*. Cassell.

Whitaker, Denis and Whitaker, Shelagh (1985) *The Battle of the Scheldt*. Souvenir Press.

Williams, Jeffery (1988) *Long Left Flank: The Hard-fought Way to the Reich 1944–45*. Leo Cooper.

Wilmot, Chester (1954) *The Struggle for Europe*. Reprint Society.

Winterbottom, F.W. (1974) *The Ultra Secret*. Weidenfeld & Nicolson.

Woodham-Smith, Cecil (1953) *The Reason Why*. Constable.

Young, Desmond (1955) *Rommel, The Desert Fox*. Fontana.

Index